Still Lovin' the Ride
The Janet McBride Story

Mary Neal Schutz
and

Janet McBride

with
Pat Boilesen

A Publication of Miles of Memories Productions
Texas, USA

Still Lovin' the Ride
The Janet McBride Story

A Publication of
Miles of Memories Productions/May 2011

Book design by Mary Schutz

For information about publication services:
Miles of Memories Productions,
479 FM 416, Streetman, Texas 75859
E-mail: texschutz@aol.com
www.milesofmemoriesmusic.com
www.texandmary.com
Telephone: 903-467-9545
For information about the Janet McBride Fan Club:
Pat Boilesen, President
216 So. 7th St., Albion, NE 68620
E-mail: pboiles@cablene.com
Telephone: 402-395-6558

To purchase copies of Still Lovin' the Ride, The Janet McBride Story, write
Janet McBride, PO Box 850351, Mesquite, Texas 75185-0351.
Telephone: 214-803-0829
E-mail: jmcbride.yodeler@sbcglobal.net
www.janetmcbrideyodeler.com
www.heroeswest.com/yodelqueen/

ISBN-13: 978-1461159698
ISBN-10: 1461159695

Printed in the United States of America
by CreateSpace

Acknowledgements

Those to thank could run on and on but I have to make some hard choices here.

First, may I say a huge thanks to Mama and Daddy. They gave me life and as you will read, a great life. Not full of stuff like today's kids but enough to get me ready for the real world.

To my brothers and sister who put up with me, fully knowing that I was a little off-center sometimes and a little bit of a wild child, who was addicted to yodeling.

To my three kids who kept me grounded and the Lord for holding my hand through the lessons he continues to try to teach me.

To Billy (John) Ingram who came into my life when I really needed someone who just wanted to love me. As he told me many times, it was all about me anyway! In return I found the love of my life in John Ingram.

To all of my friends from the years of working day-jobs in California, Texas and Tennessee and the many friends and fans of the Mesquite Opry where I was able to return to the music business I dreamed about, without having to leave the real world behind.

To the many, many friends I gathered after I retired from the Dallas County Sheriff's Department when John and I were able to travel to Austria, Canada and all over the United States just singing at festivals and mentoring young kids and older people alike in the art of yodeling.

Especially to Mary Schutz for taking on the job of turning my life story into a book and to her husband Tex for allowing it all to happen; to Pat and Wayne Boilesen for taking on the job of Fan Club President and for assisting Mary with this book. It wasn't an easy job. I don't think any of us had any clue what a big project it would be.

And we appreciate our photographer friends Lori Faith Merritt *(www.photographybyfaith.com)*, Ron and Glenda Shipman and Steve Covault (*www.rockmusicphotos.com*) for taking lots of fun photos along the way.

To everyone I didn't mention, I want to say please don't think I don't remember you, but there wasn't enough paper in this book to mention you all. That doesn't mean that you mean any less to me in the grand scheme of things. It's just that my life has been long and filled with so many great people that I can call friends. I have been truly blessed.

—Janet Lister McBride Ingram

Contents

Prologue

A young girl and her mother join Janet in her "music room" after driving more than 200 miles to get there. The veteran country music artist is helping the aspiring young performer to improve her skills as an entertainer and will teach her to do that unique kind of vocalization called yodeling, that fits so nicely into certain country and cowboy songs.

"It's easy," says Janet. "Regular voice on "A"...falsetto on "E"...and repeat twice, then tag it out with an "O" in regular voice...but don't let your sound be in your throat. Take the falsetto note to the front of the roof of your mouth and let the sound bounce around there. Now, put a smile on your face...and you'll know you have it right."

It may not be as easy as Janet McBride implies, but several hundred young, hopeful entertainers—the majority of them girls—have mastered the art of yodeling with precision, skill and style, thanks to Janet's passion and dedication and their determination to learn and practice.

Included in the list of "Janet protégés" is a seven-year-old LeAnn Rimes. Miss Rimes was already a veteran singer by the time she asked Janet if she would teach her a yodel that would fit into Patsy Montana's song, "I Want to Be a Cowboy's Sweetheart." LeAnn was a quick study in the art of yodeling and had the chance to prove her abilities when she was asked to sing that song several times during the Mesquite Rodeo Parade that day and again that evening at the Mesquite Opry.

When LeAnn rose to world-wide fame with her recording of Bill Mack's "Blue," she credited Janet with teaching her to yodel...and Janet's popularity as a yodeling coach grew in the young star's wake.

LeAnn is only one of 200 or more "students" who have sought out Janet for her unique coaching ability through the past several years. Maybe, like LeAnn, they'll become big-name entertainers one day and bring the joy of music to millions of people, or maybe they'll just sing and yodel for themselves and their families. Either way, helping them to gain a foothold on their dreams is a passion for Janet McBride, former West Coast country music star turned Texas recording artist and opry show owner/producer.

It's been said that "every life has a story." *Still Lovin' the Ride* is Janet McBride's.

1

The Listers of Maine...the Beginning

Aurelia and Victor Lister, soon after they were married.
(Janet McBride Collection)

Life in rural Maine wasn't glamorous. Many folks were poor and good jobs were scarce.

It was the 16th day of May, 1927. Calvin Coolidge was President of the United States, a postage stamp cost two cents, the Yankees had just won the World Series, and aviator Charles Lindbergh was preparing to make the first nonstop solo transatlantic flight. While others were making history, a young couple, small in stature and very much in love, were getting married at the courthouse in Maine's capital city of Augusta. Their names: Victor Lister, from Lawrence, Massachusetts, and Aurelia Marquis from Chelsea, Maine.

Aurelia had finished 8th grade in a one-room school in rural Maine. The nearest high school was in Gardiner, and although it was only about five miles away, without transportation, going on to high school was not a viable option. Instead she went to work at the Togus Veteran's Home as a waitress in their food service department. Her father had abandoned the family of eight children several years before, and her earnings went to help support the four younger siblings still at home.

An independent sort, Victor had left school at age 11 after his father died. He told his children he quit because he didn't have a pair of boy's shoes to wear. The only pair he had was handed down from his sister and he was not about to wear girl's shoes. He simply stopped going to school. As soon as he was old enough, he enlisted in the Army and served two years, but was given an honorable discharge because of his bad "ticker." (A photo of Victor with some Army buddies has survived the years.*)

The newlyweds made their home in Chelsea, Maine, a hilly town on the east bank of the Kennebec River. Aurelia continued working at the Veteran's Hospital where her grandmother and Victor's mother also worked, until her first pregnancy. It is not known exactly where Victor worked at the time. It may have been at the hospital or he may have had a position at a shoe factory in Augusta.

In 1928 the couple's first child was born, a son they named Richard. Sadly, the baby was destined to live only a short six days. Their second son,

---

* *Victor was married to another woman before Aurelia and together they had a son, Victor, Jr., who later fought in World War II and was the recipient of three Silver Stars, two Purple Hearts and a Bronze Star. He lives in Athens, Maine, at the time of this writing.*

Don, was born in May 1929, followed by a daughter named Barbara, born in August of 1930. Little Barbara lived only eleven days.

The loss of a second child and the promise of a new life prompted the young couple to pack up and move to California, where Victor's mother and her second husband Richard Blamey lived.

There the Lister family set up housekeeping along Imperial Highway in the Los Angeles suburb known as Lennox, in a house that was next door to the Blameys'. Getting settled and looking for work were priorities for Victor, and time would show that he was a man who was willing to work at whatever job would put food on the table for his family.

With his experience in the Maine shoe factory, he was able to pick up a job in a California shoe factory and became skilled in different locations on the shoe assembly line.

At some point Victor began working for the City of El Segundo in their vehicle repair shop. He was as an ace mechanic and could keep a car running no matter how old it was. He could tear down a motor and rebuild it without a hitch, a skill that he later passed on to both his sons.

"I remember Dad talking about taking the city's police cars out to check them out after he'd repaired them," recalls Don. "He'd drive them as fast as he thought he could get away with, then he'd turn on the sirens and flash the lights, all in the name of making sure that everything worked smoothly."

Victor may have also worked with some of the WPA public works projects in California, probably as a laborer. The kids remember that sometimes when they passed a bridge or building built by the WPA, Victor proudly said, "I helped on that!" or "The WPA built that!"

ભ

So hard were the times that when Aurelia's mother Phoebe died at home in Chelsea, Maine, in 1932, the young wife and mother couldn't afford to make the trip back to Maine for the funeral. Don had been very young when the Listers spent their early years in Maine and had not developed a relationship with his maternal grandmother, so Aurelia's grief was probably something she bore alone.

Joan was born in 1932 in Los Angeles General Hospital, a facility generally reserved for low-income patients. The care that Aurelia and baby Joan received was so inferior that she vowed never to go there again. On

April 5, 1934, when the young mother knew Janet was soon to be born, she waited until she was sure that Centinella Hospital in Inglewood could not turn her away, and thus Janet was brought into the world in a much nicer place.

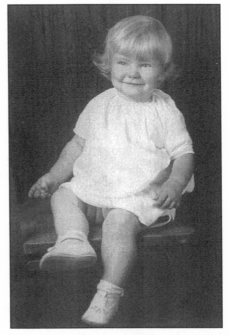

Janet at one year.
(Janet McBride Collection)

As the children grew, "Grammy and Grampy" Blamey were the only grandparents they knew. A trip over to the Blamey's house meant Jello with fruit, and two adults who were always glad to see the inquisitive young Lister children.

"I remember listening to a small radio that Grampy kept on a table next to his easy chair," said Janet. "But even more exciting than radio music was the sound of singing and guitars coming from the house across the street. Grammy said there were some 'Okies' who lived there and that was her explanation for that wonderful music." But there was something special about that music that intrigued young Janet.

Joan and Janet were sometimes allowed to stay overnight at the Blamey's house and always had a good time there. Sometimes Grammy would take the two girls to a western movie. They loved watching the horses and cowboys, and, Janet likes to think, they might have seen a Gene Autry film.

Grampy Blamey had been injured in the Army and walked with a cane. Don remembers that he had also worked as a detective for a time and would entertain the kids with some of his adventures in that line of work. He drew a pension from the Army so the couple lived reasonably well. He was a happy presence in Janet's young life and rounded out the Lister family circle in a warm and pleasant way.

"My parents told a story about me asking to go next door to hear my Grandpa Blamey's antique clock when it would 'bong,'" said Janet. "Grampy told my parents and Grammy that the clock would be given to me when they

Two-year-old Janet, with a neighbor's toy firetruck.
(Janet McBride Collection)

died. I was out of high school, working and had a car when Grammy sent the clock home with me one day when my sister Joan and I had driven to her little apartment to visit her. Now my daughter Denise has the clock. She has two daughters and I hope one day she gives it to one of them."

"The last time Joan and I stayed overnight with them, there was a fire next door and the little girl that we played with was burned to death," recalls Janet. "It upset Grammy so badly to think that it could have been us, that we were never invited to stay overnight again."

ଓ

A very small house on Mariposa Street in El Segundo became the Lister's next home. It was located just behind an elementary school, a convenient situation because young Joan was ready to start school.

Four years old, with curly hair and first-day-of-school excitement, Joan walked away with her hand in her mother's—while Janet stayed on the sidewalk in front of their home and cried her heart out.

"If only I had curly hair," Janet reasoned, "maybe I could go to school, too!"

Her disappointment soon faded into the shadows. Indeed, there would be many greater ones ahead for this pretty little girl with the un-curly hair.

Janet's younger brother, Dan, was born in 1936. He was a frail child and Aurelia worried about his health. Thin and small for his age, he had milky white skin, red hair and freckles. In spite of his slight frame, however, he would grow into a healthy, strong young man.

Two years later, the family was expecting a new addition, but one day Janet's mother returned from the hospital without "the baby." The youngsters were told that their mother had lost the child, possibly because she had been bitten by a black widow spider. After the loss of this baby, Aurelia's doctors told her that she shouldn't risk another pregnancy, and the "Lister Kids" would be forever just four.

Janet's mother was a stay-at-home mom, as were most moms in her neighborhood at that time. She didn't learn to drive and spent most of her time at home doing household chores and being with her children. Janet doesn't remember much about her mother during these early years, just that she always seemed to be working around the house.

As a very young child during her stay on Mariposa Street, Janet received a severe spanking from her father one day. It was brought on by an inappropriate gathering of older boys and little girls, but she didn't understand what all the fuss was about. She was made to stay in bed while the other kids played outside and was never told exactly why she was being punished. Not until many years later would she let loose of the pain this incident caused her. As an adult she came to realize that her father's punishment might have been more out of fear for her safety, rather than actual punishment. Whatever it was, she made sure that that situation never repeated itself.

Soon after that incident, the family moved to another house in the area, this one on Eucalyptus Street, between the Standard Oil Refinery and what is now Los Angeles International Airport.

A field around the house enabled the family to keep a goat, which provided milk for the growing youngsters. Although this home, in the town known as El Segundo, had its good points— good places to play, swings and a field—it wasn't always pleasant there.

Aurelia, Victor, with Don (on tire), Joan and Janet (inside tire) and baby Danny (in Aurelia's arms).
(Janet McBride Collection)

2

El Segundo

*Don Lister feeding a baby goat
near the Listers' El Segundo home.
(Janet McBride Collection)*

El Segundo was built in 1911-12 around the Standard Oil Refinery, by Standard Oil Company men. El Segundo, which means "the second one" in Spanish, referred to the company's second oil refinery in California.

"Certain times of the day, the fumes from Standard Oil were really bad," remembers Janet. "With all those huge tanks of oil so near, I don't believe Mama ever felt at ease, thinking that the whole plant could blow up at any time."

ભ

In about 1940, Victor and Aurelia discovered that their kids were all pretty good singers. Even without any training in music, Aurelia was able to teach each child to sing a different harmony part when they were still very young.

"Daddy was the better singer, but Mama had the time and patience to teach us, and became our coach and leader," recalled Janet. "She had us singing harmony by the time I was six, which meant that Danny was only four."

Her mother lined up the kids, oldest to youngest, and made them practice their songs. Janet most often sang lead because she was the loudest.

"Kinda like the Johnny Cash song says: 'Donnie sang bass, Danny sang tenor, me and sister Joan would join right in there'," Janet recalls.

Folks around the area began to ask the Lister youngsters to sing at various activities—and new worlds began to open up for them. People especially enjoyed watching and hearing four-year-old Danny sing tenor because his face would turn beet red, which wasn't all that unusual since he had very fair skin and freckles!

"We did a lot of church radio broadcasts. Because we could get a bit rowdy while we were waiting for our time to sing, they often made us wait in a back room. I wish I could say that the four of us were well mannered and well controlled," Janet confessed, "but I really think we might have been far from that!"

None of the siblings remembers receiving any payment for these concerts, but they may have received other goods in exchange for their performances, because it must have been worthwhile for Victor and Aurelia to take them out to their programs and spend the time required to teach them their material. On the other hand, it may have been only the joy of making

and sharing music that led the parents
to do this for the youngsters.

Regardless of the reasons why
the Lister kids were singing, they
were happily singing their hearts out
at any opportunity.

ᢙ

The kids were too young to
realize it, but while they were singing,
clouds of war were gathering on the
horizon. War has a way of changing
things and the Lister family felt many
of its effects. Where there had been
peace of mind, there now was a
feeling of insecurity and fear. Events

*The Listers at KFVD Radio, Los
Angeles, 1940.
(Janet McBride Collection)*

too close to home were suddenly changing the way they felt about where
they were living.

The Listers, as well as others in the Los Angeles area, were terrified of
the possibility of an enemy attack on the West Coast. Specifically they were
worried about an attack on the Standard Oil Refinery or the airport
nearby. The fear that either site might be attacked was ever-present and
rumors about foreign elements infiltrating California businesses were always
being discussed.

The Listers were living in that El Segundo house on December 7, 1941,
when Pearl Harbor was attacked by the Japanese.

A few days later, Aurelia and the kids saw a military plane of some
kind fly over the house. It was so low that they could see the men's faces.
Just after it disappeared beyond a hill, they heard a crash and saw plumes of
smoke. They later learned that the airplane's crew and one child on the
ground lost their lives that day.

It was just one more reason for Victor and Aurelia to begin to make
plans for leaving California and moving back to Maine. They couldn't help
but think about the possibility of a plane crashing on their house and killing
them as well.

Shortly after that incident, an explosion of some kind happened in the
field behind the house. Don can remember hearing a screaming-whistling
sound as a missile of some kind flew over the house and then exploded,

leaving a crater in
the field where it
hit. Although no
record of such an
occurrence has
surfaced, the
family indicated
that some
"authorities" came
to discuss the
incident with Victor
and Aurelia and
told them "it never
happened" and that
they should just go
on with their lives.

*Janet's kindergarten class, El Segundo, California, 1939-40.
Janet is the blonde, third from left in back row.
(Janet McBride Collection)*

"My parents never knew what really occurred," Janet said, "but they
were certainly ready to find a safer area." Don remembers that there were
Japanese submarines off the coast of California and he believes that the
screaming sound might have been caused by an artillery shell launched from
one of those vessels or even from one of our own ships.*

Victor and Aurelia decided that the best thing to do was to get out of
this dangerous area as quickly as possible, but unfortunately their trusty 1935
Ford was totally disassembled while Victor was overhauling the engine. He
sent Don (then 12) into Inglewood by himself on the bus to get the needed
parts so he could finish rebuilding the car as soon as possible.

Into that rebuilt car they packed as many of their belongings that would
fit, and the rest were left in the house. Photos of the Lister kids that have
survived through the years may have been pulled out of an album that was
left behind simply because it would not fit in the car. The back floor area of
the car was filled up level with the back seat so that the kids could sleep
along the way. Older brother Don had space made for his legs just behind the
driver's seat and little brother Dan sat up front with his parents.

"I don't know the actual day we left for Maine but it was before

---

* *Research indicates that, over a seven-day period, from December 18 to 24, 1941,
nine Japanese submarines positioned at strategic points along the U.S. west coast attacked
eight American merchant ships, of which two were sunk and two damaged, although no
evidence was found of an actual "hit" in the El Segundo area.*

Christmas in 1941," recalled Janet. "I remember Mama saying that she had ordered Shirley Temple dolls for Joan and me for Christmas, but, of course, we never received them."

3

On Rooney Road

*Church School, Whitefield, Maine,
as it looked when Janet attended there.
(Photo courtesy of David Fields.)*

It's 3,194 miles from El Segundo, California, to Chelsea, Maine. The road trip took the Lister family seven days and seven nights. Without money for hotel stops, they caught catnaps along the way. As Aurelia did not drive, all the driving was up to Victor.

One night, Victor backed off the road into what he may have thought was a field driveway so he could get a little sleep. After awhile, he woke to Aurelia screaming "Vic! Vic! A train, a train!" Whether they were actually in the path of the train, they were never certain, but for the rest of the trip they stopped to rest only during daylight hours.

When at last the family arrived in Maine they went directly to Victor's sister Madeline's home for a few days, then later to Aunt Gertie and Uncle Bill's house, both in Chelsea. Gertie and Bill had five kids of their own, plus some boarders in the house, but somehow they found space for the Listers in a room over the garage.

Although she remembers little about her Aunt's home, Janet does remember that there was a blue star in her window, signifying that their son was serving in a war zone.

As soon as they could, the family moved into a two-story house in Chelsea, the same house where Victor and Aurelia had lived when they were first married and where Don was born. The house was next door to a one-room schoolhouse where all the youngsters would attend school.

ⷀ

Janet was growing into a spunky young girl with a mind of her own and the determination to get whatever it was she was after. Not a shy child by any stretch of the imagination, she could talk many a neighbor kid into sharing their toys or coerce her brothers and sister into playing the games she wanted to play. Then one day she discovered the unique sound of yodeling. She begged her mother to wake her up early so she could listen to the cowboy singing groups on the radio and became quite annoyed when allowed to oversleep.

"It was 1942 and in those days, things were tough for sure," Janet recalls. "People were doing odd jobs to make a few bucks and Mama had told a traveling photographer that she wanted a photo of us kids. The day came and Mama had us cleaned up and waiting in the yard for the picture guy. Mama tried to keep us clean by having us play catch out front. We were using an apple because we didn't have a ball. It was going well until I missed my catch and the apple went past me into some tall grass. I let out a multi-level yell to express my dismay. That was the day I decided that I, too, could yodel like those cowboys. From that day on, I was

> *Mama was only 4'11," so regardless of how small Daddy may have appeared to others, to her he was a big man.*
>
> *--Janet McBride*

hooked. The photographer did come that day and took our picture, one of the few that has survived all these years. There we are, all cleaned up, and there I am with my braided hair, smiling like I had just won the Olympics and in a way I had...because I had discovered yodeling!"

ॐ

As World War II was raging across Europe and the South Pacific, Victor worked in a shoe factory in Gardiner and took classes in welding. Then he got a job as a welder with the Bath Ironworks Shipyard in Bath, Maine, a town about 30 miles south of the Lister home. There was a high demand for welders and others who could create and repair steel items needed for the War effort.

He would often stay in Bath all week, coming home only on weekends. It was an effort to save gasoline and wear on tires, which were inferior in quality and in short supply during those wartime years.

In addition to providing a better wage, Victor's job at the shipyard brought him a new-found level of pride in his work. With his small stature, he was often called on to do welding projects in tight places on warships, something the other guys couldn't do.

The shipyard years are the only time in Janet's life that she remembers receiving an allowance. Each child was given a generous 50 cents a week.

"I will never forget purchasing a six-pack of Coca Colas with my first 50 cents," said Janet. "The first week there was a deposit on the bottles but the second week I was really happy because then I could buy my six-pack and have a quarter left. Yep, I spent it, too...for a double dip of ice cream in a cup. It was a very happy time for an eight year old."

With his increased wages, Victor paid the tax lien on a 150-acre plot of land that included a farm house in North Whitefield, Maine, for the princely sum of $150. And, for the first and only time in his life, he was a landowner.

Soon the family was making preparations to move to the new property on Rooney Road, where there would be more room for all the Listers and they could enjoy owning their own place.

"On the day we were scheduled to move I discovered some kittens in the bushes near our Chelsea house," said Janet. "I couldn't reach them but kept trying, because I wanted a cat as a playmate when we moved to the country."

Mom and Dad stalled and Janet finally caught a kitten. She named it Tommy and he was her furry friend all during their stay on Rooney Road.

ርჄ

Janet with a group of Maine cousins, 1942. Janet is second from right in front row..
(Janet McBride Collection)

Janet enjoyed five wonderful years in North Whitefield. Her recollections are proof that bare essentials can be enough when mixed with the love of a close family.

Living conditions on Rooney Road were primitive by today's standards and rural by 1942 standards, but Victor was very proud of owning the North Whitefield home and did the best he could with what he had.

The house had no electricity and none available, as it was almost three-quarters of a mile from the electric feeder line. They did have a radio, however, and were able to play it by hooking it up to the car battery. Each Saturday evening, the kids begged their dad to bring the battery out of the car and into the house so they could listen to the Grand Ole Opry. They'd listen until the battery ran out of power, knowing that on Sunday morning they would have to help push the car until their Dad could "pop the clutch" to start it. "Daddy parked the car on an incline, headed downhill," said Janet, "and I was always the first one at the bumper, ready to push!"

The family had a good water well, situated about 40 feet from the kitchen door, but no water was accessible inside the house. As the oldest child, Don was responsible for carrying water. There was no railing around the well, just boards lying flat with a trap door, so the bucket could be dropped in upside down, filled with water then pulled up. After several trips up and down, the bucket had hit the rocky sidewall so many times that it developed some small holes. Soon water was running out through the holes faster than Don could pull it up and the bucket had to be replaced.

Toilet facilities consisted of an "outhouse" that was reached through a door off the kitchen then an uncovered walkway to the shed where the "privy" was located, about 30 feet from the house.

ᚨ

Maine can be very cold in the winter, but the Lister kids didn't really seem to mind too much. They played in the snow and had snowball fights, like any other kids who live in a snowy climate.

"Sometimes, just for fun, we'd burrow into the snow mounds left beside the road by the snowplow," remembers Janet. "This wasn't the safest thing to do, but there was always one of us watching the road in case there was anything coming."

Wood was used to heat their home and was challenging work to obtain. Because Victor was away at work much of the time, Don, Dan, Joan and Janet would bundle up and go to the woods where Don would cut down a tree. The four of them would line up in a row to carry it and they'd trudge through the snow back to the home place where Don cut it into short pieces for the potbelly stove. Aurelia cooked all the winter meals on that potbelly stove and though cooking must have been challenging, the Lister kids never missed a meal.

During the winter, part of the house was closed off and the family moved into just three rooms. Victor and Aurelia slept in what was the summer dining room, and the potbelly stove was employed to heat that room and both bedrooms. Joan and Janet shared one bedroom and Don and Dan shared the other. The doors to the bedrooms were closed all day so that the only area receiving heat was the room with the parents' bed. About an hour before bedtime, the doors of the other bedrooms were opened to let in heat. Several quilts on each bed kept the youngsters warm and flat irons, heated on the stove and wrapped in towels, were put under the covers to heat several pairs of cold feet.

One winter it snowed quite heavily and completely covered Rooney Road, making it impassable. Knowing that the County would plow the road only up to their neighbor Annie Kelly's house and no farther, Victor had parked his car by Annie's house the night before, so he was able to get to work. The kids could trudge through the snow down to Annie's house, where the school bus picked them up. Then, after Don and Victor spent several days shoveling snow by hand, the County snowplow finally arrived to clear the road. None too soon, to Victor's way of thinking!

One favorable aspect of snowfall was that it enabled Don, who was attending high school in Gardiner, to make a little extra money shoveling snow for area businesses before school in the morning.

The younger Lister kids loved waiting for the school bus inside Annie Kelly's house when it was cold or wet outside. This precious lady opened her home every weekday morning to the Lister kids, one boy from the Twist family and at least three of the Carter kids, with youngsters ranging from first graders up to eighth graders. This scenario happened over and over again for the full five years that the Listers lived on Rooney Road.

One day after school the snow was perfect for a snowman and was too much to resist when the kids got off the school bus. They rolled the wonderfully wet snow into a ball for the base of the snowman, but soon it was so large that they couldn't move it off the roadway—and they began to panic. Annie noticed that none of the kids had walked past her house at the usual time and she became concerned. She walked up over the hill and found them in the midst of a dilemma. They couldn't get the huge snowball off the road and they couldn't leave it there, in case someone came driving along too fast to stop. Annie helped them move it, and saved the day for the Lister kids and their friends!

"One night it had snowed pretty heavily and then it turned really cold and the heavy, wet snow froze on the trees," recalls Janet. "The next morning, my brothers and sister were sick and couldn't go to school, so I walked to the schoolbus alone. There was ice on the trees and the limbs formed an arch for me to walk under for most of the way between our house and Annie's. Even though I was just a kid of 10, I knew I was looking at God's great work. There were no footprints but mine that morning. The snow was perfect and clean; the road was covered so there were no ruts and no mud; the trees had no leaves, just branches heavy with ice and hanging over touching each other. I remember walking along appreciating the almost mystical sight and knowing that I probably would never see anything like that again. I was right."

Winter lasts a long time in Maine so there was nothing that measured up to the joy of the coming of spring. With its arrival, Mom Lister opened up the kitchen and once again built fires in the cook stove. A fire in the kitchen stove meant that the family would have oven-baked beans and even biscuits or some other home-cooked delight.

"Mama would put that pot of beans in the oven in the morning and that is where it stayed with the fire burning low all day," recalls Janet. "I can still remember how good those beans tasted!"

Spring on Rooney Road was especially beautiful. The snow melted and exposed the muddy ruts of the road, but along the roadside were clusters of pussywillows, wildflowers of all kinds and apple and wild cherry trees filled with blossoms. The fragrance of lilacs filled the air. According to Janet, it "truly takes your breath away."

In the spring of 1943, Victor bought an old tractor and plowed a spot for a garden. Aurelia raised young seedlings inside the house; then, when it was warm enough, planted them in the garden. Janet and her siblings planted potatoes, cucumbers and other vegetables. Victor cut grass for hay for their cows and stored it in the barn. Thanks to their work and Aurelia's canning, the family was well prepared for winter.

Victor loved a good laugh, especially when it came with a lesson attached. Blockage of the culvert a bit farther down Rooney Road brought

24

some unexpected rewards—and laughs—for Victor Lister. One time he became impatient for the road crew to clear out the roots and trash that had clogged the culvert and caused a pool of water to form. He and Don took up crowbars and shovels and dug out the big flat rocks that protected the drain, then proceeded to clean out the trash until the water ran out as it should. But when they attempted to replace the protective rocks, they didn't all fit just exactly as they originally were, which caused a rough hump that ran across the road.

There was only one family who lived past the Lister house and those folks had a habit of driving way too fast in Victor's thinking. He and the kids had a great laugh the first time the neighbor came racing down that one-lane dirt road past the Lister house and hit the bump caused by the raised rocks. His vehicle went bounding through the air until it hit the ground with a "clunk" that he'd not likely forget anytime soon. He drove a bit more slowly the rest of the days the Lister family lived on Rooney Road, and Victor and the kids chuckled each time they saw him slow down at that culvert site.

ଓ

One of the greatest gifts Victor gave his children was a knowledge and love of nature. When the springtime early growing season came, he took them into the deep woods to look for the elusive lady slippers, a member of the orchid family. He and the kids spent hours looking under logs, in brush piles and all of the other places in the woods where lady slippers might grow. The only unfortunate part of this adventure was that he often dug up the tender lady slipper plants and transplanted them up close to the house, where they invariably died. That delicate plant is nearly extinct in the area today.

Janet especially loved violets and spent hours searching for different shades and sizes of those beautiful flowers. After almost every violet-picking adventure, Janet brought home a bouquet for her mother, who acted like receiving that gift of flowers was the greatest event of her day.

"I remember watching a swampy spot near the culvert where the water would drain off slowly," Janet said. "That's where the first violets would be. Now everytime I see violets, I'm flooded with memories of my mother."

ଓ

The Listers made good use of the resources available on and around their Rooney Road home—both for earning much-needed cash and for their own consumption. As an example, they often earned extra money by harvesting wood found on their rural property. During the summer of 1944, they decided to sell timber to a local sawmill. Aurelia and Don worked with Victor as they cut down trees with a crosscut saw, then peeled the bark from the logs and hauled them home to stack in the yard. When there were enough to sell, they'd call a local lumber broker to pick them up.

One fall Victor and Aurelia gathered juniper berries that they sold to a local store in Augusta. They wore heavy gloves to strip the berries off the bushes into boxes and Aurelia spent many hours separating the purple berries from the green ones, because the purple ones brought a better price. The berry juice was used in various remedies and medicines—and some say it was used to make gin. At any rate, the family was paid well for their picking efforts.

Less painful ventures were the times they picked raspberries from under the power lines, and tiny wild strawberries (about the size of a fingernail) from the fields. They picked enough strawberries for several pints, and raspberries to make several quarts. From time to time, they bought a bushel of peaches to can. Those canned fruits were a wonderful addition to a winter's meal and gave the Lister kids a certain amount of appreciation for the work they'd done the summer before.

During their first summer on Rooney Road, Victor discovered a bee tree on the property. When it got cold enough to approach the hive, Uncle Bill and Vic gathered some of the waxy material and Aurelia warmed it up to extract the honey from the honeycomb. They also harvested maple sap and Aurelia turned it into a delicious syrup. Memories of these culinary delights add to Janet's belief that these years were some of the best ever.

The Listers also tried their hand at raising lifestock to feed the family. One spring day Victor brought home some chickens and Aurelia cared for them and gathered their eggs through the summer. But when winter came, and with no way to heat the chicken house, the chickens died. It broke Aurelia's heart that she had no way to save them.

At one point, Victor had a pig that produced a litter of piglets. Somehow, one of the young ones got an apple caught in its throat. Too tender-hearted to kill it, he turned it loose, hoping it would find a way to survive. Later, he looked for it but wasn't able to find it. He assumed it had lived since he never found a body. In the fall the neighbors started telling stories about a pig being seen under the apple trees about a mile from the Lister house. Victor was driving home one afternoon and saw that pig run across the road. The family enjoyed pork for several weeks to come.

When they had cows and milk, the family had a hand-operated cream separator, enabling Aurelia to make homemade butter, which she traded in town for sugar. During the short time that she had chickens, she was also able to trade eggs for other products the family needed.

During the late summer of 1945, the entire family picked green beans at a nearby farm in an effort to make some extra money. That particular venture evidently didn't succeed because they did it only that one time. Janet recalls that on one occasion she and Dan were punished for not doing a good job and were sent back to the car for making everyone else miserable. Fact is, Janet far preferred picking raspberries over green beans, and acting out was her way of communicating that.

Trout fishing in a little stream near the Rooney Road place was an enjoyable family pastime and gave the Listers some wonderful variation in their diet. Those trout—caught with poles made from tree saplings, household string and a hook—became a delicious suppertime treat.

Sometimes, while Victor and the youngsters were fishing, Aurelia would gather "fiddleheads" as a special addition to a meal. She had been told that the fern heads could be poisonous if they were sticking out of the water, and she was fearful of picking the bad ones, so they didn't get to enjoy that delicacy very often.

Janet likes to tell that her Daddy wouldn't stoop to eating squirrel meat. "Daddy might have thought about eating a rabbit once in a while, but I don't remember us *ever* eating a squirrel."

On one occasion Victor killed a deer. Because they had no refrigerator, the meat was stored in a snow bank outside, and, for a time, the family enjoyed the tasty venison.

All in all, the Listers ate well, with main courses that may have consisted of chicken, pork, beef or fish, plus side dishes of homegrown vegetables or wild fruits.

⑃

Going without was a way of life on Rooney Road, and that included going without medical care. Janet recalls the time her mother had to have her front tooth pulled by a dentist, but there was no money to replace it. "I remember Mama chewing a piece of gum and putting it in the hole where the tooth had been, so us kids wouldn't notice."

While all the neighbor kids were playing hide and seek one day, Janet cut her knee on a broken bottle, leaving a scar she carries to this day. "Summer was pretty much over for me," she said. "No doctor, no stitches... I just laid around with my leg elevated until the wound healed enough so I could walk without breaking it open and causing it to bleed."

The Lister wood-gathering industry was interrupted at one point when Victor cut his leg severely with an ax, an accident for which there was no money for the needed stitches. The incident put a large dent in extra income that summer and may have even caused him to miss a few days of work at his shipyard job.

One day while picking juniper berries, Aurelia jumped over a fence and landed on a rusty nail, effectively ending her career in the juniper berry business. Again, there was no money for a doctor, which meant she didn't get a tetanus shot or any treatment. She soaked her foot in Epsom salts and toughed it out, but the kids were aware that she was in constant pain.

೧೪

The war years brought their own special challenges, but for the Lister kids who knew no other life, things were normal. They were aware of rationing...such things as sugar (that Aurelia needed for canning) and silk stockings. When Aurelia finally did receive a pair of those coveted stockings one day, she put them on carefully, but immediately got a "runner," and burst into tears. They were that precious.

Low-quality car tires and inner tubes were a big challenge. On more than one occasion, flat tires ruined a family outing. One year, when Grammy Blamey was visiting from California, the family planned a picnic excursion. Grammy really wanted to go to Boothbay Harbor, a trip of about 30 miles, but because of inferior tires, Victor decided that was out of the question. Instead they chose a spot at a lake near Whitefield. On the way they had *three* flat tires.

By the time they got home they were sorry they had attempted the picnic that day...and were thankful that they hadn't attempted to go all the way to Boothbay Harbor.

4

Cellar Door Dreams

*Janet and her father loved finding
the elusive lady slipper,
a delicate wildflower found in the woods of Maine.*

The Lister kids didn't have a lot of toys of their own, but were quite creative in having fun with what they did have, or could borrow. There was a boy in the neighborhood who owned a bike and Janet often talked him into letting her use it. She learned to ride that bike one winter day when there was snow on the ground. She figured that if she fell, she wouldn't get hurt.

When some cousins gave them two adult-sized pairs of ice skates, the Lister kids wore them over their own shoes and learned to skate that way. The kids shared two sleds among the four of them, but there weren't many hills to sled down on Rooney Road.

"Unfortunately, we didn't have many books either," Janet recalled. "One Christmas Aunt Lurline sent us a beautiful book, but it didn't last long at our house. I did have a few dolls…and I do remember Mama making a beautiful angora skirt for one of them once."

As a way to keep the house warmer in the winter and cooler in the summer, Aurelia put flattened cardboard boxes on the walls and ceiling. One of the games the kids liked most was to take a word from one of the boxes and see how many other words they could make from it. Other favorite games were pinochle and poker, with match sticks as their betting currency.

School was an adventure for the Lister children and all of them were good students. Whitefield Church School, where they attended, had one teacher for grades one through eight. All the kids were in one large room so they all became friends. Janet especially remembers the Carter Family, who also lived on Rooney Road, and the Tibbetts family.

Janet's favorite subjects were geography and penmanship. Unfortunately for the young music lover, no music classes were offered, although the students sometimes put on a Christmas program for all the parents. The Lister kids were always a part of those programs and there's even a photo of Janet and Dan at one of these holiday gatherings (1946) on the "Maine Thing" website*. *(See a copy of that photo on page 32.)*

Like other kids, the Lister youngsters were sometimes ornery and even sneaky once in a while, like the summer they decided that pieces of an old wicker chair might make good cigarettes. They'd break off a piece of wicker, then go out behind the barn, light it with a stick match and attempt to

---

That photo (shown on page 32) can also be found at http://www.mainething.com/ schoolpictures/image%201946%204,5,6.htm., which is a site promoting the state of Maine and its history.

Church School, Whitefield, Maine, Christmas 1946.
Janet is fourth from right and Danny is second from right, both front row.
(Photo thanks to Francis Mooney, teacher, and David Chase for assistance.)

smoke that wicker-chair cigarette like they were really cool! "It was a *big* chair...we could have smoked it all summer that year and nobody would have known," remembers Janet. "But, oh, that stuff burned! Well, I never claimed that the Lister kids were angels, did I?"

At different times, the youngsters were taught by two different teachers during their Whitefield School days. Those particular teachers were the Mooney sisters who married the Hickey brothers, a situation that the students thought was pretty special.

Their classroom was heated by a large wood-burning stove. A long stovepipe ran to the chimney in the back of the room, which helped to heat the entire room. The oldest child usually started the fire for the day and Janet's brother Don had that assignment until he graduated. In winter, the youngsters stayed in their ski-suit pants all day, often until bedtime, to keep warm. It was difficult to keep those ski pants clean and even more difficult to wash and dry them during the winter and Aurelia did so only when absolutely necessary. She used a galvanized tub to wash them, wrung the water out of the bulky garments and hung them behind the wood stove to dry. Sometimes that took all weekend. Chances are, those heavy pants went without being washed for quite a while and weren't very fresh at the end of winter.

Water for the schoolhouse was carried from a nearby house by the older boys. In order to wash for lunch, the students lined up by the window and extended their hands outside while the teacher poured a ladle-full of water over them. Bathroom facilities were two outdoor toilets located a few feet from the school's back door and accessed by a covered walkway.

Before school let out for summer, one of the projects the teacher often gave her students was a wildflower-hunting assignment. Janet could hardly wait for the contest to see if she could bring in the biggest variety of flowers. She begged her Dad to take the whole family out to the woods so they could start gathering. Then on Monday she'd bring in her collection of flowers—and every year, the Lister kids won the competition. The teacher identified each species and made a list for the class, an exercise that taught the youngsters about Maine's bounty of beautiful wildflowers.

When kids graduated from eighth grade in any school in Maine they were given a county-wide achievement test. Janet's brother Don was the valedictorian the year he graduated and sister Joan was the top student when she graduated. "There was no doubt in my mind," recalls Janet, "that I would be Number One when it came my time, but we moved back to California so my turn never came. Dern!"

Victor, who had only a limited education, believed strongly that his children should get a high school diploma. That may have been one of the reasons he would later take his family back to California, thinking they'd be better educated there.

"As long as I can remember, my Dad always said 'If I can live long enough to see all my kids graduate from high school, I'll be happy,'" Janet recalled. "He did just that!"

○

On Rooney Road, Janet could practice her yodeling whenever she wanted, without disturbing anyone but her siblings, who didn't really count anyway, as far as she was concerned.

"During those years, what little yodeling I heard, other than my own voice," said Janet, "was on Saturday nights when we listened to the Grand Ole Opry or the shows from WWVA/Wheeling, West Virginia."

Many a day, she'd sit on the cellar door, sheltered from the wind and basking in the warmth of the sun. That cellar door was her stage, and she sang and yodeled to Mother Nature and anyone else who would listen. In the spring she'd dream about yodeling on the Grand Ole Opry in her cowboy duds or just drift off in her daydreams while smelling the lilacs blooming nearby. (That lilac bush was the only flowering plant near the house.) These were the summers and winters when she was eight, nine, ten and eleven, and she was certain that she would someday be a star, and the Grand Ole Opry was the focus of those dreams. In her mind, it was never a question of *would* she sing on the Opry, but *when*.

The Lister youngsters, especially Janet, enjoyed going in to town while their Mom did her trading. The store was near a railroad track and was situated across from the Gardiner train depot. Janet had fallen in love with trains while she was in California, and didn't miss an opportunity to drink in the majesty of those huge steam-driven machines.

But possibly as strong as her attraction to trains was the chance to hear the honky-tonk music that wafted through the doors of a nearby bar. She thrilled to the country sounds of Ernest Tubb and other hit-makers of the time during these excursions to town. It was *her* kind of music and a sound that she loved. Even at a very young age, she had found the style of music that would stay with her throughout her life.

☃

Without a doubt, Janet's favorite hobby when she was young was to practice her yodeling.

"As one of the songs that I later wrote says 'I yodeled in the fields and in the woods and even picking wild raspberries,'" she explains. "We had to walk up Rooney Road to the corner where we waited for the panel truck that was our school bus and I'd yodel at the top of my lungs as I walked along."

Her brothers and sisters quickly grew tired of the noise and often made her walk by herself. She just yodeled louder!

Her father complimented her talent in a round-about way when they were all riding in the car one day and the whole gang was singing at the top of their lungs, and Janet had a solo yodeling part. Victor leaned over and said to Aurelia, "Well, at least one of them is going to be a yodeler."

On one occasion Grammy and Grampy Blamey from California came to visit the Maine branches of their family. They stayed with the Listers for a time in that old frame house on Rooney Road and the kids loved having them there. One can only imagine how the grandparents, parents and four youngsters fared in that house with an outside toilet, no electricity and no running water.

"I remember us kids helping ourselves to Grampy's cigarettes and going out behind the barn and smoking them," recalls Janet. "There were four of us and we were all taking them. Yep…we were a bit out of control at times!"

During that visit, her grandparents bought Janet a Kay guitar. Without anyone to teach her to play and being only ten years old, she lost interest in the instrument and they decided to take it back when they left. She remembers wanting to learn to play, but didn't know how to take it to the next step, and lost this great opportunity of her young life. But the kids continued to sing and perform as a group for community activities, even though none of them had mastered the guitar, or any other instrument.

One of the first yodeling songs Janet learned to sing was "Chime Bells," a current hit. She and her siblings entered a talent contest at the Grange Hall in Whitefield and won by performing that song. Her cousin, who had been given the Kay guitar that was once Janet's, was a contestant as well, but Janet and her group beat him out in the competition. Revenge was sweet for the blonde, blue-eyed yodeling girl from Rooney Road.

In 1945, Victor and Aurelia had met a man who worked at WRDO Radio in Augusta, and decided to take the kids in to audition for a show he was hosting called *"Meet the Mike."* He heard the quartet and put the group on the radio show that very day and as often as possible in the weeks to come. They performed their gospel songs, without instruments, in full four-part harmony.

All the kids loved to sing and perform, but only Janet was obsessed with yodeling. Her determination and her love of singing, yodeling and performing would only grow stronger as she grew older.

When Joan completed eighth grade in 1946 her only option for high school was in Gardiner, about seven miles away. Victor took a job at the shoe factory there so he could take her to and from school. Having his children complete their education was very important to him, and with difficult winters and different schools for the older and younger children, he made the decision to return to California where keeping the kids in school would be somewhat easier.

Meanwhile, Victor's health wasn't improving. There were frequent coughing spells, and with the family history of tuberculosis (his father and later a brother died from complications of TB), he was deathly afraid of the possibility of contracting that terrible disease.

5

California Once Again

*This 18-feet-long, one-bed trailer
was the Listers' home from 1947 through 1953.
(Janet McBride Collection)*

It was Maine-cold and blustery that late evening of December 31st of 1946. The Listers would soon be on the road again, but this time in a 1939 two-door Chevy. Once again they took along only what they could fit in the car. They were going back west and leaving behind some of the hardest—and yet best times—that the kids could remember.

As they headed down Rooney Road for the last time, they went by Annie Kelley's house, honked the horn and waved to beat the band to their dear friend and neighbor.

"Us kids were pretty excited about going back to California," Janet recalls. "But three of us were way too small when we left California in 1941 to remember much about it."

A few days into the long trip, Aurelia was combing Joan's and Janet's hair and, much to her horror, found lice! They determined that the neighbor kids who came over to say goodbye that last night in North Whitefield must have had lice on their coats. When theirs and the Lister kids' coats were thrown together in a pile on the bed, the little critters must have crawled into the Listers' coats and later into their hair.

They stopped at the first store they could find and purchased medicated shampoo and a fine-toothed comb to treat the infestation—1947 style. "We were a sight," remembers Janet. "Mama put that smelly stuff on our hair and left it on awhile so it would work. Joan's hair was curly and mine was long and stringy, and with that soapy, oily stuff all over our heads, we looked terrible and, of course, being crammed in the car like that, we all smelled really bad!"

The trip to California took several days of driving—over pre-freeway roads through small towns, around hills and mountains. By the time they got to Uncle Jack's house they were a rag-tag bunch…and the relatively affluent California Listers could hardly believe they'd agreed to let this bunch stay at their house.

"Mama washed our hair in filling station restrooms along the way, but all she had was hand soap and that didn't work very well," recounts Janet. "We must have looked awful when we got to our Aunt and Uncle's place in California!"

Uncle Jack and Aunt Lurline lived in a different world from that of Victor and Aurelia Lister. Lurline was a seamstress for the movie studios in Hollywood, sewing for the various costumers but also for some of the actresses on a personal basis. One of her favorite customers was actress Deborah Kerr, who starred in *The King and I, An Affair to Remember* and *From Here to Eternity*. Jack worked at the studio as a lighting technician, and as a couple they brought home pretty good pay. Even with all their movie studio friends, they treated the much less affluent Victor and Aurelia and the kids well and welcomed them into their home with open arms.

Their home on Dorothy Street was beautiful and spacious for its day, considering the Listers' working-class lives. (That same area later became famous for its huge mansions, with football star O.J. Simpson one of its well-known residents.) But that two-bedroom house still would have been pretty cramped quarters when the Maine Listers moved in with their California cousins.

The money from the sale of the house on Rooney Road, less the expenditures for gasoline and food for the trip, was all that was available to Victor and Aurelia to buy a home for their transplanted family. Added to the stress of finding a suitable home was the inflated cost of houses in California. With no job on the horizon and very little cash in their pockets, they determined that a house trailer was the most viable option.

They settled into an 18-feet-long trailer home in Redondo Beach, right off Highway 101 in a lot that was not much more than a sandy field with unpaved roads. Once again the family of six was cramped into a very small space. Bathrooms, showers and laundry facilities were communal in their new trailer court home. Residents were required to sign up for use of the two wringer-type washing machines, and without dryers, the clothes were hung outside on communal clotheslines, usually by Joan and Janet.

"I remember one time my sister got shocked while she was hanging out wet clothes because some electrical wires were tied onto the clothes lines for some reason," Janet recalls. "Daddy was furious, but in those days nothing happened, except they *did* finally fix the problem."

The girls heated water for washing dishes, and the waste water from the sink drained directly into a hole dug in the sand below the trailer. Aurelia wouldn't allow the girls to cook on the small gas stove in the trailer while she was away. Quite simply, she was afraid of fire and didn't feel comfortable having the girls lighting matches without an adult around.

Aurelia and Victor slept on a bed made by folding down the dinette table, pushing the bench seats together and piling cushions on top. Joan and Janet shared a built-in bed in the back of the trailer and the two boys slept on mats on the floor. Every morning the boys had to get up early so their mats could be stored under the girls' bed, clearing space for Aurelia to make coffee and get breakfast prepared.

Safety wasn't always considered when these tiny living quarters on wheels were built during the 1940s and '50s. The Listers' trailer had only one door, and the windows were much too small for escape in case of a fire...a potential death trap. No wonder Aurelia was concerned.

With lots of kids to play with, the Lister kids enjoyed their time in the trailer camp. Without the worries parents might experience today, they were allowed to come in well after dark and no one worried about their safety. While playing "hide-and-seek" one dark night, with child-like confidence, Janet ran through an area she had been in many times. Even though she thought she knew the area well, that particular time she ran face-first straight into a wire fence. She fell backward, stunned for several minutes...and learned her lesson about running full force in the dark of night. Evidently the owner was tired of the kids running back there and had put up a fence.

Soon after their arrival, Victor was able to find work at the Fern Shoe Factory in Los Angeles, then later got a job at the Fox Theatre in Redondo Beach. He reported to work to close the theater after the last movie each evening, made sure the theater was empty and no cigarettes were left burning, and then he'd lock up. He'd clean the entire theater and make it ready for opening the next day. When one of the other janitors quit, Aurelia was asked to work there as well—and the double income was extremely welcome. The work was steady, they both enjoyed what they did and the boss appreciated their dedication.

Victor's chronic cough got worse during this time and they surmised that it had been aggravated by breathing in leather dust and glue fumes at the shoe factory. The dust he swept up at the theater only worsened his condition.

 C3

Big-city California schools were a far cry from the comfortable and personal one-room schools in Maine, and the Lister children were in no way prepared for the adjustment they would have to make.

The four youngsters attended three different schools. Aurelia walked young Danny to his school, which was close to their trailer court. Don and Joan attended another school a few blocks away and Janet walked with them as far as their school and then walked the remaining few blocks to her school alone or with some other kids she knew.

Victor and Aurelia in the lobby of the Fox Theatre.
(Janet McBride Collection)

Joan was required to wear a skirt-and-blouse uniform to school each day except Friday, when she could wear regular clothing. Don, being a boy, wasn't required to wear a uniform. Janet did not have to wear a uniform either, but for her, that wasn't a good thing. She had only one outfit and was miserable, knowing she looked very plain and poor in comparison to the other kids at school.

"Every day I wore my brown pleated skirt and fuchsia-colored sweater," she said. "I had only one sweater and one skirt to my name and soon it was obvious to all. I remember telling them once that I had several brown skirts just alike, but I'm sure they didn't believe it."

Twelve-year-old Janet felt like a fish out of water at her school and brother Don wasn't enjoying his school either. He was skipping classes and no one at home knew about it until report card time. One day Victor found him at the fishing pier when he should have been at school. He felt he just didn't fit in there, and preferred to spend his time fishing. Victor got Don to promise not to skip school anymore but allowed him to take a job as a pin-setter at the local bowling alley after school and on weekends, where he made some pretty good money. Don loved that job and the independence it gave him.

Just before school started in September of 1947, the family moved to the Victory Trailer Park, also on 101 Highway. This park had a big field across from it and sufficient sidewalk space to ride a bike, roller skate or just run free. It was larger than the one in Redondo Beach and even had paved streets. The Listers didn't own a bike or roller skates, but precocious as she was, Janet often found some boy who would loan her his skates or bicycle for as long as she wanted. There were often games of "hide and seek" after dark and many times the kids were blamed for tearing up someone's flowers or told to go home and "stop all that noise!"

Several weeks after school started that year, young Danny began having trouble with one of the teachers. Victor decided that it might be better if they just moved out of that school district into another one. All he had to do to change Danny to a different school was to move the trailer to another park, on the other side of town. Called the Lomita Lane Trailer Court, this park was also closer for the older kids to walk to school and had plenty of space to play, as well as swings and rings, making for hours of fun.

Christmas 1947 was pretty special for both Joan and Janet, because Victor bought each of the girls a Silvertone guitar from Sears. A teacher came to the trailer a few times and did his best to teach the girls how to pick out notes on the guitar. But Janet "didn't give a hoot" about how to play the *notes* for a song. What she really wanted was to play *chords* so she could accompany herself while she sang and yodeled. Although she didn't learn much about playing melody, she had learned a few chords, and that was enough to get her started. There were a couple of kids in the Lomita Lane Trailer Park who also played guitar and she learned a few more chords from them, then began to teach herself how to play rhythm as she sang.

The year 1948 passed smoothly for the Lister family. The kids stayed in school, studied hard and had a great time playing with the neighborhood kids. Victor and Aurelia continued working for the theater. And Janet continued to work on her guitar playing, singing, and, most importantly—at least in her mind—her yodeling.

Don finished high school in the spring of 1948 and joined the Army. He took his basic training at Fort Ord in California, then settled at Fort McPherson near Atlanta, Georgia, where he met Dorothy Whitmire at a USO dance and married her in 1949. Once Don moved out, there was a little more space in the trailer home for the Lister siblings and their parents. The Lister kids—now without Don—continued to do performances, receiving more offers and improving their talent at each engagement.

Sometime in 1948-49, Janet and the kids learned about a radio program hosted by a popular Los Angeles DJ who called himself "The Squeakin' Deacon." He seemed to know everyone in the country music business and his special guests often included The Maddox Brothers and Rose, Eddie Dean, Tex Williams and the like. Broadcast from the Riverside Rancho Dance Hall, half of the show was for professional singers and the other half was for amateurs. The trio performed on the amateur portion several times and, on one occasion, they won third place.

In October 1949, the Lister Trio won a contest presented at the Community Hall in Harbor City and was given an appointment with a photographer for their first professional publicity photos as their prize. This was pretty heady stuff for the siblings, and for their parents as well. With each performance they did, the dream of someday being in the big time seemed closer to reality, especially for Janet.

When Don bought the family a television set in late 1949, Janet fell in love with the various western music shows like *Gene Autry's Melody Ranch*, the *Smokey Rogers Show*, *The Tex Williams Show*, Cliffie Stone's *Hometown Jamboree*, *Town Hall Party* and others. Her teenage world revolved around country and western music. She knew who every radio DJ was, learned every song they played and knew who sang each song. She often did her school homework sitting in the car out in front of the trailer while listening to the music she loved on the car radio. Her dream of being there with all those music stars only grew stronger as she grew older.

☙

The family moved again in late 1949, this time to the Oasis Trailer Court. With private toilet and shower facilities, this one was a real step up for the Listers. Janet remembers two avocado trees and several apricot trees on the property. When she'd find an avocado that had fallen from the tree she'd pick it up before anyone else saw it and run for home. Mr. Nutter, the park owner, often complained about the kids climbing the apricot trees and eating the fruit. Some of the kids were just too heavy and were breaking limbs and damaging the shed roofs that they climbed on, so he had reason to complain.

Janet and school friends, 1949.
(Janet McBride Collection)

Victor and Aurelia believed that there just might be a chance that the Lister kids would have a place in the world of professional country music one day, and, for Christmas 1949, they thrilled the girls by giving them each a Martin 000-15 guitar! Martin guitars have never been inexpensive, but whatever the cost, this double gift would certainly have meant significant sacrifice on the part of the Lister parents and it's evident that they were pretty sure that at least one of the girls would have a future in music someday.

Janet, Joan & Danny in their first promo shot.
(Janet McBride Collection)

As was the case back in Maine, at the Oasis Park, Janet could take advantage of having hardly any close neighbors...and yodel as loud and as often as she chose. On more than one occasion, when the trailer site on either side of the Listers' was vacant, she'd watch while the owner showed the space to a potential renter. Inside her family's trailer, Janet would grab her guitar, sit on the bed and sing and yodel as loud as she could, hoping to scare the potential tenant away. "I didn't think I was being mean or anything," she recalls. "I just figured it would save a lot of time for all concerned because no one ever stayed next to us for very long after hearing me yodel," she now explains. "They would just move somewhere else in the trailer court. It never occurred to me that the owner might have asked Daddy to shut me up, but if he did, Daddy never mentioned it to me."

Don and his wife Dot moved to California when he was transferred back to Fort Ord about 80 miles south of San Francisco to spend his remaining Army hitch there. When he was discharged in February of 1950, he searched diligently but was unable to find work, so the young couple made the decision to go back to Maine where Don had friends.

Joan graduated from high school that spring, and early that fall, Victor and Aurelia decided that the family should be together, and they once again

*Janet, Danny & Joan, (The Lister Trio) after winning the Harbor City Talent
Contest but before Janet and Joan received their Martin 000-15 guitars.
(Janet McBride Collection)*

made plans to return to their beloved New England home. "Daddy must have
thought it would work this time and he and Mama would be home at last,"
said Janet. "I loved the 'feel' of Maine, and was really happy to be going
back."

Just a few weeks before they left California, the kids entered a talent
contest sponsored by a local TV station. They appeared on the popular
television show called *The Hollywood Road to Fame* and won first place
for their efforts. They each received a nice quality watch as their prize.

6

Maine and Back Again

*Towing their trailer home with their 1946 Buick,
the Listers made their way back to Maine.
(Janet McBride Collection)*

The Listers arrived back in Maine with their trailer in tow in mid-September 1950. They parked it in Uncle Bill's driveway in Chelsea. Not wishing to spend a long Maine winter in a trailer, they moved into a three-room apartment on the second floor of Janet's cousin Christine's house in Gardiner, located within walking distance to the school that Janet and Danny would be attending.

When Don and Dot first arrived in Maine they had lived in a cabin on Rooney Road for a short time, then moved into a small apartment. Soon they found a nicer apartment in a lady's home where Dot was to babysit for the owner in exchange for their rent. Some of their belongings were already moved into the apartment when it and everything inside were destroyed by fire. There was nothing left to do but move in with Victor, Aurelia and the kids. That meant those three rooms that were already full of beds and people became even more crowded. The young couple slept on a small bed on a ledge beside the stairway.

Once they were settled again in Maine, the youngsters went right back to singing as The Lister Trio over the "Meet the Mike" radio show in Augusta and picked up gigs playing for their supper at potluck get-togethers. The group became The Lister Quartet when Don sang with them, this time playing an oil-drum bass. Joan and Janet were playing guitar well enough to accompany the group and, with the addition of Don's bass, they had a full, rounded-out sound. Singing for their supper meant that seven people would sit down

Janet, Danny & Joan as The Lister Trio. (Janet McBride Collection)

to a good meal. Janet remembers eating a "a lot of beans and meat loaf, but it was wonderful."

On her first day at Gardiner High, Janet settled in to her new classes without a hitch. Lunchtime came and she was making new friends when she asked someone if they knew her cousin Norman Marquis who was in the same school. There was a gasp or two and then someone explained that her cousin had told some of the guys that Norman was anxious to meet the new girl. They couldn't wait to tell him that Janet was his *cousin*.

Bob and Marie Paulin became new friends of the Listers during this stay in Maine. Bob had been a member of Hank Snow's band for a short time and maintained his friendship with Hank his entire life. He read about The Listers in the newspaper, looked them up and soon was booking appearances for the group and presenting shows with The Listers as headliners. They were gaining good experience in entertaining various types of audiences—and for the first time, they were being paid real money to perform. One particular highlight of their career in Maine came when they were invited to perform for the Governor's Christmas Party.

ଓ

By then, three members of the Lister family—Joan, Don and Victor—were working at the shoe factory in Gardiner and the kids were singing whenever they could. But making ends meet seemed harder than ever and Victor's hopes for a better life for his family weren't working out well. They were all crowded into that small apartment and were barely able to keep food on the table, let alone do anything special or buy anything new.

Christmas 1950 came, and their only Christmas gifts were some items that Joan bought each of them with her Christmas bonus from her shoe factory job. Janet recalls choosing underwear as her gift.

Even with his job at the shoe factory, Don was unable to make a decent living in Maine, barely enough to pay their part of the rent, and he grew restless. Don and two of his friends, Norman Carter and a young

Hank Snow and Bob Paulin
(Janet McBride Collection)

Micmac Indian man named Barney, pooled their money, loaded up Dot and what belongings they could in their 1940 two-door Dodge and left Maine for the last time. They traveled through Atlanta to visit Dot's family, where they were given sandwiches and drinks enough to make it to California without having to spend any of their $70 on food. They got just outside of San Bernardino and spent the last of their cash—plus traded two quarts of oil they had brought along—on gas. It was just enough to get them to Norman's Dad's house in Ojai where the car ran out of gas in the driveway.

෪

Back in Maine, Victor realized that this trip back to New England had been a mistake. "Daddy decided when Don left, that he and the family would also return to California," said Janet. "My mother's youngest sister had married her second husband Norman McCracken and it was Uncle Norman who sent Daddy and Mama enough money to make the trip back to California."

So, in January of 1951, the family made preparations to move yet again, this time on a sad note, because they all thought that they had returned to Maine to stay, but it had lasted only six months.

A favorite story of Janet's is about an incident that happened when the Listers approached Dallas, Texas, on their way back to California. The kids knew all about the Big D Jamboree from radio and figured that maybe they could appear on that famous stage if their dad could just get a job at a nearby shoe factory that Victor knew about. For miles and miles they begged him to give it a try. Possibly to quiet the kids down, Victor stopped at the factory and went in but came out saying "They said they don't need me." He started up the Buick (with the trailer towed behind) and headed on west. The youngsters' hearts were broken, for awhile at least, as they watched Dallas—and their Big D Jamboree dream—fade away in the rear view mirror.

Victor pulled their trailer clear across the country once again and the family settled in the Victory Trailer Park on Highway 101, where they had lived in 1947 and 1948.

The youngsters were enrolled again in Narbonne High School in Lomita; Janet was a junior and Danny was a freshman. Aurelia and Victor went back to work at the Fern Shoe Factory in downtown Los Angeles.

When Aurelia had worked at the theater before the move to Maine, and now as she worked in the factory, she was gaining a new sense of purpose and independence. She was earning a paycheck and was no longer just a housewife who rarely saw anyone other than her children and her husband. She enjoyed talking with the other women who had different experiences and lives and it made a difference in how she felt about herself. Not only did she begin making her own friends, but she could also buy things for the children. Working outside her home made her life fuller.

cx

One afternoon their trailer court on Highway 101 was the scene of a heated argument. A neighbor had a habit of beating on his pregnant wife and one day Victor had had enough and confronted him. Victor, who was only 5'7" at best, told him to pick on somebody his own size, and some shoving ensued. It became serious enough that Aurelia ran to the phone booth to call for help. Somebody tried to pull Aurelia out—remember she was only 4'11"—which angered Victor even more, and the brawl intensified. Janet ran into their trailer and grabbed Victor's gun, made sure it was loaded and then ran out amidst the combatants, held the gun in the air and told everyone that they'd better stop fighting and not to hurt her Mama! Someone wrestled the gun away from Janet and threw it in the bushes. About that time the police arrived, retrieved the gun and gave it to Victor advising him to "keep it away from that kid!" No one went to jail or was ticketed, but it was an exciting afternoon for certain, and was probably discussed for years to come. Little did Janet know that a few years later she would have to explain her part in "the trailer court brawl" when she applied for her job with the F.B.I.

Before the War and even before the first trip back to Maine, Victor had come to enjoy horse racing (or at least betting on the horses). He often took

One of Janet's first "beauty queen" shots, taken in 1950. (Janet McBride Collection) (Janet McBride Collection)

Aurelia and the kids to the Hollywood Park Racetrack, where Don spent his time gathering discarded tickets. "From early on I can remember Mama taking home a big bag or two of old tickets to check against the day's race program to see if anyone ever threw away a winning ticket," recalls Janet. "Once she *did* find a winner, but that was when I was very young."

The men who worked with Victor at the shoe factory had access to a
bookie, and he and the boys liked to bet a few bucks each week if they
could. "Daddy bought a racing form almost every day as long as he lived,"
Janet remembers.

଎

The Listers hadn't been in California long when, one wonderful day,
Bob and Marie Paulin unexpectedly showed up on their California doorstep.
"We were all really surprised and happy to see them," Janet recalls. "Bob
was my mentor; he taught me the guitar chords to my songs and he always
invited me to be on any show where he was playing."

Midway through high school, Janet began to make plans for a fall-back
career in case her music dream was slow in coming. In her junior and senior
years she emphasized business courses: typing, bookkeeping and shorthand.
She made plans to go to work after high school to help her parents with the
bills and work on her music career on the side. She needed to be able to
support herself whether she lived in her parents' home or moved out and
went on her own—and music might not pay the bills.

"Most of my high school friends went on to college and became
teachers after we graduated," Janet said, "and I am so proud of them, but my
life was going down a different path from theirs. Many would say 'Boy, did it
ever!'"

Generally ill at ease in social situations with boys, Janet didn't actually
date until well after she graduated from high school. When a boy from her
trailer park asked Janet to his senior prom during her junior year, she chose
not to go, for a lot of reasons but mostly because her parents would have to
buy a dress and all the trimmings. She was 17 at the time, a pretty and
engaging girl, but totally frightened of being out on a date with a boy. She had
no idea how to act and it was easier to say "no," so she did.

Janet did have several close girlfriends, one of whom was Carol
Franklin. Carol's family had a cabin at Big Bear Lake in the San Bernardino
National Forest, where several mothers took a group of the girls for a get-
away during the summer of 1951. Janet was thrilled to be invited because
she had never done anything like that before. The mothers fed the girls
wonderful meals and took them to the local pool every day, a real treat for a
young trailer park resident. After graduation the next year, the Franklin
family took the girls one last time before they went on to work or college.
That time, Bob Paulin and his brother rented a truck and hauled several bikes
up to Big Bear for the girls.

Janet, her brother Danny and their friend Don Snow got together often to practice their songs and played a gig or two. Snow's girlfriend's mother managed the snack bar at the Harbor Drive-in Theatre and Don was able to get a part time job there. Joe Greene, owner of the drive-in, devised a way to entertain the people who came early by having an auction with play money called "Greene Bucks." Don asked Greene if the trio could sing a few songs before and after the auction. Before long, several other young musicians joined them in this endeavor and Bob Paulin was added on lead guitar. Don Snow played steel guitar, Al Poston sang and played rhythm guitar and Stew Magoo (aka Gerald Sanford) was the drummer. They called themselves "The Harbor Playboys." Again, Janet was gaining "lots of experience" and enjoyed "hanging out" with music friends on Sunday nights. Their pay was a hotdog, a Coke and a candy bar.

Two weeks after graduation from high school, Janet took a job with the FBI in Los Angeles, where her sister and a friend were working. She was a clerk there from 1952 until 1954. Still naïve in the ways of the world, Janet learned a great lesson there: to keep her mouth shut and not make waves if she wanted to keep her job. It was a government job and some of the workers who had been there several years were doing nothing more than holding down a chair, while the newer workers were left to do the work, at least in Janet's opinion. She asked management why so many people didn't have *anything* to do and others had *more* than they could do. She was quickly reassigned to another position where she worked alone in the mimeograph room. Among other tasks, she was responsible for addressing and mailing the FBI's "Ten Most Wanted" flyers. Generally, she

Janet and Danny in a promo shot
taken in 1954.
(Janet McBride Collection)

54

*Bob Paulin (second from right, on guitar) with Janet
and The Harbor Playboys, 1953.
(Janet McBride Collection)*

liked the job and even got to see John Wayne once when he was in the
building. But the FBI wasn't something she wanted to stay with for a long
time and she began to look for other opportunities.

In late 1952, brother Don and his wife Dorothy were living in a trailer
but decided to buy a home in nearby Redondo Beach. Victor and Aurelia
took over their trailer payments so the family could move into this larger,
nicer trailer. It was a one-bedroom unit with a bathroom and shower, a nice
kitchen and living room with a couch that made into a bed. Janet and Joan,
now 19 and 21, were given the bedroom, since both girls were paying rent.
Victor and Aurelia slept on the couch bed and Danny slept in the old trailer,
which was parked next door.

Janet found a position in the mail room at Northrop Aircraft, a plant
where missiles and trainer aircraft were built, and went to work there as
soon as she left the FBI. She started out as a messenger, making more
money than she had at her previous job and was able to work significantly
closer to home. Extra hours on Saturday morning meant overtime and a little
more money in her paycheck. She worked in the mail room for ten years,
and, for much of that time, was in charge of incoming and outgoing mail,
including top secret mail, for the whole plant. She loved her job and did it well
and met some wonderful people there—and began to grow into a decisive,
more confident young adult.

At home, the family dynamic was changing. Joan married Lawrence
Dearborn in June of 1954 and the couple moved to a small apartment on his
grandmother's property and lived there while they built their home in Lomita.

Now, with both Don and Joan off on their own, only Janet and Danny were left at home, and, at last, there was a bit of space for stretching.

7

Tall, Dark and Handsome

*Handsome and a fan of country music,
young Claude McBride stepped into
Janet's life in 1954.
(Janet McBride Collection)*

JoAnn Russell, Janet's new friend and her co-worker at Northrop, asked her one day in the summer of 1954 if she'd like to fly with her down to San Diego to meet some guys she knew from Arkansas.

Janet had never even been in an airplane and she certainly didn't want to pass up an opportunity like this one, even if her ticket was going to cost $18, quite a bit of money for a young working woman. When they arrived at the San Diego Airport, the guys who were supposed to meet them were nowhere in sight. Janet was frightened and had no clue what to do next, but JoAnn grabbed a shuttle and into San Diego they went. "Thank goodness JoAnn was braver than me," said Janet, "because I'd still be standing at the airport waiting for someone to pick us up."

While they were waiting for a connecting bus, they ran into one of the guys who was supposed to have met them at the airport. He was a tall, good-looking sailor named Claude McBride, who seemed to be noticeably hung-over at the time.

"JoAnn jumped all over him for not meeting us like he was supposed to," Janet recalls. "That should have been a clue for me but I was way too green to see the signs."

McBride had not made a favorable first impression on Janet and she even had a fleeting feeling that she should maybe put some distance between herself and this young man.

After that trip to San Diego, Janet and JoAnn started hanging out with a bunch of JoAnn's friends, including the McBride boys (Claude and his brother Mac). Janet often took her guitar along when they went to the park, the beach, or wherever the gang would gather. After a while, feelings began to change and soon Claude and Janet were showing signs of become a couple. He loved country music and that may have been what initially encouraged their relationship to gain a foothold. Victor didn't care much for Claude and made no bones about it, but Janet was hard-headed and began to date this new tall, dark and handsome man in her life.

Janet, with her Martin guitar, entertains Claude (left) and other friends. (Janet McBride Collection)

Claude Mcbride, Janet admits, "was the first boy I had ever gone out with more than once and I just didn't know much about boys. But he loved my country music and that was important to me! He was extremely good-looking and I was smitten big-time!"

Claude and Janet, young sweethearts.
(Janet McBride Collection)

Walks on the beach or in the park, sing-alongs with friends, or parties at someone's house occupied the couple's courting period, as neither could afford to go to movies or out to dinner.

Soon they began talking about getting married. On November 2 that year, Claude turned 18, but even then, he couldn't get married without parental consent and they refused to give it.

ભ

Meanwhile, Victor's cough and bronchial problems were progressively becoming worse. Then, in 1954, he was diagnosed with tuberculosis. All those years of bloody coughing spells finally began to make sense and his fears of following in his father's footsteps had come true.

He was placed in quarantine at what was then Harbor General Hospital in Torrance. They would have quarantined him at home, but because Danny was a minor, they had to remove Victor from his home. Of course, his illness meant that his paycheck stopped. "I had never felt sorry for my folks before then," said Janet, "but when they took Daddy away and told him he couldn't come home again until he was cured, he really seemed to lose his spark."

Without Victor's income, Aurelia was unable to keep up the payments on the trailer they were buying. She sold it and rented another one in Torrance so she would be on the bus route into Los Angeles and could get to work at the shoe factory on her own. Janet continued to live with her mother, paying rent and helping out with the chores.

Victor and Aurelia had lived so many years side by side that Victor just couldn't handle being without her. She had a phone put in the trailer, her first one ever, so at least he could call and talk to her. After a while, he became so homesick and restless that many times he called Aurelia and asked her to send Janet to meet him. He'd slide under the fence and sneak off the hospital grounds. Janet sneaked him into the car and took him home to stay as long as he dared. Aurelia didn't seem able to refuse him these unauthorized

Aurelia and Victor relaxing during a camping excursion, 1954.
(Janet McBride Collection)

visits…and they did give him a degree of happiness. Janet remembers seeing the two of them just sitting quietly holding hands during his short stays at the house. Sometimes he'd call her by his nickname for her: "Reallie." It was obvious to Janet that they truly loved each other.

ભ

Claude and Janet took Aurelia with them to Quartzsite, Arizona, one night in December of 1954 with the intention of having Aurelia sign for Claude so they could get married. But she, like his mother, refused to sign so the trio drove back home without accomplishing the young couple's hidden agenda for the trip.

In January of 1955, with a more workable plan in mind, Claude and Janet picked up his brother Bill and his wife Joyce who lived in San Diego, and drove to Ensenada, Baja California, to be married. They drove the extra miles down to Ensenada because some of Claude's sailor buddies found out the hard way that Tijuana marriages weren't always legal. If Janet was to receive Claude's allotment check, the marriage had to be legally recognized.

Once in Ensenada they found a place where the townsfolk said they could get married. After handing over money to first one person and then another, someone finally agreed to marry them. The marriage certificate was in Spanish but it had an official seal and a number, and they needed that number. A clerk wrote their names and the certificate number into a large book and they both signed it. That book was to be sent to Mexico City where each entry would be registered. The catch was that the book had to be full before it would be sent.

After the ceremony they headed back toward Torrance where Janet was living with her mother. They had enough money for a cheap motel room or a tank of gas, but not both. They chose to get a room and after that expense had only twenty-five cents between them. No money for breakfast and the car was running on fumes, but somehow they made it to the Lister trailer. Claude wanted some breakfast and, even though Janet didn't have a clue about how to fix an egg, Aurelia didn't offer to help. Her daughter was married now and on her own and had to learn to take care of her new husband... and the egg was a disaster!

Janet went to work the next day and Claude had to be back on base before Sunday night, and as for many a newlywed couple, there was no time or money for a honeymoon.

Claude was stationed 120 miles away in San Diego. There was no freeway to San Diego in those days, only Highway 101. Without a car on base, if he wanted to get home to spend time with Janet, he either caught a ride with other sailors or hitched a ride with anyone who was heading that way.

At first, when he was able to get home for the weekend, he and Janet would visit with friends and family, and on Sunday night when he had to return, she'd drive him as far down Highway 101 as she dared, all the time watching the gas gauge. She knew how much gas she'd need for the drive home and how much she'd need to get to work all week. She'd let him out along the highway and he'd thumb his way back to the base, a scenario that was carried out by many a serviceman across the country. That routine started the very first weekend after they were married and continued for a long time. Surprisingly, Claude always managed to be back on base in time.

Only 18 years old when they married, Claude was accustomed to a life of partying and running around. Unable or unwilling to accept the responsibility of having a wife, he couldn't seem to give up his single lifestyle and turn himself into a dependable husband. His lack of maturity and inability to handle responsibility hurt Janet deeply during this vulnerable period in her life, but it was only a preview of things to come.

Soon after their marriage, Claude decided that he wanted to be a medical corpsman and took classes to that end while he was in San Diego. Janet was all for it and had hopes that this field of study would help him find work in the medical field when he got out of the Navy. He began working as an X-ray technician at the San Diego Medical Center in Balboa.

The young wife soon realized that that hospital became Claude's garden, full of fresh fruit in the form of young, unattached women. Claude was handsome and had a great personality and he was able to talk his way into just about anything he wanted—and often that meant the company of pretty, young nurses.

Janet's family members were concerned about the situation with Claude and Janet and probably had many conversations about it. She still hadn't admitted to anyone that there were any problems, not her friends and not her family. Everyone around her knew about Claude's wandering eye...but Janet clung to the hope that things would get better.

Just a few weeks after they married, Janet found out she was pregnant. She looked forward with excitement to her baby's birth, but had no idea how the bills were going to get paid. Like many first-time mothers-to-be, she had no clue about the huge responsibilities that come with having a baby.

She was working as a messenger at the aircraft plant and the rules were pretty plain. She broke those rules, however, when she delayed going out on pregnancy leave because she feared living without her paycheck. She was able to conceal her condition until late April and decided if she pushed it any longer she would risk being fired and could lose her job and the healthcare benefits that went with it.

Janet managed the family's finances alone...and money was tight. She had carefully budgeted for her car payment and other bills. In addition, they still owed on their wedding rings and she paid rent to her mother for staying in the family home.

"I grew up understanding that the bills had to be paid first and many times it would mean there wasn't much left," recalled Janet. "More than once I borrowed $5 from Mama for gas until payday."

Even with their combined salaries, there was no money to buy another car for Claude to use on the naval base. He started driving Janet's car to base and she rode to work with some other gals. She hated their cigarette smoke, but by then she had no choice but to ride with the others since Victor's car had been sold.

Janet and Claude had been married only about three months and she was pregnant with Denise when her brother Dan saw Janet's car one Friday night over by the honky-tonks in Lomita. Claude was driving it. Dan called Janet wondering what was up. She told him he must be mistaken because she hadn't seen Claude or heard from him. He had told her he wasn't able to come home that weekend and she said it couldn't have been him. Late that Sunday night, Claude came by the trailer acting like he had just arrived in town and only had a minute to say "hi and goodbye." That was the beginning of a pattern.

Finally Janet's maternity leave began and she could leave the smoky air of her co-worker's car behind. But leave meant no paycheck and when that first allotment check arrived, five months after their marriage, it was no doubt extremely welcomed by the young mother-to-be!

Instead of going to San Diego and the naval hospital for free prenatal care, Janet chose instead to take advantage of her medical insurance from work and use a doctor who was closer to home. Staying near her family was more important to her than receiving free care.

On the evening of March 16, 1955, Janet, brother Dan and his new wife Jean visited Victor in the hospital and found him looking extremely frail. They talked about the grandchild that she and Claude would be giving him and Dan and Jean talked about their new marriage. Victor seemed happy to hear the family's good news, but hated being in the hospital and seemed to understand that he might never be well again.

That night he suffered a massive heart attack and died.

Although not altogether unexpected, Victor's death was devastating to Janet who hated that he would never see any of his grandchildren. She was deeply concerned about her mother's future without Victor—about both the emotional and economic impact that his death would bring.

After living several years in tight quarters with Victor, one might think that Aurelia and the Lister kids could have had a tendency toward tuberculosis, and indeed they were given chest x-rays by the County of Los Angeles. Only Janet's lungs showed anything questionable. They found a scar on one lung, but decided it was from something other than TB, and evidently they were correct in their diagnosis, because she has never had any pulmonary problems, although she carries that scar yet today.

CB

Janet and The Harbor Playboys continued to sing at local night clubs on Friday and Saturday nights for many months, even after she was pregnant. They were paid $5.00 each per night and were thrilled to get it. Bob Paulin was able to arrange a dance gig or two for the Playboys during that time, which brought in some much-needed cash. But nothing happened that would give the group the break it needed to move up in the music business.

Their longest running gig was at Bill's Inn, located on Western Avenue in Los Angeles. A truly hometown group of people patronized the place and Janet counts this gig as one of the more enjoyable ones she experienced during this time.

In late May, while she was on maternity leave, Janet heard they were auditioning talent for a big housewives' talent show to be held on Cliffie Stone's TV show called *Hometown Jamboree*. Stone was a well known DJ, entertainer and promoter in the Los Angeles area. His *Hometown Jamboree* was second in line only to *Town Hall Party* in popularity. Women interested in becoming a contestant were invited to come to the radio station in Pasadena. Janet decided to give it a try.

She arrived early so she could watch the program as it was broadcast and then do her audition after the broadcast went off the air. "I had watched that television show for years and secretly wanted to go watch the entertainers perform," she recalls. "Even if I didn't win anything, I would have realized one of my dreams."

She was thrilled to be able to see some of the best known southern California country and western artists of the day on that program. Her audition went well and she was asked to be on their first night of the housewives' talent competition shows.

The contest lasted over a twelve-week period and Janet was a bit concerned about being quite pregnant when the finals would happen later. Women in advanced pregnancy weren't usually seen on television and she hoped that this wouldn't cause any problems.

Janet & The Harbor Playboys.
(Left to right) Stew, Al, Janet, Don and John)
(Janet McBride Collection)

With no real thoughts of winning the entire contest, Janet was "there for the party" and certainly wanted to see how far she could go. She did her homework by watching all of the programs and checking out the competitors as the contest progressed.

At last, finals night came. To Janet's pleasant surprise, country star Faron Young was the special guest that night.

"Faron Young was the Garth Brooks or Alan Jackson of my day," said Janet. Being a country performer and having a well-known country singer as a special guest gave her a few extra doses of confidence. "I was the only country singer in the contest," smiled Janet. "I walked out on stage, sang and yodeled "Chime Bells" and it was all over for those other ladies." The crowd was "standing room only" that night and the other two ladies just didn't have a chance with that Faron Young crowd. It was Janet's contest to win.

Even six months pregnant and "big as a barrel" (her words), she stood out above the competition that night and won a houseful of furniture...with no house to put it in! Among her gifts were a stove, refrigerator, washer, kitchen table and chairs, a sofa and chair, a rocker, a television set and a two-piece bedroom set. Janet felt it was truly a gift from God.

She had put most of her allotment money in a savings account and it was that money that made the down payment on a three-bedroom house in the town of Wilmington. It was a tract home that had been a rental. She bought the house on a sales contract with $200 down and a payment of $58 per month. In mid-October, 1955, she and Claude moved into their new house.

Janet hadn't lived in a real house since the move from North Whitefield, Maine, in December of 1946, and hadn't had the luxury of a bathtub since 1942.

8

Peaks and Valleys

*Pregnant and still performing. Janet
with Don Snow of The Harbor Playboys
at "Bill's Inn," 1955.
(Janet McBride Collection)*

*Janet, Claude, Bob and Joyce Holliman, Jim and Joann Davis,
out for dinner, celebrating some unknown occasion, 1955.*

On November 8th, 1955, friends took Janet to the hospital and called her husband to let him know that their baby was coming. He arrived at almost the same time that the baby was born, a little girl they named Denise.

Because Aurelia had to work, they decided that Janet would go to Claude's parents' house when she left the hospital. Her parents-in-law took care of her until she was strong enough to take the baby home to her own house, just a few blocks away.

Janet sang at the Harbor Drive-In with the band until after Denise was born.* She took a week off from singing to have the baby and a few times even took the baby with her when she was performing there, but eventually quit the gig so she could take better care of little Denise.

In June of 1956, she was fed up with her marriage and visited a lawyer with plans to begin divorce proceedings. Her motivation wasn't only to get out of her marriage to Claude. There was another man in the picture. Janet had become infatuated with a married musician who was driving her to their gigs. They found each other easy to talk to, and no doubt they discussed

---

*A photo of Janet and the Harbor Playboys singing at the Harbor Drive-In appears in the
Yodel Aa Eeee Oooo book by Bart Plantenga (Released internationally in 2004.)*

many personal problems. "I was pretty easy pickings for anyone who gave me some special attention," she explained. When Janet began to talk about getting a divorce, the guy backed off, warning her that if they were ever to be together, her child wasn't welcome and wouldn't be part of the picture. With those few words, the relationship was over.

As the weeks moved on, she came to realize that this man had had no real interest in her as a person and she vowed never to allow herself to be taken in like that again. That experience would come to mind anytime some man started talking to her about some great music opportunity and she felt like there were strings attached.

"Anyway, I wanted to believe that one magic day, Claude would change like he promised," Janet said.

In late '56 or early '57, Claude was transferred to a small Naval hospital in Corona, California. Janet was excited to learn that her husband would have weekends off and could come home. But he would need a car.

"He chose a 1956 T-bird hardtop convertible!" recalls Janet. "I can just imagine how cool he looked as he was cruising in to work in a car that was nicer than most of the officers' cars. I can't believe I agreed to that car, but I did. You'll do a lot of things to let someone know how much you care for them."

Janet had a beautiful daughter to love—but wished with all her heart that Claude would spend more time at home being a husband and father. "I spent many lonely Friday and Saturday nights going crazy with my visions of what was happening," Janet recollected. "I'd rock Denise and we'd both cry for hours. I had to work Saturday morning, and many times went in with little sleep and with red, swollen eyes."

Unfortunately Claude's ways only got worse. Janet can't explain why she didn't just leave him, but she had watched other young mothers struggle to get by without a husband and was fearful of going that route, so she stayed married.

൙

When Claude was discharged from the Navy in October of 1957, a neighbor helped him get a job with the company he worked for, but it didn't last long. In 1958 he found a manufacturing job in a plant not too far from their house. He liked this job and the guys he worked with, but soon transferred to second shift without discussing it with Janet. After work, he started hanging around the honky-tonks on Highway 101 in Lomita. These clubs were country to the core and he was a nightly customer, drinking and talking with entertainers and flirting with gals. Afterwards he came home and slept until it was time to go to work again in mid-afternoon. Life was relatively easy for Claude while Janet worked and took care of the kids, the house and the finances.

Claude met a local songwriter gal named Rusty Nail at one of the clubs, and the talk came around to Janet and her singing. They arranged a meeting at Rusty's house and the songwriter invited Janet to "demo" some of her songs for Capitol Records. Janet especially liked one song called "Let Those Brown Eyes Smile at Me" and let Rusty know that she wanted to record it. Shortly thereafter, she was driving home from work one evening and heard Rose Maddox singing that song on the radio. Evidently Rusty's intention was to pitch the song to Capitol Records but Janet was wanting Capitol to hear *her* singing it, hoping that her voice and that song would be seen as a package. She was heartbroken because she had hoped to put the song out herself, but Capitol already had Maddox under contract and it was given to her.

ଔ

Los Angeles was experiencing a heat wave on September 15, 1958 and Janet, pregnant with her second baby, was on her first day of maternity leave from Northrop. She planned to spend the day with her daughter and Claude. But her sister-in-law Dorothy had called the evening before and asked if Janet would drive her to the Moulin Rouge Supper Club in Hollywood to see the *Queen for a Day* show. Originally Janet's sister Joan had planned to go with Dorothy, but Joan was having problems with her own pregnancy and couldn't go. They asked Janet if she would like to use Joan's ticket and do the driving. Dot agreed to pay for the gas and the plan was a go.

As someone who worked days, Janet wasn't familiar with the popular daytime TV show and how it worked. Each ticket had a small area for the audience members to write out a wish and Janet couldn't think of an appropriate wish so Claude wrote one for her. His two teenage brothers, who lived with the family back in Arkansas, were in serious need of school clothes and supplies, and his wish was for them.

Dressed for hot weather, with no hose, high heels or make-up and sporting a ponytail, Janet took her place in line outside the building where the audience members were asked to wait. Attendants came out and picked up the "wish" ends of their tickets, and finally the large group of ladies was ushered into the cool theater. The women ordered salads and cool drinks and found a table. Someone on the stage announced that if he called their ticket number they were to come down to the front. Surprisingly, Janet's ticket number was the first one called!

About 20 ladies were brought to the stage. Each contestant was interviewed about their wishes and each semi-finalist was given a clock radio as a prize. Then five finalists were chosen...and Janet was one of them.

Jack Bailey, the host of the popular daytime television program, asked each finalist about her wish. Janet told about Claude's Arkansas brothers, their living conditions and how they were trying to save up for clothes, shoes and other items for school. She added that Claude had left some of his own clothes for them the last time they'd been there.

Each of the finalists had very worthwhile wishes but none were quite like Janet's. The applause meter was brought out and Jack Bailey put his hand above each lady's head and asked for the audience's reaction to each wish.

To her surprise, Janet was named "Queen for a Day!" "They came and got me, put that beautiful robe on me, put flowers in my arms and sat me down in that throne on the middle of the stage."

They gave her certificates for shoes and clothes from the Speigel catalog and a check to cover school items for the brothers. Then, to her astonishment, they starting bringing out prizes for Janet herself...a refrigerator, some small appliances, clothes, jewelry, a trip, a seven-piece bedroom set, luggage, a recliner and fancy new stove that hung on the wall, plus a Speigel's gift certificate.

"The delivery trucks brought stuff to our home for weeks after that," Janet laughed. "It was awesome!" They were living in the tract home in Wilmington and the wiring was inadequate for the stove, so they sold it and put the money on their car loan. They sold the chair and refrigerator and used the Speigel gift certificate to buy a baby crib.

"When I think of all the good luck I had in those days I should have known that it was the Lord's will and that He was watching out for me," Janet said. "But I wasn't really thinking along those lines during those times."

ⓒⓈ

On February 1, 1959, the couple's second child, Claude Jr., was born. He was a big, healthy baby, 8 lbs, 4 oz., and a sweet-mannered baby as well.

On a warm September day in 1958, Janet was crowned "Queen for a Day" and won appliances, furniture, clothing and more. The popular daytime show was broadcast nationally on radio from 1945-1957 and on NBC television from 1956 through 1964.
Janet is shown with TV host Jack Bailey.
(Janet McBride Collection)

In about six weeks, just enough time to regain her strength, Janet returned to work. She needed that paycheck.

In April of that year, Janet received a note from the folks at *Town Hall Party* saying she was accepted to appear on their talent contest show. She performed on the show twice, once singing and yodeling "Chime Bells" and won that round, but was beat out on her second appearance, when she sang a George Morgan song, "I'm in Love Again," which had only a very short yodel break and she wasn't able to "wow" the audience in any way with that number. By that time Janet knew that "just a yodeler" wasn't going to make it in the business so she wanted them to know she could sing a ballad, too.

It was sometime in 1959 that Claude's brother Mac talked him into applying for work at Standard Oil Company of California. When he got the job, Janet was thrilled because the pay was good and the position included insurance, a pension and security. She believed that it was a job for a lifetime, with retirement benefits, and would provide a better life for her and the kids. At Standard Oil, Claude once again chose to work the second shift, so he could "go clubbing" after he got off work.

In 1960 the couple bought a nicer home that was closer to their jobs and in a better school district. Denise started school in Redondo Beach the September before she turned five years old in November.

Life was relatively comfortable for the McBride family. They had good paychecks, a nice home, and were close to Janet's brother Don, whose wife Dorothy often babysat Denise and Claude Jr. But the picture was not entirely rosy as Janet continued to spend lots of time at home with only the two kids for company, and her husband seldom there.

9
The Pro Stage

A publicity photo from 1962.
(Janet McBride Collection)

Throughout 1959, Claude continued to hang out at clubs. He enjoyed meeting the entertainers who were performing there, always promoting his singing-and-yodeling wife. Johnny and Jonie Mosby, who would become known to national audiences in the 1960s and '70s, were playing the LA club circuit at that time and were performing at one of the clubs that Claude frequented in Lomita. He talked them into letting Janet perform with them on one of their sets. When the invitation came she accepted joyfully, and, after singing with the duo, they invited her to sing for a new show that Johnny and his band were starting in the area.

"Johnny taught me to move with the rhythm of the song, clap my hands and enjoy myself on stage, not to just stand there and sing," recalled Janet. "I was scared to death and it showed, but I was so excited about that gig because I knew being on a show with Johnny Mosby and his band would get me noticed!"

But the joy lasted only that one weekend. Apparently Claude had done something that upset Johnny and, by the time Janet got home and into bed, Johnny called Claude and told him that he wouldn't be needing Janet's services after all.

In late 1959, Claude started hanging out at a club called George's Round-up, where West Coast country star Wynn Stewart and his band were playing. Wynn was one of the hottest artists in the area, and the club was full every weekend. Stewart's band featured Ralph Mooney, who was to become one of the true steel guitar innovators in country music.

Claude was convinced that Janet was "as good as Kitty Wells" and thought that she should make records and be heard on radio, too. After a few weeks of talking with Stewart, Claude asked if Janet could sing on his stage with him sometime. Stewart was quick to tell him that he didn't normally let people get up to sing, especially girls. Claude used the fact that she had sung with the Mosbys to gain some credibility with Stewart and he finally said "if she's good enough to sing with Johnny Mosby, she's good enough to sing for me."

Janet had been a fan of Wynn Stewart's since she had first heard him sing on the radio a few years back. She was nervous that night but thrilled as she stood on the stage of the George's Round-up club, with Wynn Stewart's band behind her and sang "Keeper of the Keys," an early Stewart song. "I could see that I was impressing the heck out of him," Janet reminisced. "He wasn't much bigger than me and was standing there grinning from ear to ear.

Ralph Mooney took a steel ride and I was a happy girl. With those great musicians playing, I felt like I just might be good enough to make it in the music business. I was on cloud nine that night!"

But how could a young working wife with two kids at home ever become a recording star? Janet now understood that she had to be the steady provider in the family, but hoped she could figure out how she could do all that and still follow her dream.

After she sang with Stewart's band a few times, Claude asked him if he would produce a recording session with Janet. Stewart said he would arrange for the studio and let her use his band, but the McBrides had to pay the bill, a whopping $600, one heck of a lot of money in 1959!

They decided to go ahead with the project, meeting first with songwriter Rusty Nail and choosing three of her songs: "I'm in Love with Another Woman's Man," "Is it Pity?" and "I Just Can't Stop Loving You." Claude wrote an additional song, ironically called "Help Me Forget Him," for the fourth cut.

The musicians were excellent and the session went well, from Mooney's first steel guitar kickoff to the last note of the last song on the four-song session. Janet felt she was realizing a dream. "I was hearing my voice singing a great song being played by a wonderful band and there was one of my favorite singers turning the knobs," Janet remembers. "Yep, I thought I had arrived, even if it did cost $600."

A local DJ friend of Claude and Janet's had advised them not to spend the money on any recording session, because it was extremely difficult to get anywhere in the business without a major record label on your side. He felt that recording on a minor label was simply a waste of time. But once the record was out, that DJ played Janet's songs over and over again on his show, helping her to build a following in his listening area.

∛

Ever the dreamer, Claude wrote a letter to Chet Atkins, c/o RCA Victor Records in Nashville, evidently thinking that Atkins couldn't wait to hear Janet McBride sing and yodel. The letter Chet sent back to them, dated January 26, 1960, indicated that he had a lot of appointments and was very busy, but to give him a call when they were in town.

"You didn't give Claude McBride an opening like that," laughed Janet, "because he was going to take you up on it for sure."

In February of 1960, they both took some time off work and drove to Arkansas where Claude's parents were living. They left the kids there and took off for Nashville and Chet Atkins. On a cold morning at about 4 a.m. they arrived in Music City, parked in a neighborhood park and slept until daylight.

Claude had no idea what to do with his tape of the "next Kitty Wells," but he was resourceful. He scanned the phone book and found a listing for Cedarwood Publishing Company, then drove around until he found the place and went in with tape in hand. He found himself face-to-face with well known star Webb Pierce. Pierce listened to the tape and said he liked the songs but his was a publishing company, and publishing songs was all he would be interested in. He wanted good songs to publish so they could get them recorded by established stars...and they wanted to own the songs, and these particular songs weren't the McBrides' to give away.

"Claude talked with him a little while but wanted to move on," said Janet. "After all, he felt like he had the next female country music star waiting in the car."

That evening Claude wanted to check out Tootsie's Bar, the famous hang-out to the stars located near the Ryman Auditorium, but when they drove by, Janet thought it looked too rough and rowdy and wouldn't go in. She remembers Tootsie's looking even worse than the low-rent motel that they were staying in, which was all they could afford. (As it happened, Janet didn't sleep at all that night. The motel room had a wall heater with an open gas flame and she was afraid it might start a fire or even worse, poison them with carbon monoxide fumes.)

The next day Claude walked into RCA Records and asked if Chet Atkins was in. The receptionist explained that people didn't just get in to see Chet without an appointment, that she'd give the tape to him to listen to when he had time. Claude showed her the letter from Chet and she asked them to wait. Atkins came out with the tape in his hand, told them he liked Janet's singing but he wasn't looking for any girl singers, and graciously thanked them for stopping by.

Disappointed that they'd spent their hard-earned money and vacation days on this trip that amounted to nothing, they headed back to Arkansas, picked up the kids and drove home.

Not one to give up, Claude heard about a midnight-to-morning disc jockey named Jack Morris on radio station KFOX in Long Beach who had an independent record company and he figured that he might be interested in the tapes. Morris had released one of Rusty Nail's songs also, so he was familiar with her name and her work. Claude started hanging around the radio station after he got off work and wangled an agreement for Janet to record with Toppa Records. Her first release was "I'm in Love with Another Woman's Man" and "Help Me Forget Him." Morris wanted harmony added to the songs before they were released and arranged for Janet to arrive at the studio in time to do her own harmony tracks. She took a half day off work and was excited about doing this type of studio work. When she arrived at the studio they informed her that the first session had ended early and because they didn't want to buy more studio time, they had

Performing with Biff Collie, a top DJ with KFOX Radio, (circa 1964). (Janet McBride Collection)

asked Jonie Mosby to do the harmony for Janet's tracks. She was disappointed but since Morris was paying the studio bills, there was nothing she could do.

Released in early 1960, this was Janet's first professional record. She received significant airplay with it across the area and even saw it show up on some of the radio charts. Soon Morris started talking about releasing another Janet McBride record.

She went back into the studio in late 1960 and recorded "Sweethearts by Night" and "Can You Love Us Both?" Both songs were recorded in keys that Janet felt were too low for her but she was too shy to ask for a key change. Again Jonie Mosby sang harmony and once again, the songs received good radio play and garnered significant attention.

10

Hurdles and Hope

A too-thin Janet with no answers,
but still singing.
(Janet McBride Collection)

Janet's third and last child, Mark, was born on January 15, 1961. She returned to work six weeks later and life moved along pretty much as it always had.

Then in June of 1961, she began having health problems. She was feeling extremely tired much of the time, but her doctor didn't seem to be worried and didn't do any particular tests. With her recordings playing up and down the coast, she was working all week, then performing at clubs around the area on the weekends. Her doctor assumed that her busy lifestyle was causing her fatigue.

Back in Arkansas, Claude's mother, Ruth, decided to end her long-time marriage to Claude T. McBride, and Janet invited her to come to California, move in with them and take on the job of live-in babysitter for seven-month-old Mark and the other two children. It was a win-win situation for both women. Ruth lived at Janet and Claude's house rent-free and earned a small salary, and Janet no longer had to take the kids to an outside sitter when she was working or performing.

Meanwhile, her health got worse, and one day late in November 1961, when she became seriously dizzy and nearly passed out at her desk, her boss told her that she had to make an appointment to see her doctor or get fired. Her regular doctor (Dr. O'Neill) was on vacation and his calls were routed to a substitute doctor (Dr. Peek). That new doctor gave her a battery of tests. She went home in tears, not knowing what was wrong and fearing the worst. She was simply tired of being sick and fatigued all the time.

"All I could think about is that I had wasted money on that office visit that we could have used for Christmas gifts for the kids," she explained. "And I still didn't know any more than I had before."

The aircraft plant where she worked closed down during the Christmas and New Year's holidays, and when she returned to work on January 3, 1962, the phone on her desk was ringing. Dr. Peek was calling to say he had made arrangements for her to go into the hospital the next day for a biopsy...that the hospital staff would be expecting her. Before she left the hospital that day, he told her he was almost certain that it was cancer. Later, the results of the biopsy confirmed it. She had cervical cancer.

Her doctor wanted the affected area to heal as much as possible before her surgery, so she went back to work from late January until the middle of April. The day of her surgery she weighed 97 pounds and needed a blood transfusion before they'd operate. When the surgery was over, she was anxious to regain her strength and move on with her life.

Because she'd already had her three children, who meant the world to her, she wasn't upset about not being able to have more. Her hands were full as it was, with her kids, her job and her promising music career.

Things were looking up for that dream. Janet's records were receiving airplay all over the country and she was making inroads into the West Coast music scene. Her singing only improved with her added confidence and for the first time in a few years, she was feeling good, both physically and emotionally. Having Claude's mother in the house greatly lightened her at-home workload and life was looking better.

CB

From early 1960 when Janet was recording and receiving good airplay in the Southern California area, her personal appearances and recording sessions picked up.

During her time with Toppa Records, Janet met Vern Stovall and Bobby George, singer/songwriters who had written some of the songs she was recording. Stovall and George were already well known on the West Coast club circuit. These two entertainers often asked her to sing a song or two during their performances at the clubs in the area. So, in addition to performing her own shows, she was increasing her exposure through these guest appearances.

She did her last Toppa recording session in November of 1962. Those sessions usually included lead guitarist Gene Davis who was also the band leader at the popular Palomino Club in the Los Angeles area. Davis was in a position to know everyone and everything that was happening in the entertainment business on the West Coast.

When he learned that Paramount was looking for a female country singer for the new movie in production, *Hud*, starring Paul Newman, he called Janet and encouraged her to audition.

"I was there at the appointed time along with Skeets McDonald who was trying out for a male singing part," said Janet. "We auditioned, went our separate ways and by the time I got home that day, the phone was ringing. It was the studio telling me I got the 'girl' part and Skeets got the 'guy' part. Yes, Gene Davis got the ten percent talent fee for his part in the deal and I gladly paid it."

The songs Janet and Skeets recorded can be heard in the background in several areas of the film. There is also a song by Skeets on the car radio and you can hear Skeets and Janet singing on a jukebox in the cafe. "A couple of times during the movie, you can hear me singing 'I'm Just Driftwood on the River' and at one point you can hear Skeets and me singing 'Honey Love' in the background," she recalls. Janet's name was not included in the *Hud* credits, but the nice paycheck she earned softened her disappointment in the omission.

In 1963, she cut a session of four songs at a top Hollywood studio with the hope of getting them on Capitol Records. The session went well but Capitol wasn't interested in signing Janet. Two of the songs were later picked up by Sammy Masters' Galahad label. (Masters was the writer who penned "If I Could See the World Through the Eyes of a Child.")

Through his acquaintance with Stovall and George, Claude met Curtis Leach, a songwriting truck driver. Recognizing Leach's potential as a songwriter, Claude recorded several of his songs onto a demo tape. With that cassette in hand, he went to Nashville in search of a label for Janet and a publisher for Leach's songs. Although he didn't find either a label or a publisher, he did come back with an offer from Starday Records. Starday's Tommy Hill wanted to create an LP of yodeling songs as a tribute to Patsy Montana and asked if Janet could come up with enough strong yodeling songs to make an album on this theme. She recorded five yodeling songs with this project in mind, but without enough material, the project eventually fell through.

By this time, Janet's records were being played on radio stations in several regional markets and her music career was showing promise. Claude began hanging out with songwriters and DJs in Pomona, and one day KWOW Radio offered him a Sunday DJ spot. The position didn't pay much but he loved it and did a good job. Soon he was playing music on both Saturday and Sunday. As was his habit, he often left the house on Friday nights and stayed gone all weekend. He liked the "show biz" aspect of radio DJ-ing so well that he quit his job at Standard Oil and started selling advertising for the station. His pay was a percentage of each ad sale, so the bigger the account, the better.

Through the contacts he was making, he procured a performance slot for Janet on the Sunday *Cal Worthington Show* on television. Worthington was a giant in the West Coast car-selling industry and presented this show live from one of his car lots as a public relations tool. The show had a strong

Janet appeared on the Cal Worthington Show on various occasions for several seasons. Janet is shown here performing with the Eddy Drake Band. (Janet McBride Collection)

audience and offered a wonderful opportunity for Janet. Worthington also presented a nightly country music television show airing on a local TV station and invited Janet to appear on that as well. To accomplish this, Janet had to take off work on Friday at noon, then drive to North Hollywood to tape the shows that would be broadcast that week, meaning that her Saturday hours at work were no longer overtime. The shows were seen statewide and in other states, thanks to "bicycling" copies of the program to other stations across the country. She did the shows for several months and saw her recognition and fan base increase dramatically because of it. For a time, Claude even sold cars for this car dealer/show producer/advertising genius.

೦೩

Meanwhile, Janet was learning about the darker side of country music entertainment during the 1960s. It wasn't called "drug abuse" then, but it was happening just the same. "Bennies" from Mexico and "Dexedrine" (obtained by prescription) and "Black Mollies" were the popular drugs that were being used by some of the folks associated with the entertainment industry...and Claude used his share.

Janet first became aware that he was occasionally using something while he was still in the Navy. As a corpsman he had quite a bit of "stuff" at his fingertips. He once told her about an officer who sent him and others under his command down to pick up codeine that was for his personal use, but Janet wondered if maybe Claude was the one who sometimes might be using the drug.

After the Navy years but before their move to Dallas, Janet began to put two and two together. His getting high wasn't just drinking; he was using something else as well. Sometimes he'd come home with his speech slurred, giving excuses that were a rambling mess. "He'd say he was hanging out with some pretty big names," recalled Janet, "and it got to the point that if he wasn't home, he was at a party and a 'party' usually meant he was writing songs, drinking and probably taking a pill or two."

One may wonder if Janet herself ever tried using drugs. After all, her husband did, and she saw a lot of it in the entertainment business on the West Coast. Not one to try potentially dangerous things, she knew that drug users often had trouble holding down a job and she couldn't afford to risk that. She does admit, however, to knowing how to take a portion of a Dexedrine diet pill to keep awake if she had to drive all night to a gig.

Claude loved the nightlife and it did yield some good opportunities for Janet. He was promoting her the best way he knew how. She wasn't always sure she wanted her talent linked to his type of behavior, but she knew it wasn't going to change anytime soon.

With her conservative background, Janet just hadn't been prepared for a dynamo like Claude McBride. She had no idea that someone could act the way Claude did after getting married and having children. She didn't expect a "rose garden," but wasn't prepared for the hand she was dealt. Claude was so different from Victor Lister, who was at home being a father when he wasn't working...the man of the house, and always there. She could handle tough times but living with Claude was tougher than she had expected.

ಀ

Janet recalls that Vern Stovall helped her get her first paying gig, at the Fred Maddox Playhouse in Upland. Once she signed with Hollywood booking agent Steve Stebbins, she began working steadily in night clubs and theaters up and down the California Coast, all the while hanging on to her day job. She performed regularly at such nightspots as the 101 Club, The Blackboard, The Crow's Nest, The Falls, National City and several others. From time to time she was offered some good out-of-the-area opportunities that she couldn't take because of her job. One was a nice-paying gig in Anchorage, Alaska, but she couldn't be away from her job as long as the trip would require and Jeannie Seely took the job. She was also offered a large fair gig in Northern California but forfeited it because she wouldn't be able to make

Receiving the 1963 "Female Vocalist of the Year" from DJ's Digest, *presented by Tex Williams. This award ceremony and the group that organized it later became the Academy of Country Music. (Janet McBride Collection)*

it back in time to do her Saturday morning shift at Northrop. The aircraft plant was already bending over backward to allow Janet to do her singing and she didn't want to push her luck.

One weekend she took a Friday and Saturday night gig in Santa Maria, California. A girlfriend planned to go with her and they would stay overnight Saturday in a room provided by the club. But plans changed and both Claude and the other gal's husband came along. Claude didn't like the idea of the two women staying there alone, so the plan was changed to having Janet drive Claude back home Saturday after the show so he could get to his DJ job on Sunday morning. The girlfriend and her husband took the motel room. During the night two men broke into that room. They were promptly kicked out, thanks to the girl's husband, but Janet counts herself lucky over that change in plans, figuring that the intruders probably knew that two women were supposed to have been in that room alone.

Claude returned to Nashville and met with Russell Sims, who had a pretty hot label at the time. In 1964, Sims released two cuts from the session meant for Starday, "Almost Three" and "Swiss Cheese." He invited Claude and Janet to come back to Nashville where he would introduce her around in hopes of catching someone's attention. Under Sim's direction, she recorded four songs at a studio in Alabama during that trip. She did not get to perform on the Grand Ole Opry, but they did attend Ernest Tubb's Midnight Jamboree, and that night, they also spent time in Tootsie's Orchid Lounge, which was crowded with country music stars. "It was all very exciting," recalls Janet, "but nothing of promise came from that trip to Music City." Sims would later release two of the Alabama cuts, "Letter to a Fool" and "The Arms of a Child," on a single.

One night in 1964 Janet and Claude dropped in to visit a DJ at KWOW Radio in Pomona and met a man named Dewey Groom, who owned Longhorn Records and Ballroom in Texas. He invited them to come see him when they were in Dallas sometime and promised to get Janet a spot on the Big D Jamboree.

Soon Claude and Janet were on their way to Dallas to check it out. The Jamboree was held in a building called the Sportatorium and the stage was actually a boxing ring. The headliner on the show that night—March 28, 1964—was George Jones and the place was packed. Janet got to sing a couple of songs and when she yodeled, the crowd went wild.

Meanwhile, Claude, Vern Stovall and Bobby George decided to start up their own label, calling it Brookhurst Records. The label's first release was "Highway Man" with Curtis Leach, followed by a release of two of Janet's cuts, "Cannonball Yodel" (from the Starday project) and "You'd Better Go" (from the Capitol session). Stovall and George released a couple of songs, then Brookhurst released "Country Guitar," written by Stovall and Phil Baugh and sung by Stovall with Baugh on guitar. That song was generating excitement in the club where they were playing and Claude hoped to catch that energy on vinyl. They accomplished just that and soon the record was being played nationally and steadily climbed up the charts. Leach's "Highway Man" became a regional hit and was showing promise nationally as well. Brookhurst also released Janet's cuts of "What Did She Do?" (from the Capitol session) and "Cowboy's Sweetheart" (from the Starday project) on the Brookhurst label.

Janet was working her day job and running the office part of Brookhurst during her off-work time. Soon the success of "Country Guitar" and "Highway Man" became more than they could handle and Claude sought out his Texas friend Dewey Groom for help. Groom's organization had the necessary money and connections to promote the songs and he was excited by the promise these two cuts were showing. Envisioning a package show featuring Stovall, Leach and Janet, he signed the three of them, as well as Phil Baugh, to Longhorn Records.

At that point, Stovall and George relinquished any claim to the Brookhurst label and McBride became the sole owner.

Stovall, Leach and the McBrides all moved to Dallas in 1965.

11

Dreams as Big as Texas

An early Texas-days publicity shot.
(Janet McBride Collection)

Janet left her job of 12 years to give her singing career a serious chance to grow in the Lone Star State. She had hopes that the move to Dallas and the Longhorn recording contract would make a difference in Claude's behavior and, of course, further her own career. They would be totally immersed in the music business, a dream both she and Claude had long shared.

An added benefit of the move was that she could remove her children from the fast-paced and sometimes weird West Coast lifestyle.

The kids really loved Texas and were happy in the Dallas school system. Janet enjoyed her day job as a receptionist/secretary in the Longhorn Records office. Her job consisted of answering the phone, opening the mail and packaging and sending out record orders. On Friday and Saturday nights she sang at the Longhorn Ballroom, plus performed a few other gigs from time to time. She was happy, at least in this part of her life.

Claude's mother, Ruth, moved with them to Dallas and seemed happy in the new surroundings, and the kids loved having her there. Janet and Ruth McBride were not close like girlfriends, but there was a mutual respect between them. Ruth, however, thought her son Claude could do no wrong.

After a few weeks, Dewey Groom put Claude to work behind the bar at the ballroom. Janet had been working while Claude was out running around and Dewey did what he could to change that situation. He paid Janet $2 an hour for clerical services and Claude earned about the same as his hourly base pay, plus he received tips tending bar. Groom knew how badly the young couple needed the extra paycheck.

"Putting Claude McBride to work tending bar at one of the biggest night spots in the country was like throwing a T-bone steak to a hungry dog," said Janet. "He was in heaven, with cute waitresses and beautiful female patrons all around him. Nothing had really changed."

Many of the singers, pickers, songwriters and police officers who worked in the Dallas area gathered after hours at the Longhorn Ballroom. Once the doors were locked for the night, the real party began. Janet joined the fun when she could and hung out with such celebrities as George Jones, Lefty Frizzell, Ray Price, Conway Twitty, Charlie Pride, Connie Smith, Jan Howard and others. No matter where they had performed earlier in the evening, many of the professional entertainers who were in the area came to the Longhorn to unwind. Unfortunately, this partying only served as a fun way to fill time for a man who wasn't inclined to go home anyway.

Dewey Groom didn't allow anyone to call the Longhorn Ballroom a "honky-tonk," but rather preferred the phrase "Texas Dance Hall." There was never any trouble inside or outside the Longhorn and if anyone should ever hint that they were looking to cause some kind of disruption, they were in for a ride to the Dallas police station. Off-duty police officers were always admitted free to the club and employees knew who they were, so if a hostess, waitress or bartender needed assistance, all they had to do was shine their flashlight up toward the ceiling and that would be the last you saw of that troublemaker.

Groom put together a package show featuring Janet, Curtis Leach and Vern Stovall. The trio was added to "Bam" Bamford's large, three-day tour promoting his radio stations across Texas. During these gigs, Janet was thrilled to perform with such greats as George Jones, Roy Clark, Marty Robbins, Hank Snow, Little Jimmy Dickens, Don Gibson and some of the popular DJs from the area. They were frequently booked on the Big D Jamboree in Dallas as well.

After only one tour with the major acts, one night in December of 1965, Leach got into a fight with his girlfriend after he got home from a club gig. She grabbed a kitchen knife during the scuffle and somehow cut an artery in his leg. Curtis was dead before an ambulance could get there. In a matter of minutes he was gone and, without Curtis Leach as the headliner, so were the bookings for the package show. He had been on the verge of having his first radio hit with his self-penned "Golden Guitar" and many thought he was destined to be a big name in the music business.

After Leach's death, Janet and Stovall began to work as a duo act. From early on, Dewey Groom had done everything he could to

Groom's Longhorn Ballroom was one of the largest country music ballrooms in the United States during its heyday during the 1950s, 1960s and 1970s.

make stars of them both. He advertised their appearances in the big music magazines, consistently sent good promo materials to radio stations and booked the act as much as he could. He helped them purchase sound equipment and a band trailer (that had once belonged to Willie Nelson).

For one of their first bookings with their new back-up band, they headed out of Dallas to a night club in Silver City, New Mexico. Janet, Claude, Vern and his wife and the band members were piled into a station wagon, with the trailer full of sound equipment and band instruments behind it. Once again, Janet felt like she was on her way in the entertainment business.

The Silver City gig went well, and the next morning they headed for a New Year's Eve gig in Tucson. Unfortunately the pay was based on a percentage of the door and someone forgot to promote the show. Only about 50 people showed up. Jimmy Dickens, who was the star of the show that night, had a contract that said he was to be paid his guaranteed fee first. There wasn't even enough to pay Little Jimmy's fee. So Janet and the band were not paid. It wasn't a laughing matter, but they did have a laughing, good time all the way to Phoenix where they were scheduled to join a Grand Ole Opry show on New Year's Day. That night and the ride to Phoenix— with the band in the front seats of the station wagon, Jimmy, Vern's wife and Janet all in the back cargo area, and the equipment trailer towed behind—is definitely one of the treasured memories of

Janet and Vern Stovall teamed up for a successful, touring duo. (Janet McBride Collection)

Janet's career. After the Phoenix show, they actually got paid! That was the way the business went in those days—sometimes the band got paid, sometimes it didn't.

Another tour, this one booked by a different Texas agent, took the group to Lovington, New Mexico, and then up to Colorado for shows at the NCO (Non-commissioned Officers) clubs at Fort Collins, Fort Carson and Trinidad. The club in New Mexico said they hadn't even heard of the band, so they didn't even play that gig, but they still had to scratch up money for motel rooms so they could rest up before traveling to the next stop.

The next morning they drove to the first Army base and were welcomed. The band set up even though the NCO club people were expecting two go-go dancers to be part of the show. Claude and Vern explained to the manager that there was surely a mistake, but the guy said that without the dancers there would be no show—and no pay. Claude and Vern decided that if they weren't going to get paid, they weren't going to play so he motioned to the band to pull the plug and sent the girls to the car. Again they had to spring for motel rooms without being paid. The second NCO club gig went well but they were given a check as payment. By the time the band was packed up and ready to leave, it was too late to cash that check anywhere. So again they were without cash.

Janet, Vern and Curtis (fourth from left) were included in a high-end tour promoting "Bam" Bamford's various Texas radio stations. She worked with Roy Clark and George Jones (far left), Hank Snow, Little Jimmy Dickens, Marty Robbins and a host of others.

Snow was falling hard the next morning, and, with no cash in hand, they wired Groom for money. By the time they got the money, they were late getting on the road to their next gig in Trinidad, Colorado. The weather was worsening, they were late, and although they saw flyers advertising their show, they decided they'd had enough, skipped the show and went on down the road.

With Roy Clark on one of the Hap Peebles shows. (Janet McBride Collection)

಄

Janet and Stovall released a recording of a song called "I'm Wild Bill Tonight" in the summer of 1966. Good bookings and great memories followed throughout that year and the next. They worked a full week at the Golden Nugget in Las Vegas with the Compton Brothers, and again Janet felt like she was just possibly on the way to becoming a star. Their single made the national charts, and fans all over the country were beginning to take notice.

In 1966, Vern and Janet joined two Grand Ole Opry touring groups performing throughout Kansas, Nebraska and South Dakota, organized by package-show promoter Hap Peebles.

The first was in June. Some of the Grand Ole Opry stars who were on that first tour were Ferlin Husky (aka "Simon Crum"), Stringbean, Wilma Lee and Stoney Cooper, The Taylor Sisters, Mavis Thompson, The Clinch Mountain Clan and Leon Douglas.

The second was in October and on the night they were to perform in Topeka, the city was hit by a tornado and the show that night was canceled. But the television station in Topeka put on a telethon involving the various stars and it turned into an all-night extravaganza. Stars on that show included Johnny Western, Roy Clark, LaVon Lear, Gary Van and his band, Jimmy Gately, Buddy Cagle and Red Simpson.

"Roy Clark was a hoot," said Janet. "I have since performed on a lot of stages and a lot of live shows, but this tour was the only one where all of the acts who were not on the stage at the time that Roy Clark was entertaining were in the front row or standing where they could watch this man do his act."

Being part of the Hap Peebles tours was a great experience for Janet. After all, she was a nightclub singer who was now permitted to perform with the "big boys" and she was hungry to learn all she could about this part of country music entertainment. "There was no bus on these particular Hap Peebles tours," recalls Janet. "We traveled in a seven-passenger Pontiac station wagon filled with guitars and clothes. We just had to show up on time and put on as good a show as possible. We used the band provided for us and since we did the same show night after night plus matinees, it was a breeze."

Janet worked on occasion with Jan Howard during the Longhorn days. (Janet McBride Collection)

They sang "I'm Wild Bill Tonight," a comedy song that was a moderate hit on the national charts. Vern sang the "Wild Bill" part, and Janet sang the "You'll be Sweet William in the Morning" part. "It was pretty dern funny every time we did it," Janet laughs. "It was a good song for me to get my entertainment legs under me because it was guaranteed to get the crowd's attention."

Vern and Janet were on that tour because they had a Nashville booking agent named Bob Neal who was able to book them all over the country, but in order to keep them solidly booked, they needed a follow-up hit. It didn't happen and they lost their ties to Bob Neal.

Unfortunately, touring with its stars was as close as Janet came to appearing on the Grand Ole Opry. Even with all her dreams and hard work, she would never perform on the stage of the Ryman Auditorium in Nashville, Tennessee.

In addition to the Peebles tours, Janet and Stovall appeared at several other impressive venues, among them the Old Edison Hotel in Toronto, the Flame Café in Minneapolis, and the better clubs in Southern California, where they both had an impressive group of fans and were treated like stars. Janet enjoyed working with Stovall and appreciated his "big brother" way of watching out for her. Stovall is co-writer, along with Bobby George, on "Long Black Limousine," a song since recorded by several major stars including Elvis Presley, Glen Campbell, Merle Haggard and Keith Whitley. Low key and always a professional, Vern Stovall was ever the gentleman and Janet treasures their friendship.

*Vern Stovall, Janet and Jack Greene, taken after a show in
Fort Worth, mid-'60s. (Janet McBride Collection)*

She got used to having the support of a performing partner and never
was totally comfortable with the thought of doing a booking alone. Most of
the club owners were decent men, but every so often one of them thought
that Janet's pay included some private time with him. That's when a
supportive man like Vern was really nice to have around.

Between tours, she returned to work at the Longhorn Record
Company, mailing out records, corresponding with disc jockeys and
sometimes selling tickets for the Longhorn Ballroom shows.

Meanwhile, Janet and Vern were learning that the quality they were
getting through Longhorn's recording studio wasn't acceptable to many of

the radio stations across the country. This prompted a couple of trips to Nashville for recording sessions at the original Columbia Studios. Those sessions yielded six cuts for Janet, which she released on the Longhorn and Metromedia labels.

While Claude and Janet were still living in California, Victor's sister Lee, who had lived in Florida, passed away. She left ten of her nieces and nephews $5,000 each but Janet didn't receive her check until well after she and Claude had moved to Dallas. By that time, the amount had grown to $6,000. That money helped pay for two and a half acres of land in Dallas County near Seagoville, Texas. They used the land as collateral and a down payment for a four-bedroom brick home they built on the property. They moved into their new home in November of 1967.

Around that time Claude and Vern went to Nashville and came back with a recording contract on Monument Records for Vern. Claude was managing Vern at the time and they were all thrilled at this big slice of success.

Performing with Vern Stovall at the Cotillion Ballroom in Wichita, Kansas. (Janet McBride Collection)

12
The Nashville Experience

Janet and Claude, all dolled up
to attend the CMA Award ceremonies in 1969.
(Janet McBride Collection)

In mid-1969, thanks to Metromedia's A&R man Tommy Allsup, Claude had an opportunity dropped in his lap when he was hired to work for the Sunbeam Publishing Company in Nashville. It was a new name in publishing for Nashville but the parent company had been around for a long time and was located in New York City. They wanted to give country music a try and hired Claude to promote songs to artists and sign songwriters to publishing contracts. He would then cut demos on the new songs, and for that he was guaranteed more money than he had ever earned in his life. This position looked like everything he had been looking for since the day he quit his job at the Standard Oil Company.

Claude told Janet that "all those years of hanging out to meet people in the business" prepared him for a job like this. As an added benefit, Janet would be able to record for the Metromedia label that was part of the company. Claude finally would have a real job in the music business and that meant a lot to Janet. She truly wanted it to work for him. So they would both have positions in Nashville, Dewey Groom arranged for Janet to work in his newly opened Nashville office of Saran Publishing.

Groom also bought their house in Texas. The best part, from Janet's perspective, was that they wouldn't receive the money from the sale of the house until Groom's own house sold. It was a good way to keep the money from slipping through their fingers before they were ready to buy another house themselves.

By the time school had started in 1969, Claude and Janet had packed up the kids and the furniture and moved to Nashville, for one more try at making it in the music business.

Although the move was primarily for Claude's job, it was also Janet's chance to try, once and for all, to gain the support of a major recording label. She signed a contract with Metromedia Records as one of their first artists.

Janet & Claude's children: Claude Jr., Denise and Mark, during their time in Nashville. (Janet McBride Collection)

By now, Janet was in her mid-30s and getting close to being too old to be taken seriously as star material.

"I wasn't real sure I had a chance at a singing career any longer," Janet recalls, "but I thought if Claude could find his calling, and with my work in the Nashville music publishing office, we'd do just fine and still be associated with the business that I loved."

She did have a couple of good bookings while they lived in Nashville, both of them out of town. Bob Neal, the agent who had booked Vern and Janet with the Hap Peebles tours, had a client named Morrie Shapiro who had a big club in Colorado. She had worked for Shapiro before and was booked into his club as a solo act. They arranged to have Janet picked up at the airport and taken back—basically escorted—so she didn't have to get around on her own. Unfortunately the paycheck from the Colorado booking agent bounced. He was immediately blacklisted by the Nashville country entertainer community. Shapiro also had Jeannie C. Riley booked with that same Colorado agent and the Nashville agent said to the Colorado agent, "Make this check good immediately or Jeannie C. Riley won't be there!" Before the bank closed that day, Janet had her money.

On Veterans' Day, 1969, Janet joined a busload of Nashville-based entertainers and headed for Washington D.C. for a show hosted by Senator Tower from Texas, to be held on the plaza of the Washington Monument. The Compton Brothers were the headliners and it was their bus that the group used. On the way, the water line on the bus heater broke and flooded the bus. For the rest of the trip there was no heat, but Janet was thrilled to be on the road with these big-time Nashville entertainers, and felt the trip was well worth the cold bus ride.

Even with his fulfilling new job, Claude didn't really change his ways when the couple got to Nashville. His "song plugger" title and the fact that he worked for a publishing company gave him even more reason to hang out, only now it was with people with bigger names. This kind of networking was an accepted way to find good songs and talent during this time, and for the first time ever, Janet felt like he had a reason to be "hanging out."

Janet's two Nashville-recorded singles were released on the Metromedia label, but received no real reaction around the country, and it didn't look like they were going to release any more.

By that time, Claude had started flying back to Dallas every other weekend, presumably on business, but these trips were costing money that the couple couldn't spare. Janet suspected that he went back to Dallas to see his friends there and let them know just how "big" and successful he was...but figured that it was also likely that he had a girlfriend there.

cs

When Claude had first become a DJ back in California, he and Janet began attending the Nashville-based National Disc Jockey Convention. It was a wild party where disc jockeys and station owners from across the country gathered to meet artists and record company executives. Claude and Janet attended this major Nashville publicity activity each year for several years.

Janet and Claude at their Nashville house.
(Janet McBride Collection)

At that time, most of the radio stations were owned by individuals, not by the large corporations common today. Each record company and radio station hosted hospitality rooms, and the booze "flowed like water," according to Janet. During the convention, there was always an outstanding show at the Ryman Auditorium, and Claude and Janet especially enjoyed that part of the festivities.

Each record company would pass out complimentary records for the DJs to take back to their stations (and hopefully play them), and the DJs looked for stars who would consent to an interview or who would agree to record a station plug.

Once Janet was signed with Metromedia, she was invited to "hang out" in their hospitality room, along with the other Metromedia talent. "One of the people I remember being there that year was Chill Wills," said Janet. "He had an album released on Metromedia also and what a hoot he was to be around!" Among her souvenirs are the large format photos of both Chill Wills and herself that were used to decorate the hospitality room that year.

Soon thereafter, the wild-party atmosphere of the DJ Convention event ended, because the CMA (Country Music Association) and others wanted to clean up the image of country music.

cs

The McBrides looked at property and homes in the Nashville area and even as far as 50 miles out. Janet wanted a place that had room for the kids to run, but soon determined that they didn't have enough money to purchase anything like she had in mind.

The prospect for Janet finding work if necessary was always good, but if Claude lost his job—and it looked like he might—it would be more difficult to find something he liked and would stay with. "To be honest," said Janet, "by then I had given up the idea that Claude would ever work a normal day job again."

Janet and Claude had been married nearly 15 years by this time and she was only too familiar with his weak work ethic. She'd often wonder if it might even be her fault; maybe she had made things too easy for him. He knew early on that no matter what happened, Janet would have a job or could easily find one.

When the Sunbeam Music Publishing Company was dissolved and Claude no longer had a job, the decision to close Dewey Groom's Nashville office was made. Janet and Claude decided they would return to Dallas.

They had spent only six months in Nashville, but finally Janet was ready to admit that life with Claude was never going to be the way she wanted. He was never going to have much time for her and the kids.There were just enough good times to make her think that things could get better, but then he'd be off again until he grew tired of that outside world and would come home where his other life was waiting.

"I just smile now when I hear TV's Judge Judy say, 'You picked him,'" laughs Janet. "I was like so many young women—I thought I could change him."

One Friday before Claude was let go from his publishing company job, Janet took off work and joined him for his every-other-weekend trip to Dallas. She bought a new outfit and was ready for a weekend away from the kids, who stayed in Nashville with Claude's mom. She was sure that he had girlfriends in Dallas and was determined to keep him from seeing any of those gals, at least for a couple of days. First stop was the Longhorn Ballroom and, as usual, everyone was really happy to see them. When the ballroom closed that night, they headed for their motel. They planned to go back to the ballroom on Saturday night to hang out with their Dallas friends, and then on Sunday they'd start back to Nashville, a twelve-hour drive. They had to leave early so Claude could get to work on Monday.

But Claude dropped Janet off at the motel, then headed back to the ballroom to "have a drink with Dewey" and said he'd be back soon. Janet didn't see him again until Sunday afternoon.

Staying alone in a motel room all weekend, without money or food, wasn't her idea of fun...and she was ready for a change in how she looked at things. Those hours alone gave her lots of time to finally face her situation. She did some serious talking to the Lord and at last made some solid decisions about where she would go from there. When she drove out of Dallas that Sunday afternoon, with Claude asleep in the back seat, she was a different person—a person with a plan.

13
Return to Seagoville

*Claude Jr. and the family cat, "FuzzyButt,"
with a fresh catch of fish from their own pond.
(Janet McBride Collection)*

After the Dallas weekend, Janet steadily gained courage and independence…and learned not to count on Claude for anything. She also let go of her lifelong dream of becoming a country music singing star.

Her kids needed more of her time and attention than she had been giving them. She had noticed that Denise would begin stuttering as soon as she knew her mom was leaving town and "it wasn't rocket science to figure it out."

"Christmas 1969 was on us by then and there wasn't much money coming in but I went down to Grant's Department Store and took out a merchandise loan for $150," said Janet. "With that money each of the kids got something, I got something, and Grandma picked out a nice dress. Yes, I got something for Claude, too. I didn't hate him…I just quit worrying about a lot of stuff and took care of Christmas for the family my way. It was a wonderful Christmas morning and a great Christmas dinner and we all knew that our next Christmas would be in Texas."

In early 1970, they found a house with five acres near Seagoville, Texas. A small, well-kept frame house, it had enough space for the boys' bunk beds and for Grandma's bed, and there was a small enclosed back porch to serve as Denise's room. Claude and Janet's bedroom was a renovated breezeway. The bathroom was located in the renovated garage.

The house wouldn't be available until the old couple living there moved out when the house they were buying was available, so the McBrides lived in a small rental house in Seagoville until they could move to the acreage.

With the money from the sale of the house that Dewey Groom had purchased, plus a small loan from the Seagoville Bank, they were able to pay the $18,500 price for the property.

The only drawback was that there was no water on the property and no city water close by. It would be costly to bring water out to the house, so they figured they could dig a well when they moved in.

Claude took up where he left off tending bar at the Longhorn Ballroom and eventually became the manager, which meant purchasing the beer and set-ups and handling the money every night. He loved the job.

Janet was happy in herself, taking charge of her own life and taking care of her children. She had acquired one of the things she wanted most: a real home for her family with lots of space for the kids to play. She was determined never to have to count on Claude for anything ever again. With no house payment, she and the kids could start re-building their lives.

Claude's mother, who was still living with the McBrides, had never had a job other than babysitting for Janet. She had a talent for country cooking and wanted to find a job as a cook so she could earn credit toward future Social Security benefits. At some point in 1970, she found a live-in cook position with a wealthy Dallas family who provided her with a small apartment on their property. They loved her and her country cooking, and she worked for them until she had enough quarters to retire and draw her own Social Security check. At that point she moved to Louisiana, to be closer to her son Clyde.

Janet loved being back in the Dallas area and, with her new mindset, felt like a new person. Even though she had given up hopes of becoming a star, she felt sure that life would have good things in store.

While Janet was working days at the Longhorn, one of Claude's waitress girlfriends attempted to stir up trouble for Janet and remove her from the Longhorn Ballroom picture, but, ultimately the woman's plan backfired and *she* was the one to get fired. Soon, however, Janet grew tired of being in constant contact with Claude's "harem" and quit her job there.

Once she'd left her job, she felt she needed new skills and thought about taking classes of some kind. A television ad for the National Beauty School caught Janet's eye one day in 1970. At age 35, she signed up to go to school again. She liked the school and the gals and, although it wasn't as exciting as singing on stage, doing hair was a satisfying endeavor and promised at least some job security.

That summer, the McBride family moved to their Seagoville property.

The McBride acreage near Seagoville was a truly rural setting, complete with geese and cattle. (Janet McBride Collection)

They were unable to find water on the property, so for several years they pumped water up from the stock tank (pond) to one of the encased dry-well holes. They added a bit of bleach before it was pumped into the house and used that water for baths and toilet water. It couldn't be used for drinking and cooking, so they had to haul water for that purpose, and laundry was done in a laundromat.

By early 1971, Janet finished her beauty school classes, passed the state test and became a licensed beautician. Her first job was for a friend who owned her own business, but it was farther from Seagoville than was convenient, so she looked for a shop closer to her new home.

She enjoyed her work and the gals she worked with, and did a good job cutting, styling and perming hair, but there were times when she *was* a bit dismayed. "There was a streak in me that wanted to tell some of those dear old gals that no matter what I did, it wasn't going to improve their looks that much," she said.

Since the beginning of their marriage Janet had made the day-to-day decisions in the household. Once the couple purchased their own home and it was paid for, the money went a little farther without that large payment looming over her head. Each year they raised a calf for beef, so the freezer usually had meat in it and the grocery bill was manageable, even with two growing boys.

 CB

Several "big boy toys" helped to feed Claude's fun factor but sometimes challenged his better judgment. He had a nice motorcycle, but crashed it and was skinned up pretty badly in the accident. He also owned a large pleasure boat that he kept on Cedar Creek Lake, until his failure to correctly ventilate the engine compartment caused it to blow up one night with him and one of his girlfriends aboard. Before long he replaced that boat with another one just like it.

After work late one night, he was leaving the Longhorn Ballroom in his '71 Mercury, when he collided with a frozen-food truck that was backed up to a loading dock and blocking the road.

Some of his friends knew that Claude had been in a pretty serious accident but, inexplicably, not one of them called to tell Janet that he was in Parkland Hospital. The accident happened at about 12:30 a.m. She finally received a call at about 10 a.m. while she was at the beauty shop.

She drove to the hospital and found Claude lying unattended on a gurney in the hall. He didn't seem to know what had happened or what was going on. They waited together until, finally, at about 3 p.m., a nurse came out to check on them. "Okay, Mrs. McBride, he can go home now," she said, "but be sure he uses a sling to protect his arm and shoulder."

When he tried to stand to get into the wheelchair he was obviously in extreme pain. The nurse again said, "He'll be fine. He's bruised, that's all. Just take him home to rest." Janet didn't trust that assessment and called an ambulance with instructions to take Claude to Baylor Hospital. They admitted him right away, then suggested that she go home and rest and come back in the morning after they had done X-rays and thorough tests.

When all was said and done, he was in the hospital 31 days and had surgery on his broken leg and multiple surgeries on his badly broken shoulder. They discovered that he had very high blood pressure and put him on medication for that problem as well. At home he stayed in bed for almost five weeks, but Janet felt good about having the kids' father at home acting like he cared about his family—with no drinking or partying.

Because of this accident, Claude was away from alcohol for almost nine weeks.

Finally, the day came when he could make it back to the Longhorn Ballroom and his friends. Janet went with him the first time because he promised there would be no partying after closing time. With all the medication he was on, he assured her that he wouldn't have any alcoholic drinks. At midnight when the ballroom closed, a group of his friends met over at one of their houses, and Janet went along, hoping she could keep him from drinking. Before long she saw him with a water glass full of whiskey and when he wouldn't leave the party with her, Janet drove off alone. That was early Saturday morning. She didn't hear from him until about 4 p.m. on Sunday afternoon when someone dropped him off, and her husband came walking in the door.

Sometime in 1972, he received a settlement of $14,000 from the car accident and put it in the bank in his name alone. Whatever he planned to do with the money, it evidently didn't include Janet.

It's not difficult to imagine the heated argument that ensued when Claude told Janet he wanted to use the money to open a bar with one of his girlfriends as a business partner.

"We don't have quite enough money, Honey," he pleaded with Janet. "Please. Let's just take out a little loan against the property and everything will work out fine." Needless to say, Janet objected vehemently!

Not one to give up easily, Claude turned to his mother and asked her to lend him the needed money. "Absolutely not!" she said, without hesitating.

Claude's health was spiraling out of control by this point. Still on blood pressure medication, he was drinking as much alcohol as before the accident, but now he was also taking "uppers" to get him going and "downers" when he needed to unwind.

౪

On their 18th anniversary on January 22, 1973, Janet and Claude went to the Longhorn to celebrate with friends. Janet sang a few songs with the band and they spent an uneventful evening visiting with friends. They started home around midnight, and Claude wanted to stop for breakfast at an all-night truck stop on the way. Janet noticed some agitation on Claude's part; he was folding the napkin over and over and sometimes not making much sense when he talked. When he went to pay the bill, she noticed he was having trouble with the money. He insisted on driving, which worried her. She sat close to him so she could watch the road and grab the wheel if anything happened. She knew he couldn't be drunk, but something just didn't seem right. When they approached a stop sign in the Balch Springs area of town, he slumped over the wheel. She insisted on driving the rest of the way and he didn't argue this time. The next morning he felt good and seemed okay. He took his medications and went on as usual.

A few days after that incident, Janet and Claude went for a walk through a wooded area across the fence from their property. As they were returning home, he picked up a piece of wood to use later as a fence post and threw it over the fence before he climbed over. Janet was concerned when he had to sit down to catch his breath. He was quite pale, but after a while his color returned and he felt better, so they continued on up to the house. He refused to be taken to a doctor, insisting he was okay.

A little after midnight on February 2, 1973, he came home from his job at the Ballroom on time, which was unusual. He ate a slice of Claude Jr.'s birthday cake, changed for bed, and he and Janet talked a little.

Without warning, Claude said "I'm not feeling well at all. I think you need to take me to the hospital!"

Janet was frightened but helped him put on his robe and get in the car. Baylor was the nearest hospital with an emergency room and off they went into the night. The hospital was about 25 minutes away. Before she was halfway there, Claude had a massive heart attack and, just like that, his life was over. He was 36 years old.

It happened that Dewey Groom's wife was also in Baylor Hospital at that time. When Janet told the emergency room staff where Claude worked, they said that Mr. Groom was upstairs with his wife. They called him and he came down to be with Janet for a while. He was very surprised to hear about Claude's death, as he had just seen him a couple of hours before. Because it was a DOA (dead on arrival), Groom let the hospital officials know that he knew Janet well and there was no possibility of foul play on her part related to Claude's death.

ભ

When Janet went to pick up Claude's mother from her job, one realization dominated her thoughts. "There would be no more nights of worry. It's finally over."

Her mother-in-law was not surprised when Janet told her about Claude's death. She knew there was always a possibility that this could happen.

The funeral chapel was full of friends and flowers for Claude's service. Janet didn't cry that day...or even for a couple of years afterward. Not until 1976 would the tears come. With the help of her daughter Denise and her two sons, Claude and Mark, she would get through the roughest times.

The money from the settlement from Claude's car accident, which was safely tucked away in the bank, was still in his name when he died. She wasn't sure that she could get access to it, as Claude had no will. In any case, she decided to leave it there and save it for some future need.

Just a few days before Claude died, their daughter Denise had married her childhood sweetheart and moved to the Fort Hood, Texas, area. Now only the two boys were at home with Janet.

14

Finding her Way

At the Seagoville house in 1974.
(Janet McBride Collection)

Hair styling may have been in Janet's fingers but it wasn't in her heart, and it wasn't easy building a large clientele in a town the size of Seagoville, Texas.

Janet often opened up her part of the business at 6:30 a.m. She stayed late to catch the gals coming home from work if that was what they needed. She was good at what she did and usually had a decent paycheck. With what Claude gave her from his salary, she and the kids had done okay. But when he died, that paycheck stopped and there was only one small insurance policy for the family in case something happened to him.

While Janet was working at the beauty shop, the boys were by themselves a lot of the time. They were 12 and 14. They lived in the country, they rode the school bus daily and they were good kids, so Janet wasn't worried about them. Mark often rode the school bus until he was the last one on, and then the driver would let him off in front of the house. As soon as Claude, Jr. was old enough to get his driver's license, he started taking Mark to school.

A new friend, one who appreciated good country music, came into Janet's life during this time. Her name was JoAnn Tucker and she was a friend of Phyllis', the woman who owned the beauty shop where Janet worked. They had first met during the time Claude was recovering from his motorcycle accident.

After Claude's death in 1973 and while she was still at the beauty shop, Janet felt she was in a state of limbo, not knowing what to do with her life. She went to the Longhorn Ballroom sometimes just to be with some of the only people she knew in Texas. She met some men there and even went on a few dates.

Sometimes JoAnn and Janet, along with JoAnn's husband Robert, Phyllis and a dear friend named Hattie Mae Harrell (their mail carrier) all went to the Longhorn together. "We'd always call ahead and get a front table and drink Cokes and just have a great time," Janet recalled.

Often they got to enjoy some of the big stars performing on stage at the Longhorn. One night the special entertainer was the legendary Lefty Frizell. He joined Janet's group at their table and they spent the evening chatting like old friends. "JoAnn even danced with Lefty and got him to autograph her arm. What fun it was!"

"Once when Conway Twitty was the special guest, the Longhorn was absolutely full!" recalled JoAnn. "Someone had given the table that Dewey Groom's wife Helen had saved for us to another party, so Helen set up another table in front of the others, and it was even closer to the bandstand. We could have reached out and touched him!"

At Christmas time in 1973, the beauticians at the shop decided to offer a little complimentary Christmas cheer to their customers. The ladies enjoyed their "happy punch" as their hair was being styled. When closing time came, the doors were locked and for those who stayed, the party continued with country music pouring from the stereo. The

JoAnn Tucker Page and Janet during a stop in Austin, Texas. (Janet McBride Collection.)

fun went on long after the town of Seagoville was closed up for the night. "At some point we ran out of ice and called JoAnn at home and asked her if she could bring us some," remembers Janet with a chuckle. "Sure enough, here came JoAnn in her pajamas and robe with ice in hand. That was a sight in itself!"

A little later, there was a knock on the (glass) front door. JoAnn, who was dancing with one of those styrofoam wig heads, opened it to find the Seagoville police. They were checking to make sure everything was alright since they weren't accustomed to seeing a light on at the beauty shop so late. When the gals told the officers that they were fine, just friends visiting, the officers wished them well and left.

The next day one of the young beauticians came in and quit. Her husband had told her that the whole town was talking about the "rowdy party" at the beauty shop and that those gals were a bad influence on her. Hattie Mae Harrell, JoAnn Tucker, Hattie's sister and the shop owner were "shamed in Seagoville" for a while, after that "wild beauty shop party!"

In early 1974, one of Janet's customers who worked at the Holiday Inn in Dallas encouraged her to apply for a front-desk job that was open there. She got the job, started out on second shift but was soon sent to day shift. It was nice to again have a regular salary. She worked there until late 1975.

"It was during that time that I came face to face with my situation," explained Janet. "My two boys were nearly grown, my daughter was already gone and I was soon going to be alone. I had never been alone. It scared me a lot!"

From the day Janet was born she had been part of a family. She lived with her mother until she married Claude, then with the three kids. She lived with Claude in turmoil for nearly 18 years and now was on her own with her two boys, who would be leaving home one day soon.

ﾨ

In 1975, while she was working at the Holiday Inn, Janet met and dated a contract telephone installation worker assigned there. Sometimes his company sent him out of town to work on special projects. If he was going to be gone for an extended period he would leave his truck at Janet's house with instructions for her to start it every now and then to keep the battery charged. She drove it to work one day and that's when his "Romeo" story started to unfold. When his other girlfriend saw the truck in the parking lot, she naturally thought he was back in town.

"Imagine her surprise (and mine) when we learned that this fella had been seeing both of us and neither of us knew about the other," exclaimed Janet. "I quit my job at the Holiday Inn. I didn't want to see this guy again for any reason so I took myself out of the picture completely. Of all the men in the world, I had to pick one who couldn't be happy with just one lady friend. We're talking about a man who would go to church with the boys and me on Sunday mornings and eat dinner with us often."

She went through some pretty heavy soul-searching after this interlude. It had been two years since Claude died and finally the tears she hadn't cried when he died started to fall. It seemed that she cried incessantly. Afraid she was losing her mind, she even made an appointment with a psychologist, but then didn't go. She knew she wasn't really crazy and finally determined that nothing but time was going to erase all the years of hurt she had endured.

"I found myself wondering why it took me so long to realize I wasn't alone at all. I was finally able to stop crying and to sleep again. I wouldn't wish for anyone to go through that, but my first advice to anyone going through anything like this is to 'start talking to the Lord.' I know that it was my prayers and my trust in the Lord—along with my kids and their wonderful support—that brought me through that terrible time."

There wasn't much music in Janet's life at this point—either figuratively or literally. She did, however, perform at times for a television show called *The Cowboy Weaver Show* that was broadcast on local stations.

In 1976, Janet got a new job at the Montgomery Ward department store, this time in an office. The wages were adequate, she had benefits and she liked the job. Working at Wards helped her on her way back to finding out who she was.

"I couldn't understand why I always picked a guy who appeared to need someone to help them," Janet lamented. "You know the kind! Well, I was a classic case, and as a grandmother in my 40s, I finally realized it. I made up my mind that I'd be a lot more careful in the future!"

By mid-1976, Janet was feeling better and was even asking her friends to help her find a "nice guy." All she wanted was a decent man with no small children, because she wasn't interested in raising another family. Of course, he had to have a job and he had to be someone who didn't want more than one girlfriend at a time.

One of the men she had dated wanted her to put him into business, one wanted to move in with her and the boys, and most didn't want any kind of commitment. It was all rather frustrating, but she never gave up on finding "that one good man."

"I talked to the Lord about it often and kept my eyes open because I knew He'd be sending someone," Janet laughed, "and I knew I'd better not miss 'Mr. Wonderful' when he came skipping along."

os

When Janet had first met JoAnn Tucker, JoAnn's husband Robert worked for a company that made batteries, then later took a job at the Dallas County Sheriff's Department. JoAnn also worked for the Sheriff's Department as a dispatcher at one of the substations.

JoAnn and Robert were having some rough times in their marriage, some of them probably brought on by the stress of losing a young daughter to cancer. They eventually divorced but still did things together with the kids, and Janet enjoyed going with them to Rangers baseball games.

Handsome young B.J. (John) Ingram came into Janet's life in 1976. (Janet McBride Collection)

JoAnn would gather as many kids as wanted to go and then pack up hot dogs, buns, chips and Cokes for all of them, always including Janet's two boys. Tickets were only $2 each and patrons could carry food into the stadium. Their seats were in the outfield bleachers, but they didn't mind, and they all had a great time. In fact, Janet claims that these were the best times she ever had at a sports event, but the real winners were the kids, who got to spend those good times with their families.

One night when Janet and the Tuckers were together, Janet asked Robert if he was sure he didn't know a deputy who was single and looking for a "good ol' girl." Not too long after she made that joking remark, Robert asked JoAnn to arrange a picnic and bring Janet along.

Robert's sergeant at the Sheriff's Department was B.J. Ingram, a divorced man who was definitely interested in meeting Janet. The prospect of meeting a widow with two teenage boys didn't bother him, since he had two boys of his own.

Janet was well aware that Robert Tucker had only one driving speed and that was full-out as fast as his car would go. On a trip with him to Fort Worth to see Merle Haggard and Bob Wills in concert one time, she had learned that his driving was unforgettable...and a bit frightening.

When B.J. Ingram climbed into Robert's car for their blind date that day, Janet's first words to him were "You'd better get on the floor, because Robert is about to show you how he drives!" They both slid down in the back seat like a couple of teenagers and laughed, as off they went for a cook-out. B.J. agreed that he had never experienced such a ride before.

Janet took her guitar with her that evening because she wanted this man to know that music was a part of her life even though she had not done much singing for a long time. They all sang songs, ate hotdogs and had an all-around fun time before packing up and heading home. They dropped B.J. off at his car, then Robert and JoAnn took Janet home at around 4 a.m.

When she got home from work that next evening she could hear the phone ringing. It was John Ingram calling to ask for a date.

From that point on, Janet and John were inseparable.

John was living in an efficiency apartment in Dallas. A short time later, he found a little apartment in Seagoville and he and Robert, who was now separated from JoAnn, shared the rent. They both worked varying shifts and when one was leaving for work, the other was coming home.

15
In Harmony

O, Happy Day!
John and Janet were married in 1976.
(Janet McBride Collection)

John and Janet started talking about getting married not long after they met. Janet was 42 and he was 46. John wanted to wait until he'd saved money to pay for all the wedding expenses, a nice dinner and a "honeymoon room." When he had saved enough, they went to the preacher's house, along with Robert, JoAnn and their three kids plus Janet's two boys, and were married on October 8, 1976.

"We ate dinner at the 'Steak & Ale' and spent the night at a nice motel. As luck would have it, 'Bevo,' the University of Texas Longhorn football team's mascot (a longhorn steer), was there and 'bellered' all night. I was used to hearing cattle 'beller' out where we lived in the country but not in that area of Dallas." That was the weekend of the annual "Red River Shootout" between the University of Texas and Oklahoma University that takes place annually in the Cotton Bowl stadium.

The next morning they went to Mineola, Texas, to John's family reunion where Janet was welcomed with open arms. Everyone in John's family was glad to see John so happy. "If they told me once, they told me a thousand times over the years how much they appreciated me being with 'Johnny.'"

John was one of nine children and they were all still living in 1976. His two sons got along well with their dad and didn't seem to have any animosity over their dad's divorce, and certainly had no hostility toward Janet, who came along several months after the divorce. Janet's daughter and her two boys took to John right away.

The newlyweds made the round of parties where deputies were involved, and sometimes Janet took her guitar along and sang for their friends. There was usually alcohol available and the parties were a lot of fun. When the deputies were off duty they all knew how to have a good time, but very seldom did anyone go overboard.

Janet and John regularly threw parties and cook-outs for the gang on their five-acre spread, often including a bit of pickin' and grinnin.' From time to time they went to the Longhorn Ballroom for special parties or sometimes just to visit Dewey Groom and the band. They were treated like family at the Longhorn, something John appreciated, and Dewey thought the world of John.

A few weeks after they were married, Janet and John made a quick trip to California to see her West Coast family and friends. They all welcomed John right away, even the McBride brothers. Janet's mother and

Emmitt, her second husband, took a liking to John as well.

John and Janet had discovered early on that they both loved to travel. Between 1976 and 1981, as often as possible they took long trips during their vacation breaks from work. In 1979 they traveled to North Whitefield, Maine, where Janet lived when she was very young. They flew to Alaska one year to visit Janet's daughter and to see the countryside. Other trips took them to Niagara Falls, Plymouth Rock, Washington D.C. and New York City. They traveled to Custer's battlefield, Mt. Rushmore and Yellowstone National Park. They walked out into the Great Salt Lake, visited the Mormon Temple and heard the Tabernacle Choir sing; they visited the Tetons, Carlsbad Caverns and the Grand Canyon.

By 1979 John had heard Janet sing at parties and get-togethers, had looked at her scrapbooks, listened to her old records and decided that she shouldn't quit singing. Janet was not interested in singing in bars and honky-tonks like she had before, but figured that might be the only outlet for her music. They had gone to a few night clubs where she knew the musicians and was invited to sing, but she felt that she might be too old to please the crowds in those places. Those crowds were mostly young people and a woman in her 40s just wasn't what they had come there to hear and see. The bar scene was rougher in the late 1970s than it had been in the late 1960s. "I didn't sing so bad and I didn't look so bad, but I was not a spring chicken any longer and my voice wasn't like Tammy Wynette's or Dolly Parton's...and I certainly didn't look like either of them."

She couldn't help but long for the days of touring with the Grand Ole Opry folks. The crowds were big and the shows were usually held in large auditoriums. What a pleasure it would be to work with such professionals, but she held no real hope for that ever happening again. She wasn't sure how she'd go over even if she did find somewhere to sing. She had to face it: she was rusty by being away from performing all those years. "I wasn't even performing at my church," Janet recalled. "I think the preacher at our little church thought a guitar was an instrument of the devil. He let me sing if someone played the piano for me, but the guitar was not welcome."

In late 1978, Janet heard about the Grapevine Opry. She had read some newspaper articles and seen a story about it on television. On a Saturday morning early in 1979, she learned that auditions were being held that day and she decided to give it a shot. The show was in an old theater with no alcohol or smoking allowed. It seemed to be just what she was looking for.

They rushed over to the theater, just in time for Janet to audition. It was full of people all waiting for their turn to perform. A man named Johnnie High was in charge of the auditions, and he alone made the decisions as to who would be chosen for the show. As Janet sat there waiting her turn, she had to kick John in the shins more than once when he nearly laughed out loud at some of the not-so-talented performers.

"It was his first lesson in how I thought he should act at an audition," said Janet. "I told him he couldn't laugh at anyone, no matter how bad they were. That was so rude and I didn't want him to be a part of that sort of action, at least where I could witness it. Besides, what if he was sitting next to that person's parents, grandparents or some other relative?"

After all her years of experience it seems inconceivable that Janet was a nervous wreck when Johnnie High called her name. She doesn't remember which song she sang, but she took her trusty Martin guitar and did her thing. When she and John left that day there was no indication whether she had made the show, but she does remember Johnnie asking about her Martin.

The audition happened at about the same time she submitted her application for a job as a deputy with the Dallas County Sheriff's Department. A position with Dallas County would mean a good salary and a pension for her retirement. It was too important to pass up for a few performance gigs.

When Johnnie High, the Grapevine Opry man, called, the Saturday they wanted her to perform fell in the middle of their planned two-week vacation to the Northeast. She worked out another date, this one in June of 1979.

Their trip that year took them first to Niagara Falls and then to Maine to visit Janet's Aunt Gertie and some cousins on her mother's side of the family. It was Aunt Gertie who told her that Annie Kelly was still alive and living in the same house out on Rooney Road where she lived when Janet was a child. Janet hadn't seen Rooney Road or Annie Kelly since they left Maine on New Year's Eve of 1946...and she could hardly wait to see her again!

She opened the door and said 'Hi, Annie, I'm Janet Lister.'"

"Oooooh, you dear girl," Annie cooed, and invited John and Janet to come in.

"I am not exaggerating when I say that nothing had changed inside her kitchen all those years," Janet said with a big smile. "The same wonderful rose dishes were in that same glass-front cupboard, and the stove was right where I remembered it being."

Janet shares her experience here:

I walked to the kitchen window where one of us kids would look out on cold and rainy mornings in the harsh Maine winters of 1942 through 1946. One of us kids would watch for the little school bus to appear and we'd all grab our stuff and run up over the little rise to the bus. When I looked out, I could almost see that panel bus coming up the road. There were four Lister kids, three Carter kids and Elwood from the Twist family who walked up that road to catch the school bus. Imagine if you can, eight kids coming in out of the rain and the snow and all tracking mud and yuck into Annie's small kitchen while we waited for the bus. I'm sure that snotty noses, along with wet shoes and boots, probably weren't her favorite things, but she never acted like we were any problem. What a treasure Miss Annie and her sister Katherine were!

"So," Janet asked, "what ever happened to George, your handyman back then?"

"Oh, he's still here," the 98-year-old Annie replied. "He lives inside the main house between the kitchen and the garage now. It's so much warmer there for his 80-year-old bones."

"You know, I still have that small brass jewelry case you gave me just before we left," Janet told her.

"I've often wondered what happened to that," Annie said.

"You also gave my sister and me a pretty clock, but it was really fragile and didn't survive all those years we lived in trailer houses!" laughed Janet. "If that jewelry box weren't brass and unbreakable, it wouldn't have survived either. My daughter has it now, and I hope she hands it down to one of her daughters or to her granddaughter someday."

Annie Kelly, Janet and George, taken during a visit to Maine in 1979. (Janet McBride Collection)

"I remember that night that you and your family left for the last time," recalled Annie wistfully. "It was so cold, and I remember your dad honking the horn and you kids waving up a storm!" Annie paused and continued thoughtfully, "You know, Janet, you were always *different* from the rest."

They all laughed when John couldn't resist jumping on that statement: "She was then and still is *very different!*"

Later that day, when John and Janet drove down Rooney Road to where the old house used to be, Janet was a little sad. It just didn't seem to be the same as she remembered it and she left thinking that it must have been replaced. Try as she could, she didn't "see" the house she knew in her youth.

During that 1979 trip, the Ingrams kept an ear to the radio because they'd heard about a gas shortage and didn't want to take any chances, so they headed home to Texas.

Back in Texas, Janet was excited about her upcoming appearance on the Grapevine Opry show and generally happy to be back in the music business, even if it was "small time." One of the songs she did for that first show was "Chime Bells," her showy yodeling tune, and she was honored by a standing ovation. Of course, she was ecstatic!

She was asked back for another Grapevine Opry appearance and then Johnnie High asked her if she'd like to perform on a more regular basis and also on other shows he was producing. But she had just signed papers to enter the Dallas County Sheriff's Office deputy training school, and when training was completed she would be a full-fledged deputy with the Sheriff's Office and needed to be available to work any shift with no guarantee of particular days off. She would be expected to be there when called, and singing gigs would not be a valid reason to take off work. So she had to tell him, "No."

There were certain jobs inside the Dallas County jail system that wouldn't require her to work on the streets unless she chose to. As it turned out, she did work the jail area for a time, but transferred to the vault (the place where inmates' personal belongings were stored) and did other jobs such as booking inmates in and out. Later she was assigned training officer status and sometimes rode along as an escort with the women inmates who were being transferred to the prison facility in Gatesville, Texas.

One day in early 1980, Janet heard about an opry show in Stephenville, Texas, and when she finally found the contact information, she called and asked about an audition. When she told the manager her name he said she didn't need to audition; they knew who she was.

It was plain that the singing bug had re-bitten hard. Janet was in her mid-40s by the time she learned about these down-home country music shows, and it was beginning to look like singing might be a wonderful hobby. She and John had to plan well when they committed to a Saturday night show, to make sure she could get home in time to get some sleep and be at work on time on Sunday if she was scheduled.

cs

When Janet had quit singing in the 1970s, she had also quit writing songs. Because the opry folks wanted her to yodel each time she appeared and she knew only five yodeling songs and new ones were hard to find, she decided to write some of her own. One was called "A Yodeling Tribute" and another was "Best Dern Yodeler." Some of the artists at the opry shows were selling their records, so John and Janet started looking for a recording studio to make one of their own.

"We figured we could get our money back at least," she said. "You'd think I would have learned something for all the years and money I had already given to a recording career."

Tommy Allsup, from the old Metromedia Company days, was back in the Dallas/Fort Worth area and Janet asked him to produce her two songs. It was in1980 when she released a 45-rpm record on her own Brookhurst label.

She mailed a few copies out to the radio stations and followed up with a phone call. But nobody was playing it. She made an appointment with a DJ at one of the big stations in Dallas that she knew from the Longhorn Records days. "He had a variety of reasons why they couldn't play my record but the real reason was the station had a playlist and if the record wasn't on it, he couldn't play it," she explained.

It was primarily the late night DJs across the country who brought Janet's name back to radio. Janet contends that "Bill Mack is still the king of the all-night radio DJs." Had it not been for Bill Mack, the midnight cowboy on WBAP Radio in Fort Worth, Janet might have given up recording altogether, but Bill was playing her record to the truckers who could hear his show from coast to coast. Bill had played her records during the 1960s and believed in her talent and wanted to share it with his listeners. It wasn't long before she started hearing from people all over the country who had heard

"Ol' Bill." Many were fans from her earlier performance days, and had wondered why they hadn't heard any Janet McBride records for nearly ten years.

Larry Scott was another DJ friend who was playing her songs on KWKH in Shreveport, Louisiana, on his country-wide nighttime show.

"In the early 1980s, I talked to Bill Mack on the air many a

Bill Mack, after a Mesquite Opry show.
(Janet McBride Collection)

night while on my break during the midnight shift at the Dallas County Jail," confesses Janet. "There were jobs inside the jail facility that were pretty quiet from midnight until about 4 a.m., and being able to talk a few minutes with Ol' Bill helped brighten my night. That's why Bill Mack was such a success. The listeners never knew who might pick up the phone and call in to talk. He's still a dear friend and I will always treasure that friendship."

ജ

John's and Janet's day jobs meant traveling was limited—usually to visiting her mom and family, and if it was possible, they'd work in a visit to a music festival as well.

Later, her singing gigs would give them opportunities to see the world, and many times they'd turn those trips into vacations. Two trips to Nova Scotia to sing at the Hank Snow Festival are among special memories. The first was in 1997 when Janet's friend and mentor Bob Paulin invited her to appear with him and his band. They stayed in Bob's very comfortable Airstream trailer on the festival grounds and enjoyed being in the midst of all the music and excitement of the event. Invited back for the 1998 event, they were to have the same accommodations, but earlier that summer Bob discovered he had cancer of the esophagus. He passed away before festival time. Janet and John stayed in a bed-and-breakfast near Caledonia, Nova Scotia, "But it just wasn't the same without Bob," Janet recalled.

The two were given an open-ended invitation to perform any year they wished at the Hank Snow Festival in Liverpool, Nova Scotia, and Janet hopes to return one day to perform at that great event and enjoy the sights in that area of the world.

Canada has a special pull for Janet because her Grandmother Myrtle Carr Lister Blamey was born and raised there. Her Grandmother Phoebe Julia Marquis' family migrated through Canada, with their ancestry traced back to France in the 1600s. "I have always heard that we were somehow related to Lord Lister," Janet commented with a smile, "but maybe that is just 'Lister lore'."

Janet and John with an old, familiar street sign. Taken 1989. (Janet McBride Collection)

As they traveled south from Nova Scotia that second time, they decided to go back to Maine and revisit the area where Janet had spent several years of her childhood. They went back out to Rooney Road and drove past the house and turned around in the area where the Twist house used to be. As they drove slowly back up the road to a point where Janet was looking at the front of the house, which was sideways from the road, she realized that the old house was still there after all. She was thrilled to see it again.

This time Janet took photos, talked to the owner and "kind of freaked her out" when she told her she had lived there in the 1940s and described where every room was. When she mentioned the two rooms that shared the same fireplace, and the three little bedrooms, the current owner smiled and invited them in. There was an additional room upstairs in what had been an attic plus indoor plumbing and electricity throughout the house. The kitchen was a bit larger than before but not much else had changed. Janet's memories of life in that house took her back to 1946!

John and Janet didn't always travel alone. They especially enjoyed traveling with their good friends Larry and Shirley Shipman. On one occasion, the two couples flew to New York City, rented a car, drove to Niagara Falls, went over to the Canadian side, drove through Canada and re-entered the US in the New England area. They visited Janet's half-brother Victor (from her father's first marriage), whom she had never before seen. The Shipmans accompanied John and Janet as they looked for her old Rooney Road house in North Whitefield, Maine. They stuffed themselves with lobster and other great New England fare, then drove to New Brunswick before turning around and heading back to New York to fly home.

16
A Stage of her Own

*John caught the performing bug
and loved being on the stage.
(Janet McBride Collection)*

As she sometimes did, one summer day in 1981 Janet stopped by the Montgomery Ward store in Mesquite, just to chat with her former co-workers.

"Did you hear about the country music theater they're starting up here in Mesquite?"one of the gals asked Janet. "I don't know much about it, but there's a guy who's planning to start an opry show in the old Texan Theatre, down on the square."

"Boy, wouldn't that be nice!" exclaimed Janet to the gals. "That's only about 15 minutes from my house. If I could sing there instead of going all the way to Grapevine or Stephenville to their opry shows, I could save a bunch of driving!"

She stopped in at the Texan to see what was going on, but her hopes fell when she entered the theater for the first time. There was quite a bit of work going on, but it looked more like a disaster area than a place preparing for a show in a few weeks. Once home to a flea market, the building had no seats in place, the floor was bare gray cement and there was scaffolding along one wall where someone had begun painting a mural. The other two walls were bare and construction of the stage had barely begun. None of this really mattered to Janet. She just wanted to sing there, whenever the place was ready!

She asked the owner about auditioning for his new Mesquite Opry, told him about her various recordings and the other two Opry shows where she had been performing and, in true Janet-fashion, told him she'd be glad to perform without pay!

The first show was on Friday, September 18, 1981, and featured The Halyards, a family gospel group, and the Saturday, September 19, show featured Brian Collins, a 1980 Grammy nominee.

Janet appeared on the show for the first time on Friday, September 25. She arrived early so she could go through her songs with the band, and when she went backstage, she noticed a large cooler with iced-down beer. When she walked onstage to rehearse her numbers, she noticed that the guitar player had a burning cigarette stuck on one of the string-ends.

"How can they call this an *opry show*?" Janet asked herself. "An opry show should be a *family* show, not a place for drinking and smoking!"

But she loved to perform and tried not to let it bother her.

The crowd was pretty light that first night and most who came were either friends of the owner or friends of hers from Montgomery Ward. The show went well and Janet loved singing for the crowd, even if it was a small one.

"I'd be interested in coming back and performing again tomorrow night, if you'll have me," Janet mentioned to the boss before she left for home that Friday night.

He hesitated a few moments and replied, "Well, sure...yeah, that would be fine."

Later Janet learned that there were several entertainers who had invested their money and time into that old theater, with the hope of getting their money back at some point and being a part of the actual show when it opened. Janet was being invited back and she hadn't done anything to earn a spot other than sing a few songs.

The first house band worked about three weekends and then didn't return. The next band was pretty good, but they, too, lasted only two or three weeks and then were gone. Janet suspected that they weren't getting paid, but kept her suspicions to herself.

For several weeks, she sang there every Saturday night, with the exception of two that she had already booked at the Grapevine Opry and The Johnnie High Show.

೧ଓ

"I'm having some pretty bad financial troubles," the owner said to Janet and John one early October afternoon. "I was wondering...would you two have any interest in buying half of the show?"

"Well, maybe," John said. "But only if half ownership of the building is part of the deal."

A verbal agreement was made, and John and Janet were intrigued by the prospect of owning an opry show. They began almost immediately to raise the money they needed to fund half of the Mesquite Opry package. Too green to bargain with him or even to check things out thoroughly, they simply looked forward to owning part of a business that they loved, and had hopes that it one day might help with their retirement. With no idea of how unprofitable such activities can be, they forged ahead, and on October 20, 1981, the deal was finalized.

At first, John and Janet chose not to make any suggestions for changes in the show. The former full owner, now their partner, was still in charge of the band and guest talent, and continued to serve as MC for the shows. Janet and John helped with clean-up and concessions.

They became troubled when the first week went by without any information provided to them about income from that week's show, a bank deposit or attendance numbers. The second weekend they asked about figures, but received only vague answers.

"We knew there wasn't much to go into the bank, but as half owners we were concerned that it hadn't been mentioned," John recalled. "The electricity, water, gas and phone bills had to be paid each month and with the obvious low attendance there was reason for us to be concerned."

One morning in November they went to the theater alone just to take a closer look at their new "baby." There was a small office area just to the right of the door and when Janet went in to take a look around she noticed the Opry checkbook lying open on the desk.

"I can't believe it!" Janet said in dismay as she began to review the various expenses for which checks had been written—such things as the owners' personal bills, personal credit card payments and rent. The most recently written check was to a woman who came in to clean the theater's restrooms, something that Janet had earlier said wasn't necessary when the owners could do that on their own to save money. She called John into the office and, upon closer inspection, they found that the Opry was renting such items as an ice machine, a water cooler, a cigarette machine and a coffee maker. She called the partner immediately and arrangements were made for John and him to go to the bank the next day to open a new Mesquite Opry account with all of their names on it. Agreements were made that there would be no household bills paid for either couple out of the Opry account and all the owners would work together to clean the bathrooms. The cigarette machine was removed and they purchased the water cooler, the ice machine and the coffee maker outright.

"There was no confrontation or anything," Janet recalled. "It was just something that had to be done."

To enable better control of the sound, they suggested moving the mixing board from behind the stage to a position in an upstairs area in the back of the theater. John took over the responsibility for sound mixing. Stage lighting and curtain movement were also improved.

By the end of 1981, they were beginning to build a viable house band.

Rocky Lennon was hired as the bandleader, and was singing and playing piano. Ricky Gene Wright began as a solo artist and back-up singer, and later was added as rhythm guitar player. A young fiddle player named Jeff Huskins and his drum-playing brother Paul became regulars in the band and, as a group, they provided the foundation the show needed.

The partner was still in charge of lining up all the special guest talent, and was producing the show each week on his own. Things were beginning to stabilize, however, and the show *was* entertaining and began to run more smoothly. But with too few paid admissions, it was not making anything resembling a profit.

"Since the weather hadn't been cold up to this point, we hadn't given any thought to the heating of the building," Janet explained. "We knew there was a big heater upstairs and the building had been there for many years, so we assumed the heater would heat up the place when the time came. Well, we were wrong!"

On New Year's Eve, which fell on a Thursday that year, they planned to gather a few friends and band members for a small party at the theater. Several ladies brought snacks and soft drinks, and everyone, including the partners, were enjoying a pleasant evening. The heater was running but wasn't doing much to heat the place, and the attendees had to wear sweaters to keep warm.

About a week later, before a show in January, Texas's coldest time, they started the heating system the night before the show just to make sure the building would be warm by show time. But when they arrived Saturday morning they could still see their breath as they talked and sadly realized that the heater just wasn't up to the task of transforming the building's space from frigid to comfortable.

"I'd been talking to the Lord all day about the situation and asking for a miracle," said Janet. "I was afraid that we'd have to cancel that night's show."

A young mother named Emma Herron had recently joined the Opry cast. When she came in for rehearsal that day, she was told that the show would most likely be canceled that evening. Herron called her husband Charlie, who brought over a huge electric heater that looked, in Janet's estimation, "like a huge silver bullet and sounded like a jet engine when it was running." Within an hour that heater had brought the temperature in the building up to the "comfortable" level. Janet thanked the Lord for bringing the Opry a miracle in the form of Charlie Herron that day.

Thankfully, the theater's own heater was able to maintain the temperature in the building that night during the show, but they kept Charlie's heater on hand for back-up for the rest of the winter of 1982. They bought their own "magic bullet heater" before the cold season arrived the next year.

ભ

On Monday, January 25, 1982, Janet was scheduled to work the afternoon shift at the county jail. That morning she walked into the foyer of their theater and saw their partner with a lost look on his face. She attempted to cheer him, but was shocked when he said, "They've shut us down."

"Who has shut us down?" Janet asked.

"The tax people," he answered painfully. "I owe some back taxes."

"I'm really sorry, but what does that have to do with John and me?" she wondered out loud.

"They're attaching the building to get their money and they will be locking the doors soon," he explained woefully.

"After he 'fessed up to everything," recalled Janet, "we found out that he owed taxes to Uncle Sam, Dallas County and the City of Mesquite, plus a brother-in-law in Oklahoma had a lien against the theater building, so he also owed him money."

The money that Janet and John had paid him for their half of the theater and the show evidently hadn't made a dent in his money troubles.

The words of the officer at the Seagoville Bank, who had told them to be careful and make sure they knew what they were doing before they entered into this partnership, hit Janet and John hard as they realized they had not investigated their purchase thoroughly enough. Even though they had worked with an attorney, they had not required title insurance, a mistake that now could cost them dearly.

Claude McBride's brother Ray had been visiting in Dallas a couple of weekends before and had come by the Opry just to visit and see the theater. Janet remembered his remark: "If this guy ever wants to sell this little jewel give me a call." She called Ray and told him that half interest in "the little jewel" was available. He was truly excited about it and soon wired half of the needed money with the stipulation that John would accompany their soon-to-be ex-partner as he paid all the outstanding bills so that the theater building and the Opry show could open its doors without fear of any more surprises.

"If Ray McBride had not stepped in when he did, we would have lost our investment," said Janet.

As of January, 1982, the Mesquite Opry and the theater building that housed the show belonged to only Ray McBride and the Ingrams. It would prove to be the vehicle that would put Janet back on stage and in the music business—singing her beloved country music, writing songs and recording once again. The Ingrams' appreciation and affection for Ray McBride and his wife Sue would last through the years.

Ray had a successful business in California, which meant that John and Janet had full control of the day-to-day workings of the Opry.

While Janet produced and emceed the shows, John handled the sound and lights. Volunteers helped with ticket sales and concessions. Behind-the-scenes work, cleaning, purchasing and other tasks were accomplished by Janet and John on their time off from their full-time jobs. Janet also worked hard to gather a good group of musicians for the band and found some good guest talent to fill her shows.

To promote the shows, Janet, John and friends passed out flyers, contacted area newspapers for free publicity, did cable TV spots and put up posters —whatever they could do that didn't cost much.

Another effort to promote the show on a shoestring was an entry in the annual Mesquite Rodeo Parade, which became a yearly activity beginning in 1982. John rigged up an inexpensive sound system on a truck bed and gathered some of the talent and other volunteers who waved to the public along the

Ray McBride, Janet in uniform, and Janet's sons Claude Jr. and Mark (1982). (Janet McBride Collection)

parade route. Others stayed at the theater and sold concessions to the crowd. Over the years, involvement in the parade (and the resultant concession income) was an activity that became vital to the theater's bottom line. On parade day, the theater's regular patrons would bring their folding chairs and gather for a great time in front of the building. By 1983, the Opry gang had built a bandstand-on-a-trailer float that was used each year in the parade.

ଔ

Once a sufficiently large volunteer pool was in place, operation of the show ran a lot more smoothly. Members of the core group of volunteers and fans founded the Mesquite Opry Association, a club that helped support the Opry through fundraising and promotional efforts. Such names as Withrow, Greer, Bittner, Shipman, Carlson, Smith, Goodman, Peerman, Baxter, Tucker, Robertson, Cliatt and Moore were some of those early supporters who joined forces to create the Association and keep the mission of the Opry alive and well through the years. The Mesquite Opry Association was patterned after the Grapevine Opry Association, and membership included a newsletter, a discounted ticket price and occasional get-togethers.

Both Janet and John were working full time jobs that involved rotating shifts, with no guarantee of weekends off. More than once Janet got into her uniform at the break, drove to work, and then stopped by after work to sweep the floors and clean up the mess made the night before. During the week John took the past week's deposit to the bank, then purchased products for the concession stand and other supplies.

Before long the couple realized that the effort, time and money that the twice-a-week Opry shows required of them might be more than they could handle. In late June of 1982, they changed from Friday and Saturday shows to only Saturday night. It was a way to save on utility costs and band payments, and they hoped that having the show only on Saturday night might make it special enough to bring increased numbers of music fans through the doors.

With the Saturday-night-only shows, attendance numbers picked up somewhat, and both Janet and John fell into the routine of presenting these amateur/semi-pro musical shows for the folks in the area. "There's nothing quite like the feeling I'd get when someone would tell me how entertaining the show was," said Janet, "and then ask what we were going to do to top it next week!"

An early shot of The Mesquite Opry building, before the large sign was installed, was taken as the audience was going in for the show.

Sometimes the joys of owning the Opry were offset by the problems of keeping up the repairs on the old theater building. At some point in 1982, a problem reared its head when, during a hard rain, the roof began leaking—directly onto the seats. They blocked off the affected seats for that night's show and made plans to get the roof repaired—because, like true entertainers, they knew that "the show must go on!"

The first roof repair company they hired came, took a lot of their money, spread some tar and left—without a guarantee. When the next rains came, the roof leaked again, although not as badly as before. Determined that he could do at least a temporary repair job, John purchased a supply of plastic sheeting and tar and attempted to fix it himself. Before John got home, the owner of the restaurant next door called and told Janet that the wind was blowing the tar-laden plastic across the windows of the restaurant and the Opry house.

"The fronts of both buildings were a mess," Janet remembers. "Needless to say, John was totally embarrassed and extremely disappointed that his whole day and his repair job had been wasted." They had to hire another company, this time with more satisfactory results.

A few years later, rain followed by freezing temperatures caused cracks in one area of the roof, which happened to be just above the sound board, by this time located downstairs in the back of the theater. The resulting leaks ruined the board and they had no choice but to replace it, creating a double hit to the budget.

The problems that occurred and recurred through Janet and John's fifteen years of owning the theater building never seemed to end, and many times the Opry didn't have the money to cover them, so they put their own money into it. Without their good jobs with the Dallas County Sheriff's Department, the dream would have ended.

When a training-officer position came open in the Sheriff's Department, Janet's supervisor approached her about taking it. After he assured her that she could work the day shift and have her weekends off to work at the Opry, she decided to take it. (She remained in that position until 1985 when she became a bailiff in the courthouse.)

As the years moved on, Janet and John got into the swing of running the theater and the show became more and more important in their audience members' lives. Fans were being truly entertained and that's what it was all about for Janet. Shows were coming off more and more smoothly, talent was increasingly stronger, crowds were picking up, and Janet absolutely loved what she was doing—and John supported her in every way.

⑳

With all the work there was to do around the Mesquite Opry, and with only John and Janet running the show, there was a tremendous need for volunteer help. Volunteers made the Opry happen each weekend, and by blending their varied talents, they gave the stage, the theater building and the overall operation an element of class.

Janet has lots of memories of some pretty special Opry volunteers who did some wonderful things over the Opry's lifetime.

The Vinyards, who ran an embroidery shop in town, made and donated a silk Mesquite Opry flag that was displayed on the stage from the beginning. Helen Nutter fashioned a beautiful Mesquite Opry Band sign made of tile that fit right in front of the steel guitar. Another talented volunteer made two stained glass signs—one saying "Mesquite Opry," the other a representation of Janet's blue guitar—that hung in the lobby.

From the beginning, an old banjo and fiddle adorned the side stage wall, and later on, so did an old Silvertone guitar, donated by Sergeant Rufus High from the Dallas County Sheriff's Office. All these pieces decorated the stage throughout the Opry's history.

There were several other gifts from Opry supporters through the years.

Comedy was an important part of the entertainment presented by the Mesquite Opry. That's John Ingram on the right (yep! sure is!), along with Jamie Shipman and Mark McBride, doing a skit about rock 'n' roll music. Junior Knight is on steel guitar. (Janet McBride Collection)

Laverne Van Hutson donated a brand new baby grand piano for the Opry stage. Cy and Pat Baxter funded the rebuilding of the women's restrooms. Monte Woods, who worked for a sign company, installed a large neon Mesquite Opry sign on the front of the building.

Many folks donated items to be raffled off to help raise funds for building maintenance or to help pay for a big-name guest performer. In addition, Maxine Tucker made wonderful pies for the Association dinners.

Several volunteers worked regularly for the Opry. Jean Wheeler Lee, Shirley Shipman and Karen Beauchler sold tickets; JoAnn Tucker and, later, Ernie Moore and Janet's daughter Denise sold concessions.

Janet's son Claude, a Dallas police officer, often came to help out— with the condition that he could leave as soon as the audience was inside the theater. "We counted on Claude a lot in the beginning, but he was a young, single guy, and the Opry wasn't the place he really wanted to be on a Friday or Saturday night," recalls Janet. Once in a while, her son Mark came to help out as well, usually when someone couldn't come in for some reason. Later, he became a regular entertainer on the show.

There was an early group of volunteers that Janet lovingly called the "Opry Work Crew." Comprised primarily of Bill Goodman, Larry Shipman, Curtis Smith, Robert Tucker, Gary Peerman and Cy Baxter, the group of men scheduled work days from time to time, and repaired and updated things in the theater building. When a benefit drive enabled Janet and John to purchase new seats, the "Opry Work Crew" installed them. They rebuilt the old air conditioner, installed new stage lights, built dressing rooms, installed a bathroom, made the public bathrooms handicapped-accessible, rebuilt the stage, and accomplished many other "handyman" duties as well.

"It was because of all the volunteers that we were able to keep the Mesquite Opry show going," explains Janet. "Plain and simple...it would not have been possible without them!"

CB

While seated on a stool and playing rhythm guitar for the band, Janet provided transitions between acts, giving the show a smooth flow, as she introduced guest after guest through the years. But what made the show special and entertaining for music fans were the many musicians and singers who spent time on her stage sharing their own individual forms of talent. Janet has fond memories of all of them.*

The band was the foundation for the show and Janet worked to find the best musicians she could get. Through the years, band members came and went as they pursued their musical aspirations elsewhere.

Once Rocky Lennon moved on, Chris Rickets played piano for a few months. Then they were without a piano player until a young Keith Kukendall came by the theater one practice night and offered to play piano, and they decided to put him in the band. He was the first to suggest a chart system of communicating chords so the band could easily learn a new song. It was a technique that added greatly to the Opry band's professionalism.

JoAnn and Robert Tucker's son Mike was just a teenager when he was invited to sit in on drums at the Opry. He was an instant hit with the audience and the rest of the band. He left the Opry when he got a job with the up-and-coming group known as "Canyon." Later he landed a full-time job as drummer for the Bellamy Brothers band and stayed with them about ten years. He is now in a back-up band for a show at the Golden Nugget in Las Vegas.

Earl Briggs, the band's steel guitar player, came to the Opry when he was still a teenager in 1982 and stayed until he left to play regularly for The Wylie Opry in north Texas.

Jim and Carla Little, country musicians from Dallas, came to the Opry at a time when they were sorely needed. Jim played lead guitar and Carla filled in on steel guitar when the regular player couldn't make it.

George Geisser's name was added to the Opry's list of musicians in 1984. George and his family were from the East Coast and took unending ribbing for being a "Yankee." A self-taught musician, George played fiddle with the band for a while and worked to familiarize himself with country music tunes. He left to take a full-time fiddle-playing job with the mountain music shows in Eureka Springs, Arkansas, and Silver Dollar City near Branson, Missouri. He was a staff musician with the largest and most successful show in Branson, "The Shoji Tabuchi Show."

The late Gary Hogue played steel guitar on a part-time basis when the Opry's regular steel player wasn't available. Janet had known Gary since he was a teenager and asked him to produce and play on some of the albums she released in the 1980s. After the Opry, Gary went on to play steel with Marty Stuart's band and was with him until his (Gary's) passing.

Steel player Junior Knight, who had been a regular band musician for the Longhorn Ballroom and also a road musician with several big name acts, played with the Mesquite Opry band for eight years. When he left the Opry, he worked at one of the largest local night spots in the Dallas area until LeAnn Rimes asked him to join her road band. Like Gary, Junior has played on several of Janet's recordings over the years and can be heard on her 2009 CD entitled "Still Loving the Ride."

Art Greenhaw was leader of the band from 1983 through 1994. "Art was the glue that held the finest bunch of Opry musicians together for all of that time," Janet recalls. "He loved being part of the Mesquite Opry Band and went on to make a name for himself when he became half owner and a full-time member of The Light Crust Doughboys." (Art recorded dozens of sessions with The Light Crust Doughboys before becoming the sole owner of the group when Smokey Montgomery passed away. Art promoted, recorded and booked the original James Blackwood gospel group and, with the combined recordings of the Doughboys and Blackwood's group, he won two Grammy Awards.)

Johnny Crawford with Janet at the Opry's ticket booth before a show in 1989. (Janet McBride Collection)

150

Paul Polish and his family came to the Opry as fans in 1984. Paul later became a regular singer and a favorite on the show. He filled in on bass when Grandpa Marvin Hitt left, then when Mike Tucker left, he slid into the drummer's seat, where he stayed, and Thomas Miller, a regular singer along with his friend Connie Faulk and her daughter Christi, began playing bass.

Polish and Miller, along with Art Greenhaw and Junior Knight, made for a solid band, and they were all quite handsome, according to Janet, and the gals in the audience loved that!

Jerl Welch auditioned at the Opry on March 31, 1990. He was a strong harmonica player and fit into the band perfectly as a lead player. As good fiddle players were difficult to find and Janet had had little luck in finding one who would stay, she asked Jerl to play lead on harmonica. He could take the place of a fiddler, playing the "kick-offs" and lead breaks for any song thrown at him, and he could do solo features whenever the band was performing an instrumental.

"Jerl was good-looking and the ladies added him to the list of reasons to come to the Opry," recalls Janet with a smile. "Those ladies loved the band members and the band loved them back."

Jerl stayed with the show until the last song was played on December 30, 1995. Welch's music can be heard on many of Janet's recordings and he and his wife Ann will always be regarded as dear friends of John and Janet's.

Joe Degelia was recommended by Jerl Welch as a lead guitar player. At first rehearsal, Joe showed up with long hair and a beard, but those two things disappeared before the first show. "Joe had been a club musician for so many years and when his kids could come and see their dad on stage, that was just the greatest, as far as Joe was concerned," remembers Janet. "And the ladies loved Joe, too."

One part-time drummer, Jamie Lynn Slayton, stands out in the Opry's list of musicians. She loved the Opry and came to play whenever she was summoned. She was especially thrilled the night she got to play for Grand Ole Opry star Connie Smith.

Included in the long list of players who were part of the Mesquite Opry band at one time or another are fiddler Willie Van Hook, steel player Milo Deering (who would go on to become band leader for LeAnn Rimes in her early career), Skip Pilgrim (a steel-guitar-playing preacher), pianist Terry Tosch and singer/piano player Vincent Worley.

Many different guest artists graced the Opry stage as well, some with famous names and others (like James Farmer) who were local or regional favorites. The goal each week was to fill the seats, and John and Janet worked hard to choose artists who could do that.

Patsy Montana, cowgirl singer/yodeler who was best known for her song, "I Want to Be a Cowboy's Sweetheart," was one of the first famous artists who appeared on the Opry. She appeared ten different times and was one of the top favorites.

Connie Faulk, who started on the Opry as a single, soon added her daughter Christi and later Thomas Miller to form a trio they called "Country Flair." Sometimes she invited Thomas's brother Matt to perform as well. When they performed as a group, they consistently brought the house down. Encores and standing ovations were common for this trio. Then one Saturday night after the show, Connie and Thomas exchanged marriage vows on the stage of the Opry. Both Connie and Thomas continued to perform with the Opry until the last show.

Bill Callahan of The Callahan Brothers appeared once. Bill Phillips was a screaming success and one of the best all-around entertainers on the Opry stage. Charlie Louvin appeared twice with his son Sonny playing lead guitar for him. Pretty Miss Norma Jean appeared twice and was a true favorite. Melba Montgomery was a hit with her "No Charge" song, and Claude Gray of "Family Bible" fame was a guest on at least one show. Connie Smith was a huge success, and right in the front row for her show, sat the world famous singer-songwriter and disc jockey Bill Mack. Even Johnny Crawford, from TV's *The Rifleman* series, put on a show for the Opry crowd. The Light Crust Doughboys appeared twice. Grand Ole Opry star Jack Greene gave an

The Opry regulars at a show at the Mesquite Championship Rodeo arena. Front row: Connie Faulk, Christi Faulk, Janet, Karon Shipman and Emma Tucker. Back row: Paul Polish, Jr. Knight, Art Greenhaw, Jamie Shipman, Thomas Miller, Robert Tucker and Larry Shipman. (Janet McBride Collection)

excellent performance and thrilled everyone when he went to breakfast with the band and staff of the Opry and joined in the conversation like he had known everyone for years. Walter Nevada brought the "Salty Dogs" band from Europe and put on a memorable show for Opry crowds.

Connie Smith was featured in a 1994 Opry show.

The various members of the Shipman family became a major part of the Mesquite Opry from the first night their youngest child, 15-year-old Jamie, appeared on the show with dad Larry playing guitar behind her. In a letter included in the scrapbook that Larry was to give Janet and John many years later when the Opry was closing, Larry told a heartwarming story about Jamie's first time on the show. Jamie sang "Some Days Are Diamonds" that night and when the crowd responded with really warm applause, Janet asked her to sing another song. The youngster explained that she had performed the only song she knew and Janet said, "Well, sing it again!" The second time she was on the show she brought along her sister Karon, and soon both girls became regulars on the Opry. Later on, brother Zane performed with them as well.

"It wasn't unusual for Larry and all the Shipman offspring to be onstage performing as a group," recalls Janet. Zane sometimes brought along his barbershop quartet and often provided some good family comedy with his portrayal of "a perfect nerd." Karon performed until she married and started her family and Jamie sang there until the end of the Opry's run. Dad Larry and mom Shirley were dedicated Opry volunteers from the day they walked in the door in 1982. Larry Shipman worked for AT&T in Mesquite at the time and regularly "talked up" the Opry to his co-workers at AT&T. Jamie later joined the Light Crust Doughboys as a singer, the first and only female to be a member of that legendary group.

A gal who made a big impact on the Opry fans was Emma Herron, otherwise known as "Miss Emma." She was a pure country singer-songwriter who sang and wrote from the hurt she'd experienced in her life. Her time with the Opry, however, helped her to blossom, from Janet's perspective. She was especially good at comedy routines that involved dressing up like Dolly Parton or portraying "Fatsy" Montana in a parody of Patsy Montana. The crowd howled when she attempted to yodel like the most famous yodeler of all! Emma and her husband Charlie divorced along the way and her comedy routines began to use Robert Tucker, one of the volunteers, as the "straight man." Robert already had a great following as his "Elmer Dean, the Plumber" act. The two became a huge hit as "Elmer Dean and Geraldine Dean."

Tucker had been married to Janet's friend JoAnn, and as a couple they had introduced Janet to John Ingram, the man she would marry. During their time at the Opry, Tucker and Emma Herron became a couple and eventually got married. In addition to her role as comedian, Emma served as president of the Mesquite Opry Association for several years.

Young steel guitarist Sarah Jory from the United Kingdom was featured annually from 1987 through 1990 when she came to the Dallas area for the Steel Guitar Association's yearly convention. "We watched a teenage Sarah progress into one of the leading steel guitar players whose name is now known worldwide," recalled Janet.

Joe Paul Nichols appeared several times and became a Mesquite Opry favorite. The Pfiffer Brothers presented a program of cowboy music and The Palmer Family Band, who also sang western music, appeared twice. Bob Everhart, director of the big National Old-Time Music Festival, came by twice on his way to spending the winter in old Mexico. A couple who were to become dear friends of Janet and John's, Ed and Jolene Bullard from Oklahoma, appeared with a group of friends and entertained the crowd with some great bluegrass music from time to time. Ed was a very popular disc jockey in Atoka, Oklahoma, and promoted the Opry by playing Janet McBride songs on-air during the weeks leading up to their appearance.

Other early stand-out talent appearing on the Mesquite Opry included:

Dave Cash....known as "Little Willie" because of his likeness to Willie Nelson. Singer/guitarist who now lives in Colorado.

Rita and Lori Anderson...known as The Anderson Sisters. They also sometimes sang with their mother. Lori has a family now and is no longer in the music business. Rita continues her singing and is raising a family.

Craig Arnold...Singer who lives in Mesquite and works with "The Christian Pickers."

Shawn Bailey...Fiddle player who went on to appear with a group of Texas youth in Branson, Missouri.

Jan Barker...Singer who appeared on the Big D Jamboree during its early days and later appeared at the Mesquite Opry.

Ken Berry...Singer who later went on to work in Branson.

Nathan Belt...Currently in the "Fifties" and "Elvis" shows at the Grapevine Opry.

Robert Blackburn...Singer who went on to work in Branson.

David Bradley... Singing cowboy who performed with "The Sons of the Pioneers" for five years as lead singer, harmony singer, yodeler, rhythm guitar and even comedian. He currently performs as a solo act.

Larry Bradfute...Singer/guitarist who plays with "The Studebakers" and "Just Country" bands in North Texas.

Wanda Clark...Singer with a band called "Southern Spur," based in Mesquite.

Randy Erwin...Cowboy singer who lives in Illinois and continues to perform.

Freddie Eskridge...Singer/songwriter based in Texas.

Tommy Horton...Singer who performs at festivals, fairs, theaters across the US, in Europe and Canada.

Woody Leath...Singer who has released material on major labels.

Shawn Lee...Early yodeling protégé who enjoyed early success on recordings, now a motivational speaker and raising a family in Mt. Juliet, Tennessee.

Willie Mack ...A singer/songwriter who went on to work with Marty Stuart. He has had songs recorded by well-known performers, and has charted with five singles on Canadian country music charts.

The Marie Sisters...Chaz and Kessie Marie, recorded one album for

Universal/Republic Records, charted one single on the *Billboard* Hot Country Singles & Tracks charts ("Real Bad Mood," peaked at #46). Still performing in the Dallas/Fort Worth area.

Ed Parker... Known as "The Singing Sheriff," Ed performed at festivals and theaters across the country. He has now passed away.

Stephen Pride...Brother of Charlie Pride, known for

Patsy Montana watches with appreciation as a young LeAnn Rimes performs "I Want to Be a Cowboy's Sweetheart" at the Opry on August 13, 1994. (Janet McBride Collection)

singing his brother's songs, continues to perform at festivals and events.

Keith Sewell...Singer/songwriter/multi-instrumentalist who went on to work for Ricky Skaggs, continues writing and performing for Skaggs and has toured with several major artists as well.

Brian Spradlin...Singer/musician who went on to perform in Branson.

Teri Travis...Singer who went on to work at Opryland in Nashville.

Scott Whittaker...This singing police officer formed his own band and went on to win the Colgate Country Showdown.

Lee Ann Womack...Singer who went on to have several chart hits, and continues to be very active in the music industry. (She recently recorded one of Kacey Musgrave's songs, not yet released. Kacey was a member of the Buckaroos group of young entertainers founded by the Cowtown Opry of Forth Worth.)

The following were all strong performers at The Mesquite Opry, but their activities after the Opry years are unknown: Chaz Avery, Clyde Creel, C.C. Dozier, Reverend Mike Edmondson, The Fancy Pants Cloggers, Jon Henderson, Nisha Jackson, Lisa Lassig, Keith Van Treese, The Purtles, Ed Post, Mark Manley, J. D. Munson, Andy Neugent, Jennifer Raynor, Stacy Burke, Chris Dotson and Sammy Sadler.

ങ

Young talent was a big part of the Opry's show schedule—for several reasons. Janet loved to help them get started on the stage, they often brought lots of paying family members with them, and the audience loved them. Many of those youngsters have gone on to accomplish big things in Branson, Nashville, Dollywood and other well known music venues.

One of those youngsters was **Lani Bartley**, who has been a regular entertainer at the Texas State Fair for several years. **Nathan Belt** and **Doug Ashby** were entertainers at the Mesquite Opry who went on to win many awards at the Grapevine Opry.

Jeff Huskins, just 14 when he began playing fiddle regularly on the Opry, stayed until 1983 when he left to play for such groups and single acts as "The Shoppe," Clint Black, Gene Watson and "Little Texas." He later headed up a Nashville-based record company. Jeff's brother Paul was the drummer with the band off and on for some time.

David Norris, the youngest son of legendary steel player Charlie Norris, played drums in the band for a while then moved on to play in various local bands.

Eleven-year-old **Robert Blackburn** did his first show with the Mesquite Opry on January 15, 1982. Blackburn would later take his talent to the Branson shows. On March 5, 1982, 14-year-old **Tim Rushlow** appeared on the Opry for the first time. He and his mom Patti were on often that year and soon had progressed to performing on Johnnie High's show on a regular basis. Tim Rushlow was a founding member of the "Little Texas" band and enjoyed several hit records through the years. When that band broke up in 1997, Tim formed his own group known simply as "Rushlow."

Allison Moore and **Karen Rhodes** were 11 and 13 respectively when they joined the Opry. They both moved up to the Johnnie High Show and then on to the Shoji Tabuchi Show in Branson. Karen is currently working in Nashville and Allison is a motivational speaker and very involved in her church in Springfield, Missouri.

A four-year-old **Josh Owen** started appearing on the Opry along with his dad and brother in 1990. Later Josh was a finalist on both the *Ed McMahan's Star Search* and *Nashville Star* television shows. He was a regular on several Branson shows over the years and still makes the Texas opry circuit with his brother and dad from time to time.

LeAnn Rimes, Steve Holy, Chris Rodriguez, Blake Barnes and **Hillary Bergman** also found their footing on the Mesquite Opry before moving to bigger things in the entertainment industry.

Along the way, Janet encouraged the parents of young aspiring entertainers to be there for their children, meaning that they needed to make the commitment to take them to the shows that would let them get up in front of an audience to perform. Many parents over the years have let Janet know what a difference being on the Mesquite Opry made in their child's ability to get up in front of a school class or assembly and speak, a comment that only strengthened Janet's devotion to helping young entertainers.

While the Mesquite Opry many times gave the youngest of the talent a stage where they could find their footing before they advanced to the bigger shows, Johnnie High, who operated a well-produced country show in Arlington, Texas, served as a springboard for more developed local talent. The Grapevine Opry in nearby Grapevine, Texas, was another springboard for youngsters who found their first footing on The Mesquite Opry.

ca

All the Opry fans were special and oh-so-appreciated but certain ones brought a little extra fun to the Opry house when they showed up in the audience. Some of these were Dewey Groom from the Longhorn Ballroom; Walter Nevada from Vienna, Austria, who often brought a group of tourists visiting the United States; Gene Davis, Janet's long-time friend from California; Canadian yodeler Shirley Fields; New Hampshire yodeler Paul Belanger and even Barbara Mandrell's dad Irby, who came by a couple of times and just sat and watched the show. Johnny Horton's manager, Tilman Franks (who was in the car accident that killed Johnny) once visited the show with a new artist that he was promoting (Gene Snow). The then Chief of the Cherokee Nation Wilma Mankiller visited one Saturday night. Others were just special, ordinary folks, such as two regular fans: Doug Weaver (who sat in the front row) and Maxine Tucker, who were there every Saturday and helped wherever they could. Karen Beauchler was one of those fans who lit up the hall when she came during those early Opry days.

Here are a couple of Janet's favorite fan stories:

One year a group of Mesquite Opry talent and fans went to Fan Fair in Nashville. While Ernie Moore (an avid fan from Mesquite who also volunteered at the concession booth) was in the men's room, a stranger struck up a conversation with him about his Mesquite Opry T-shirt. Ernie told Marc DeNicolai, a country music fan from the West Coast, that the

Mesquite Opry was the "best country music show around" and suggested that Marc stop by on his way back to California. Marc and his wife Carol attended the Opry that next Saturday night as they headed back home in their RV. The DeNicolais became instant fans of the Opry and fast friends of John and Janet's. Later, the Ingrams often visited the DeNicolai family and stayed at their home while they were seeing family in California. Marc and his wife Carol even hosted concerts featuring Janet in their home or their local community center from time to time. They also traveled back to Texas many times just to attend the "best country music show around!"

Another time, John and Janet and about 20 other Mesquite Opry people went to Fan Fair all wearing—as planned—their brightly colored Mesquite Opry T-shirts each day of the event. A man approached Janet on the Fan Fair grounds and asked her if she knew Janet McBride, to which Janet answered, "Why yes, *I'm* Janet McBride." They both laughed and the gentleman introduced himself as Pete Lenloy, the DJ from Austria with whom Janet had been corresponding for several years. (In 1996, John and Janet reconnected with Lenloy when they were on tour in Austria.)

❧

In November of 1994, while John and Janet were attending the Western Music Association (WMA) festival in Tucson, John suffered a heart attack and returned to Texas where he underwent quadruple bypass surgery. He had complained only of shortness of breath, but this episode and the surgery took a toll on his energy level. For several weeks, he was not even able to attend the Opry much less work the sound board.

Somewhere in the middle of 1995, they found themselves thinking that all the work and expense of the Opry were going to have to end. Even with two hundred paying folks each week, the income too often fell short of the "outgo." "We really needed to raise the admission price," Janet mused, "but we knew our audience members just couldn't pay any more."

In addition, John needed some serious rest and time without stress so he could fully recover from his heart problems.

"I'm not sure when John was able to return to the Opry sound board, but for sure he didn't bounce back all that fast," recalled Janet.

Janet was hoping to retire from the Sheriff's Department in April of 1996, but felt she couldn't leave her job and still continue making payments on the Opry building at the same time. After heart-breaking deliberation, she and John settled on December 30, 1995 as their last Mesquite Opry show.

Dozens of artists who had appeared on the Opry through the years asked to be on that last show, and they were all stars! Finally the big night came. The show was allowed to go on as long as needed as each entertainer shared his or her special talent and comments with the fans.

There was a little sadness in the air, but also an air of celebration, as if it were a reunion of a family whose members all had a connection to the Opry.

The guest artists that night were Doug Ashby, The Marie Sisters, Laverne Van Hutson, Mike Shirley, Mark Manley, Jennifer Sanford, Glenn Kelly, Trish Atwater, Tommy Horton, Randi Crawford, Aaron Rodriguez, Nathan Belt, Brian Cline, Vickie Gatling, Gayla Dawn, Wanda Clark, Bill Rogers, Bob Skaggs, Curtis Smith, Bill Goodman, Eric Phillips, Marilyn McConnell, Kevin James and Jamie Travis. Regular performers were Robert and Emma Tucker, The Shipman Family and Country Flair.

The band was comprised of Thomas Miller, Connie Miller, Jerl Welch, Paul Polish and Joe Degelia, with Junior Knight as guest steel player. Junior said, "I just *had* to be there!"

But the real stars were Janet McBride and John Ingram, the couple who had given life to this weekly, family-style country music show.

ଔ

Owning and operating the Mesquite Opry, even with its many expenses and headaches, gave Janet the chance to own the stage she performed on.

"That show started a fire in me that still hasn't burned out," Janet recounts. "I saw some of the most talented kids and they didn't even know how much it was helping me to help them," Janet reminisces. "I could see myself in them and I cherished the ability to put out my hand for them to hang on to. By keeping the kids coming, we kept a crowd coming, because all those kids had aunts, uncles and friends from school. It was a win/win situation for the Opry, for those youngsters and their families as well, not to mention for me personally."

The Opry also helped Janet sell her various recordings from the early days and gave her credibility as she recorded new projects. During this period, she continued to write songs as well, and credits her involvement with the Opry for helping to make that possible. Such Janet McBride songs as "The Gospel Yodel" and "Yodeling at the Grand Ole Opry" (co-written with Gwen Young) were created during this period of her life.

She also gained expanded exposure for her various recordings. Janet was in the process of recording a cassette of all original songs for her Brookhurst record label when she was contacted by Binge Records of West Germany. She agreed to let them re-release all of her old recordings on an LP. A second LP of Janet recordings was released the next year. Cattle Records, another company owned by the same people who owned Binge, approached Janet in 1986 to record a project with Alabama country legend Dexter Johnson and his band. Two yodeling LPs from those sessions were released on Cattle Records, one in 1986 and another in 1988.

The Opry also broadened Janet's knowledge of other aspects of the entertainment industry as well. She served as MC from the day she and John took over the show in February 1982. She booked and coordinated the talent and produced each week's show. For the majority of those shows, she played rhythm guitar in the band as well.

cs

Soon everyone in the Dallas metroplex knew that the show had closed and the building was for sale. Rocky Gribble from the Grapevine Opry was the first person serious about buying. John and Janet worked with him for several months and finally in October 1996, the papers were all signed and the McBride/Ingram team was out of the opry business.

Once Gribble purchased the operation, he turned it over to Mike and Elizabeth Edmonson to manage, as he was still running the Grapevine Opry. Janet sang at the new Mesquite Opry each Saturday night in October and twice in November of that year, in an effort to help the new owner hold some of the old crowd. She appeared almost every Saturday through June of 1997, but by then was more than ready to walk away.

"The Opry had its ups and downs, but the experience was a perfect lesson of 'Don't ever give up!' and 'Quit while you're ahead!' and I was ready to move on," said Janet. "We were worn out with the hard work of it, not to mention the financial worry!"

"When we hosted various stars who were appearing on the Opry, we really got to know them well," recalls Janet. "Johnny Crawford from *The Rifleman*, the Light Crust Doughboys, Charlie Louvin, Norma Jean, Claude Gray, Melba Montgomery, Connie Smith, Jack Greene, Patsy Montana and LeAnn Rimes became more than just Opry guests. They became friends!"

"How many times did I hear John say 'I can't believe that a little boy from Mineola, Texas, has been able to meet and get to know this many famous people!'" she laughingly shares as she recalls John's enthusiasm for the lives they were leading.

"So many wonderful people became our friends—and friends of each other," Janet remembers. "There were marriages, divorces, deaths, births and some real bumps in the road, but we usually came out of them alright. It was almost 15 years of having the most fun I've ever had!"

17

Sing Me a Story

Johnny Western presents Janet the
2002 WMA Award for Song of the Year
(for "Wyoming Rose").
(Janet McBride Collection)

Janet's father wrote his one and only song when she was a teenager. She helped by putting it to a tune and adding a yodel. They called it "My Echo and I." "Daddy sent for a copyright," said Janet, "and my love for writing songs started right then and there." She recorded that first-ever song twice, in 1951 and 1953, each with a different yodel, then, many years later used one of the cuts on her "50 Years of Yodeling" CD.

When Janet began to record professionally in 1959, Claude was writing songs and Janet would add her ideas along the way. One of Janet's own early songwriting efforts, "That's Not Like Me," was recorded by Freddie Hart in the early 1970s on an LP he did for Capitol Records. She had given up half the writing rights, but did receive royalties from it.

Janet wrote two songs that were tributes to her parents, Aurelia and Victor Lister, shown in this shot taken at Joan's wedding in 1954.
(Janet McBride Collection)

Since Janet wasn't registered with BMI* in her early recording days, they put the songs in Claude's name, who was a registered writer. Dewey Groom asked her one day why her name wasn't on her songs, and she told him she wasn't a BMI writer. He laughed and had her fill out the BMI registration papers...and her name was added to all the songs she wrote after that.

Although not as prolific as some songwriters, Janet has certainly written a varied style of songs: gospel, honky-tonk, yodeling, heartbreak, love songs, cheatin' songs and ballads. She's written songs about her own personal experiences and about things that she just imagined.

In the 1960s, when Janet was keeping company with other entertainers

_____

* *BMI (Broadcast Music, Inc.) is an organization that collects license fees on behalf of its songwriters, composers and music publishers and distributes them as royalties.*

like Vern Stovall, Bobby George and Curtis Leach, writing songs became a way of life. "We'd hear a clever line and start thinking about how to work it into a song," she recalled. When she stepped away from the music business, she stopped writing. Once she stepped back onto the stage, she started writing again. The first two were "Best Dern Yodeler," which tells of her Maine experiences as she was first learning to yodel, and "The Yodeling Tribute," which honors the many yodelers she holds in high esteem.

Best Dern Yodeler

I can't tell you how I felt, the first time I heard somebody yodel.
I wasn't very old, but it was something I knew I had to do.
I lived in New England at the time,
And they weren't that big on country,
But if I got up early, I could hear the yodeling theme song
Of the early morning country music shows.

I yodeled in the fields, and in the woods
And even picking wild raspberries and I had dreams of being
The best dern country yodeler in the land.
My lessons came from records, I heard them playing on the radio.
"Chime Bells" was my favorite.
I learned the "Cowboy's Sweetheart"
But "He Taught Me how to Yodel" stole the show
(Yodel)

We moved back to California,
Where Dad bought me a Silvertone guitar,
And with the few chords that I knew,
I entered singing contests near and far.
And when someone yodeled something new,
I practiced till I knew that I had learned it,
'Cause to get the title of "the best dern yodeler in the land"
I knew that I was gonna have to earn it!

I sang around the country for a while
And this poor girl really tried
To make it to the top, but I quit, it was just too rough a ride.
There's not much yodeling anymore,
And though I quit a while, I still can!
So I'm going to yodel country-style, and maybe for a little while,
I'll be the best dern yodeler in the land!
(Yodel)

Like most songwriters, Janet finds her inspiration in the situations around her. For example, after working a full day in divorce court (as a bailiff), she felt like everyone there wished that it wasn't happening and that there would be no real winner. She went home and wrote a song called "If It Hurts this Much to Win (I'm Glad I Didn't Lose)."

"Mom, Can I Come Home?" was also inspired by her job as bailiff in the felony court. "I'd pull inmates from the 'tank' to see the judge or the lawyer and they'd never fail to ask, 'Is my Mama out there?'" said Janet. "They would promise the judge, their lawyer and their families that they would change if they just had one more chance and out they'd go, only to mess up again and come right back to my 'tank' to ask the same question: 'Is my Mama out there?'"

Sometimes Janet would use the songs she wrote as a release of some of the anger she held from her waiting-for-Claude-to-come-home days. Songs like "Alone Again," "A Little at a Time," "I'm Leaving this Time" and "Why'd Ya Do It?" are in that category.

"This One's for Daddy" was written for a recording session with Dexter Johnson for the Cattle label and was released in 1986 on the "Yodeling at the Grand Ole Opry" LP. It's Janet's tribute to her father.

An interesting story about that song: Brother Don and his wife—on a trip home from Maine, stopped at an RV park in South Dakota, right outside of Deadwood. Don signed in at the office and went to set up, and soon the lady from the office was knocking on their RV asking if he was Janet McBride's brother. The lady's daughter, an aspiring yodeler, had Janet's LP and particularly like the "Daddy" song. She knew the Lister name from the liner notes and was excited to meet the brother of her favorite yodeler.

This One's for Daddy

I remember singing for the church on Sunday morning.
As best I can remember, I was four.
My brothers and my sister and I harmonized together
And everybody always wanted more.

Mama made us practice and how we used to hate it,
But daddy always seemed to be so proud.
My little brother Dan would stand and sing the real high tenor.
As I remember I just sang real loud!
(Yodel)

Daddy kept us singing as the years went slowly by.
Our harmony got better as we grew.
I had learned to yodel some and with my daddy's help
I learned to play a guitar chord or two.

Daddy really hoped that we could make it to the big time,
But Don and Joan both went their separate ways.
That left me and Dan to sing and we did for a while.
Then Danny quit and I saw Dad's hopes fade.

Daddy died before I ever made a country record
And it kinda breaks my heart he never knew.
If you don't mind, I think that I'll just sing this one for Daddy.
So Victor Lister, this one's just for you!

Of the seventy-plus songs she's written, Janet's most requested is "The Gospel Yodel." It was written because she received requests for yodels when she was singing for church services. There were very few gospel yodeling songs to choose from, so she wrote her own. Jim and Jeanne Martin ("The Rockin' M Wranglers") recorded "The Gospel Yodel" on two of their albums and young Alexa Whipple included it on her debut album.

The Gospel Yodel

My destiny is heaven, I'm here to say
I've made my reservation, and I'll soon be on my way.
I can't wait to hear the angel voices when they sing.
I'll do the gospel yodel, and make the heavens ring!
(Yodel)...

If you've read your Bible, I'm sure you know,
You're either bound for heaven, or somewhere down below.
It's time you decided, what it's going to be.
Why don't you be an angel, and come along with me?
(Yodel)..

If you can't make up your mind, old Satan's standing by.
The fires of hell are burning hot, on this you can rely.
Still the choice is up to you, you're running out of time.
Tell the Lord you want to go, or you'll be left behind.

Heaven's waiting, what will be your fate?
Will you walk the streets of gold, or will you hesitate?
When this world has ended, and when the angels sing,
We'll do the gospel yodel, and make the heavens ring.
(Yodel)...

In 1991, she went to the Western Music Association Festival in Arizona to enter the yodeling competition and found that she wanted to become more involved in that organization. Because the WMA has as its mission preserving the purity of western music, Janet's country music background was holding her back. She learned to emphasize her cowboy songs and spiced them up with cowboy-style yodeling and in that way became a stronger presence in the WMA.

She wanted to write a western song, and often sat in on Hal Spencer's songwriting seminars and, with his teachings under her belt, she "painted a picture" with "Wyoming Rose," a cowboy love song as told by a girl. That song won WMA "Song of the Year" in 2002. It is the title song of a 2001 Janet McBride CD and was also recorded by Pat Boilesen on her "Keepin' It Simple" album in 2004.

Wyoming Rose

(First Chorus)
Her eyes were as gray as the skies of Montana
Just before winter's first snow.
Those eyes had a sparkle that nothing could match
Except maybe a mountain stream's flow.
Her hair was the color of aspen in fall
And the light of the moon made it glow.
She told me she'd wait, but I never returned
To my beautiful Wyoming Rose.

I saw him as he sat alone on his bunk.
It was plain he would ride nevermore.
His skin was like leather from riding the range
And as rough as the boots that he wore.
He motioned for me to come sit down beside him.
It seemed he had something to say.
I figured he'd talk about horses and roundups,
So I sat down to hear what he'd say.

He said, "You remind me of someone I knew
In the days when my age didn't matter.
I met her that spring, when I worked the spread
Where she was the landowner's daughter.
We spent that summer, in each other's arms
And made plans to live our lives together.
I left her to earn us a place of our own
And I promised I'd come back to get her."

He said, "Time slipped away, and though I saved my pay,
It seemed it was never enough.
'Cause she was a lady, and I just a cowboy
And life on the ranch would be tough.
I couldn't see her wasting away
With less than the life she was used to.
But when I saw you there, with your long aspen hair,
I thought heaven had come into view.

(Bridge)
'Cause her hair was the color of aspen in fall
And the light of the moon made it glow.
She told me she'd wait, but I never returned
To my beautiful Wyoming Rose."

His words sent a chill all the way to my toes
As my mind hurried back to the days
When I watched my mother, as she watched the road,
The same road that took him away.
And I knew right away, that he was the man
My mother had loved all her life.
And I wanted to tell him, she would have been happy
In a cabin, just being his wife.

(Second Chorus)
'Cause her eyes were as gray as the skies of Montana
Just before winter's first snow.
Those eyes had a sparkle that nothing could match
Except maybe a mountain stream's flow.
Her hair was the color of aspen in fall
And the light of the moon made it glow.
She told him she'd wait, but he never returned
To his beautiful Wyoming Rose.

Now I know she waits at heaven's gate,
His beautiful Wyoming Rose.

"A Cowgirls' Dream," a song that includes an inserted segment from a Patsy Montana unpublished tape, received significant airplay on western stations across the country and was a finalist for WMA's "Song of the Year," in addition to receiving a Grammy nomination in 2005. Janet assigned 50 percent of the song to Michael Losey, who allowed her to use the segment of his grandmother's (Patsy's) recording within her song. (It was also recorded by Pat Boilesen on her "Hats Off to the Ladies" CD in 2008.)

Janet started to write "Mama (I Got Here as Fast as I Could)" soon after her mother died in 1999, but didn't finish it until much later. When she first started the song, she was thinking in generic, non-specific terms. The words were misplaced during a move, then found again in about 2008. John often asked her "Have you finished 'Mama' yet?" When she put *herself* into the song, she found that the words began to flow much more smoothly.

In early 2009, she made the decision to record one more time (at age 75), primarily to put the "Mama" song on CD. She had shared the words with Judy Hamilton, Sherry Trosper and Pat Boilesen for their critique...and finally had the song with just the right impact she was looking for. She recorded "Mama" on the "Still Loving the Ride" project.

This project also included four songs from her cassette days, recorded in '89, '90, '91 and '95, that had never been released on CD. In addition, she included two unreleased cuts from her 1959 session with Wynn Stewart and his band. When she took the old vinyl recording of those cuts to Phil York at Yorktown Digital Works in Irving, Texas, and heard the sound he was able to achieve, she was convinced that those cuts had to be included on the CD.

The "Still Loving the Ride" CD has received the greatest response of any of Janet's albums, partially because of the strength of the "Mama" song, and partly because folks are intrigued by the cuts from the Wynn Stewart/ Ralph Mooney sessions. Janet feels that "Mama" is one of her strongest songs, but it did not receive significant radio airplay, most likely because it doesn't fit into current radio programmers' missions. The response she gets from folks who buy the album at country festivals, however, is phenomenal, and "Mama" is one of her most-requested songs. Francine Roark Robison, Oklahoma's Cowboy Poet Laureate, included "Mama" as a poem on her "Prairie Tales from the Heart" album in 2010 and receives an especially strong response when she performs it.

Mama (I Got Here as Fast as I Could)

I could hear her calling me from the garden gate.
Her voice meant I should hurry home and I knew not to wait.
I'd tell my friends goodbye and wave, then I'd run all the way,
'Til I was wrapped in Mama's arms
Then she'd hear me say...

(First Chorus)
I got here as fast as I could, Mama.
I wish I could have played a little longer.
Then Mom would tell me
I would always be her little girl
And every day my love for her grew stronger!

Mama's hands were always there to hold as time went on.
Her arms were always open wide to keep me from all harm.
She often told me to be careful when I picked my friends.
But when he said he loved me, I threw caution to the winds!

I knew he had a wild streak but I followed right along.
I never gave another thought to what was right or wrong.
I think Mama always knew some day I'd have to pay.
Still it was Mama to the rescue, when I called her that day.

(Second Chorus)
I said "Get here as fast as you can, Mama.
There's no one else to help me, Mom.
So please come set me free."
I'm sure Mama knew I'd never
Do those things again.
And when we left there, Mama held my hand.

(Recitation)
I got a call to hurry to her home the day she died.
I sat down beside her bed, as teardrops filled my eyes.
I know she knew that it was me who held her hands that day.
'Cause I saw a smile on Mama's face when she heard me say...

(Third Chorus)
"I got here as fast as I could, Mama!"
I hope she knew how proud I was
To be her little girl.

I couldn't help but wish
She could have stayed a little longer.
How could I live without her in my world.

(Recitation)
Tho she's been gone for years now,
The other day I heard her voice.
I swear—it sounded like she had never gone away.
She told me she'd be waiting for me by heaven's garden gate,
And I know when I see her face what I'm going to say...

I got here as fast as I could, Mama!
I got here as fast as I could.

Several of Janet's songs were collaborative efforts. Two are her most-recorded songs: "Santa's Yodelin' Song" (written with Dell D'Lizarraga) and "Yodeling at the Grand Ole Opry" (written with Gwen Young). In addition to co-writing with Vern Stovall and Claude McBride during the 1960s, she also co-wrote with Emma Tucker, Christy Honea and Thomas Woodall during the Opry days.

For Janet, the yodeling songs came first. She needed new songs so she wrote them. Then she went through her hurting period and wrote pain songs. They were songs she could relate to and it made her feel better to "let the pain go" through her songs. And that's what makes a lot of country songs work.

"Writing things down in songs was a great way to get them off my chest and even out of my mind," said Janet.

Her gospel songs, on the other hand, seem to be saying "if you don't change your ways, this is what can happen."

She wrote a song for John called "You Do, I Do!" and included it on the "Still Loving the Ride" CD.

At least two of Janet's songs have been included in film/theater projects: one for a musical stage production called *Honky Tonk Laundry* and another for a documentary film about lady wrestlers called *Lipstick and Dynamite*. See Appendix D for more on these odd but wonderful uses of a good country song.

18

Two Passions Merge

*Janet, Terrina Hope and John
relax during a visit to Dollywood,
Terrina's workplace, in 1998.
(Janet McBride Collection)*

Long a passion for Janet, maybe as much as her music, was traveling. Now, for the first time without the constraints of jobs or an opry show, she could enjoy both of her strongest passions—music and travel—at the same time. And she had John, who loved it as much as she did.

John had retired in 1991 and Janet retired from her job on April 30, 1997. Not ones to "switch off" during retirement, they jumped full force into a schedule of traveling and performing that many younger folks might have trouble handling. Their duo consisted of Janet on guitar and John on upright bass, with Janet yodeling and doing most of the singing, and John jumping in with his "two cents' worth," from time to time, usually with novelty or comedy selections. They both loved to travel and enjoyed mixing music performances as they "sight-saw" themselves across the country.

For their first post-retirement trip, they lined up a chuckwagon gig in Cody, Wyoming, with Kate Taylor and "The Circuit Riders." They drove across the northern states to Niagara Falls to visit that national landmark before continuing to a friend's beach house at Ship Bottom, New Jersey. They visited Janet's brother Victor in Maine, and then headed for Nova Scotia and the Hank Snow Festival at Caledonia that year. Janet's long-time friend and mentor, Bob Paulin, showed them around before taking them to his camping trailer where they would stay during the festival. Afterwards, they were taken on a whale-watching excursion in the Bay of Fundy by longtime fan Boyd Brydon.

The Ingrams returned home to Texas just in time for LeAnn Rimes' 16th birthday party at a club in Dallas called "The Velvet E." A few days later they left for a cowboy festival in Bandera, Texas, a town northwest of San Antonio known as the "cowboy capital of the world."

With the Opry experience behind them, Janet and John decided that this was the time to take Walter Nevada up on his repeated invitation to perform in Vienna, Austria. In August 1996, they embarked on a 14-day musical tour of Austria, performing for a variety of concerts and festivals, sightseeing and visiting fans. Sponsored by the Vienna Country Music Club, John and Janet were booked on several concerts around the country and members served as tour guides to such sights as Shoenbrunn, St. Stephen's Cathedral, the Danube River, numerous sidewalk cafes, and even on a trek into the forest to pick mushrooms.

It was in Freitag at the Buffalo Western Saloon where they met "Snake," a bearded, tattooed, Harley-riding, chain-decorated, rough-looking devoted fan of Janet's, who had a huge smile on his face when he left that night with a personally autographed photo of his favorite country singer.

Austrian fans wanted a photo with Janet.
(Janet McBride Collection)

"One of the spots where we were booked was at 'Jorgi's Bar.' We got a chuckle from the poster on the door," said Janet. "It read 'Texas Jodler Tonight.'" Their room was above the patio of the bar area of Jorgi's and the rather loud party went on all night, giving this Texas couple a night to remember forever.

ఆ

In 1997 these two gypsy entertainers began to participate in a full range of annual events across the country, plus local theaters, churches and senior centers, and conducted yodeling clinics wherever Janet was asked...either on location or in her own home. That year, she was presented the Academy of Western Artists "Yodeler of the Year" Award.

They often visited Janet's mother in northern California, along with her brother Don and sister Joan. Both siblings lived at that time in the mountains of Big Bar, California, which also made it easy to take side trips to Yreka to visit longtime friend Ginger Jackson and her mother, Mazi.

By now, John had fully developed his act and was doing a few serious songs along with his silly songs and that outrageous Tarzan-style yodel of his. "He was a ham," Janet said. "He loved being on stage, and it became much more fun when it was the both of us making the crowd smile, laugh, cry or just applaud!" He had learned to play upright bass and, later when his doctors advised him not to be carrying around that big bass, he taught himself to play harmonica, and if he, for some reason, didn't go on stage with Janet, everyone wanted to know "Where's John?"

From 1997 through 2000, John and Janet attended Fan Fair in Nashville where she performed at the "Reunion of Pioneers Show."

From 1998 through 2009, the duo performed, often annually, at the National Cowboy Symposium in Lubbock, Texas (Alvin Davis); the

Cheyenne (Wyoming) Cowboy Symposium (Pat McKelvey); Cowboy Days in Las Cruces, New Mexico; the Gene Autry Oklahoma Film & Music Festival in Gene Autry, Oklahoma (Elvin and Flo Sweeten); the WMA (Western Music Association) Festival, the Patsy Montana Festival in Pineville-Havenhurst, Missouri (Jane and Larry Frost); Prairieville Farm Days in Delton, Michigan (Bill Ackerman); Festival of the West in Scottsdale, Arizona (Mary Brown); the San Antonio Livestock Show; Cowboy Songs & Range Ballads Festival in Cody, Wyoming (Lillian Turner); the Elton Britt/ Patsy Montana Celebration at the Mountain View, Arkansas, Folk Center; Old-Time Music Festival in Iowa (Bob Everhart); and Rex Allen Days in Wilcox, Arizona (Lowell Lydic).

Janet enjoyed "giving back" some of what had been given to her over the years so chose to do most of her gigs without pay—and these performing commitments also gave them a perfect excuse to travel. They were putting lots of miles on their car traveling to festivals, celebrations, churches and senior citizen centers as they performed their cowboy and country music but, oh, how they were loving the ride!

In March of 2000 she and John were asked to sing for a benefit to restore the Star Select Theatre in Mineola, Texas, John's hometown. They also participated in the Festival of the West in Arizona, Patsy Montana Festival in Missouri, Fan Fair in Nashville, and performed on Ernest Tubb's Midnight Jamboree. Back in Texas, they participated in the Academy of Western Artists convention in Dallas.

August found the couple in Clifton, Kansas, for the Clifton-Vining Country Music Festival hosted by John Wray, then on to Avoca, Iowa, for Everhart's festival again. September events that filled out their schedule included appearances at the Gene Autry Oklahoma Film & Music Festival and the National Cowboy Symposium in Lubbock, Texas, followed by a return to Wilcox, Arizona, for Rex Allen Days in October.

In January of 2001, an all-day music clinic was held in Fort Worth for the benefit of the Buckaroos organization that helps young entertainers improve their skills, and Janet was the yodeling instructor.

The couple traveled to Florida early in 2001, and on their way to a square dance rally in Florida (set up by Otis and Linda Lutz), they picked up a gig in Polk City at an RV resort. After the Florida gigs, Janet conducted a series of yodeling clinics in northern Georgia (organized by Kaye Whitener). At this clinic, she met young Mallary Hope, who became one of her protégés and would go on to win a recording contract with a major label.

In June of 2001, the old Mesquite Opry building was renovated as the Rodeo City Music Hall, owned by Clara Walker and featuring "Klassic Kountry Saturday Nights" with Karol Dyess and friends. Janet has an open invitation to perform anytime on their stage.

 appropriate symbol

In August of 2001, Janet received an e-mail from Annie Von Trapp of the famous Von Trapp family of singers, who asked if Janet could help her four children with their yodeling. Rather than have the family spend lots of money on flights to Texas from Montana where they were living, Janet offered to drive up to Montana before doing a scheduled performance in Cheyenne, Wyoming, over Labor Day weekend.

Janet and John met with the Von Trapps at their home not far from the entrance to Glacier National Park. "Mom Von Trapp and four kids, all grinning from ear-to-ear, came running out to greet us when we approached their beautiful lodge-style home," recalls Janet. "And we grinned right back!"

Janet spent the afternoon working with all four young Von Trapps, who were already veteran entertainers and fast learners when it came to yodeling. Annie prepared a wonderful meal for them and after supper, several church friends came over to meet the "yodeling lady from Texas" and then the real fun began...with singing, yodeling, laughing, eating and visiting the evening away. "It was the thrill of a lifetime to meet and spend time with the Von Trapps!" said Janet.

Later, when the Von Trapp Singers were scheduled to perform in Richardson, Texas, in 2009, Janet contacted Annie, who obtained two tickets for her and John to the already sold-out concert. "I couldn't have been more pleased with their performance," said Janet, "but when they sang "The Lonely Goat-herd" and yodeled, I could hardly hold myself down in the seat! They were wonderful!" After the show, John and Janet waited for everyone to leave the lobby so they could have photos taken with the Von Trapp kids. She treasures those photos yet today.

In October of 2001, Janet was hospitalized after experiencing stroke-like symptoms. The doctors gave her no real answers for her condition, and when they released her from the hospital, she and John drove to Beaumont, Texas, where she picked up her Lone Star State Country Music Hall of Fame Award. But Monday found her back in the hospital again, this time complaining of dizziness and numbness in her arm, but still no real answers for her symptoms came to light.

*Watching the Von Trapp Singers perform and hearing the
kids yodel were especially gratifying for Janet.
(Janet McBride Collection)*

Later that month, they traveled to Las Cruces, New Mexico, for that
city's Cowboy Days event, and in November returned to Tucson for the
WMA festival.

cs

Janet returned to Georgia in January 2002 to conduct another series of
yodeling clinics, this time in Dalton. On the way, they visited Paige Parnell in
Leeds, Alabama, a ventriloquist who was a former Miss Alabama and first
runner-up for Miss America. She had asked Janet to help her teach her
"dummies" to yodel.

That spring Janet began work on her "50 Years of Yodeling" CD
project. She had long wanted to gather together some of her signature
yodeling songs for a project that would serve as a retrospective of her
career. It was an effort that would require several months of work.

On the way to San Diego to perform at the Adams Avenue Roots
Festival, they stopped in Lancaster, California, to visit Rosalie Allen, one of
the top female yodelers of the 1940s and '50s. "I was aware that Rosalie
had become very reclusive and hard to get to know," said Janet, "so I felt
very honored to be able to spend time with her. She showed us her WMA
Hall of Fame Award and DJ Hall of Fame Award. I had listened to and

picked up yodeling patterns from Rosalie Allen records all my life. What a thrill!"

Then in Hemet, California, she met up with Beverly Losey and Michael Losey, Patsy Montana's daughter and grandson, who were preparing Patsy and Paul's home for sale. Patsy had passed away in May of 1996, and her husband was in a nursing home at this time. Janet and John felt privileged to entertain Patsy's husband and the others at his care facility.

While they were in California, they visited with Janet's brother Don and his family (who now lived in Southern California), and had the opportunity to meet with western film star/yodeler Carolina Cotton's daughter Sharon Marie and Janet's long-time pen pal and yodeling hero Betsy Gay.

Memorial Day weekend that year found John and Janet at the first annual Cedar, Kansas, Depot Festival, an event she was instrumental in forming, along with coordinators Lowell and Nan Lydic.

In June they returned to Georgia to do some coaching. They stayed with Woody and Shirley Wilson and worked with their son Justin and Mallary Hope, both of whom later were in the finals of the Colgate Country Countdown at Disney World in Florida.

In July they drove to Branson, Missouri, to take part in a "Riders in the Sky" concert that featured the Prairie Twins, two of Janet's "students." Janet was thrilled when "The Riders" asked if she would sing a song during their show.

In October, Janet and John's traveling slowed down significantly, as John had to see doctors for a nagging case of shingles. They did attend the WMA Festival in Las Vegas in November, but John's shingles kept him uncomfortable most of the time.

That year, Janet won the WMA's "Western Song of the Year" Award for "Wyoming Rose," a cowboy love song from an intriguing perspective. (See pages 169 for lyrics to "Wyoming Rose.")

଒

Their travel schedule was quiet for the early part of 2003; then in March they went to Mineola, Texas, to perform, followed by a trip to Scottsdale, Arizona, for the Festival of the West. Other events during the year included all the annual festivals where they usually performed.

Recovering from a back injury, Janet chose not to attend WMA that year, but in December, while she was still on crutches, they made a trip to

Hot Springs, Arkansas, for the induction ceremonies for Patsy Montana's addition to that city's Walk of Fame. Because Janet held Patsy in such high regard, she counts her participation in that event a highlight of her life.

In January of 2004, John and Janet hosted a large Mesquite Opry reunion show with the proceeds to go to The Rodeo City Music Hall. The old theater building was overflowing, and everyone there had a wonderful time. But the evening ended on a sour note when it was discovered that the man who had collected the ticket money had left town with it.

During a doctor's visit on July 28, 2004, John suffered a stroke in the doctor's office, and was hospitalized for three days. After just a couple of weeks of recovery time, he felt fine and said he was "anxious to go again."

In August they traveled to Los Angeles to participate in the Autry National Center's celebration of cowboy music. Janet was part of the yodeling cowgirls' tribute program, and honored Carolina Cotton with her songs.

Janet's "yodel story" was included in a book titled *Yodel-Ay-Ee-Oooo,* written by Dutch writer Bart Plantenga and published and released in 2004. The author calls Janet a "yodel missionary of the most effective kind...a wonderful entertainer with a vibrant yodel." *(Routledge, New York, London)*

In August, John Pronk, a producer from a local television station, came out to the house to do a feature on Janet and John. As it turned out, the feature segment

John and Janet were having fun with friends at the Cash Country Opry in Cash, Texas. Photo by Brule Carleson, 2004. (Janet McBride Collection)

ultimately centered on John, his bass playing and his yodeling. This time it *was* "all about John!"

September, October and November of that year were again filled with their usual schedule of gigs and festivals.

℅

In March, 2005, after participating in the Festival of the West in Scottsdale, Arizona, and the Saguaro Music Festival east of Phoenix, they went to the Adams Avenue Roots Festival in San Diego, then attended some of their standard festivals and yodel camps, but did not take on anything extra. In November of that year, Janet received the Hall of Fame Pioneer Award from the Western Music Association.

Then in March of 2006, after they performed in Mineola, Texas, and the Festival of the West in Scottsdale, Arizona, John entered the hospital for treatment of a staph infection. It was a very serious incident and required several weeks of recovery. They were, however, able to attend the Cedar Festival the end of May. In June they participated in the first annual McBride Family Reunion in Lake Village, Arkansas, where Janet re-acquainted herself with some of Claude's cousins and met many others who comprised the family of her first husband, the father of her children. During that and subsequent reunions, she enjoyed spending time with Ray and Sue McBride, June McBride, former wife of Armand (Claude's brother "Mac" who had passed away earlier) as well as Claude's brother Clyde and his wife Jackie.

August took the couple up to Cedar, Kansas, to clean up the house and property they had purchased in that small town. While they were in Cedar, Janet noticed that John's heart seemed to be "racing," although there were no other indications of any problems. Afterwards, they left for Cheyenne and Pat McKelvey's Symposium there. When they were packing up the car to leave Cheyenne for Lubbock, John complained of shortness of breath, but attributed it to the altitude. After Lubbock, they picked up Janet's AWA "Yodeler of the Year" award in Dallas and then traveled on to Gene Autry, Oklahoma, for that event.

The first week of October, John entered the hospital once again, after suffering what was determined to be a heart attack that damaged the back side of his heart. The doctors put him on blood-thinning medication but okayed him to travel to Albuquerque for the WMA Festival in November. He spent the remainder of November and all of December resting up at home.

℅

By late January 2007, John was anxious to perform at some of their local venues, including the Fort Worth Stock Show and the Star Select Theatre in Mineola, Texas, and then began a limited version of their standard national festival circuit, being careful not to let John become over-tired.

The more they traveled to events across the country, the more John loved the opportunities to rub elbows with celebrities, from the worlds of television, film and music. At the various festivals, they met and spent time with such stars as Dale Evans, Jack Palance, Ernest Borgnine, Ronnie Robbins, Rusty Richards, Rex Allen, Clint Walker, James Drury, Donna Douglas, Roberta Shore, Wes and Marilyn Tuttle, Betsy Gay, Sharon Marie (Carolina Cotton's daughter) and Rosalie Allen.

March of 2008 found Janet performing at the Star Select Theatre in Mineola and Festival of the West, and then, for the first time, they entertained several weekends at the Dallas Arboretum performing in front of the DeGolyer Estate. "The Arboretum was following a western theme," Janet recalled, "and we were perfect in our western shirts and boots!"

In mid-April they drove to the Gene Autry Oklahoma Museum to showcase some of the young talent from Texas and Oklahoma. They performed at several local shows in late April and early May, including The GermanFest in Euless, Texas, before heading out to the Cedar Depot Festival in Kansas, then on to the Patsy Montana International Yodeling Competition in Missouri. On June 14th they drove to Hope, Arkansas, for that community's first annual Patsy Montana Celebration and the next weekend they performed for a fundraiser event at the Gene Autry Oklahoma Museum.

Although John was not complaining, he was definitely showing signs of slowing down, but the doctors could find no real reason behind it. He was taking all his meds and kept saying he was "good to go." So they went ahead with

Janet, James Drury from TV's The Virginian, *and John, in a photo taken by Jerry Baumann at one of the Gene Autry fans' "lunch bunch" activities. (Janet McBride Collection)*

plans to perform at Six Flags Over Texas in September. The first day went fine, although he was tired from setting up and striking their sound equipment. The second day, he didn't feel up to participating and stayed home. The second week, he had rested sufficiently and was able to perform both Saturday and Sunday.

Before the third weekend, a doctor's appointment indicated no particular problems, except possibly that he was anemic. On Saturday it was obvious to Janet that something was wrong, although they did complete their performance that day. Then on Sunday, John was unable to go at all. Monday morning, Janet took him to the emergency room where doctors gave him a blood transfusion. After several appointments with a blood specialist, no one was able to give any reason for his ailment.

For the first time since they had discovered the Gene Autry Oklahoma Film & Music Festival, she and John were not able to attend this favorite event.

On October 11, 2008, they entertained at the Athens (Texas) Pea Festival, but other than the monthly Buckaroos performances, they did not entertain for the rest of the year.

Then in December, John suffered congestive heart failure and was again admitted to the hospital and spent two nights there. A few days later, Janet herself was admitted to the hospital with an amnesia episode that later proved to be insignificant, and she was fine after a bit of rest. No cause was ever found, but the doctors assumed it was a result of the stress she was experiencing over John's health issues.

○8

With rest they were both doing fine, and in January 2009 they resumed their usual schedule of gigs at the Fort Worth Stock Show and the Buckaroos plus they attended the Von Trapp Singer's performance in Richardson, Texas. In March, Janet began recording her new CD, entitled "Still Loving the Ride," at Yorktown Studios in Irving, Texas, for her own Brookhurst label. In May, they attended the usual festivals and conducted the usual yodeling clinics. In June, they returned to the McBride Family Reunion in Arkansas, hosted by Claude's brother Ray and his wife, Sue, along with his brother Clyde and wife Jackie.

In September they performed at the Cowboy Symposium in Lubbock and, later, the Gene Autry Oklahoma Film & Music Festival, where Janet was awarded the Museum's prestigious "Lifetime Achievement Award" for her continuing work with young people in the field of traditional music.

Near the end of February in 2010, John was hospitalized again for congestive heart failure. This time the situation was more serious than previously, and in March he began a period of intense rest as he recovered from this latest episode of heart trouble.

In late April, the couple traveled the short distance to Streetman, Texas, where Janet recorded a couple of duets for a CD being produced by fellow entertainer Buck Helton. She also performed that weekend at the Trinity River Jamboree in Trinidad, Texas.

Just before they went to perform at the Cedar festival in June, Janet took John to the doctor because of a recurring infection, and they were referred to a urologist. He improved, but still wasn't his usual, spunky self for several weeks.

In late July of 2010, they traveled to Holbrook, Nebraska, where Janet was honored with a "Living Legend Award" at the first Burton's Bend Music Festival. In a hilarious reenactment of her "Queen for a Day" experience on television some years earlier, Janet was officially crowned "Queen of the Yodelers" at this inaugural event. The presentation was complete with a large spray of roses presented by her "attendants" and Lowell Lydic, sporting a pencil-thin, black mustache, portraying TV host Jack Bailey. The Burton's Bend Music Festival is presented by Christine and Rodney Whipple of Arapahoe, Nebraska.

In September, John and Janet were honored by the Star Select Theatre in Mineola and were included in a documentary project about the theater: John, for having worked there beginning at age 12 in 1943 and Janet for her help in raising funds for the theater's restoration.

In October, Janet received the Rural Roots Commission "Yodeler CD of the Year" award for "Still Loving the Ride," and later that month she learned that many of her protégés had been selected to appear in a new television series called *Shotgun Red's Variety Show,* broadcast on RFD-TV in 2011. She and John met friends Lowell and Nan Lydic and Jack and Marge Hennenfent in Branson where they attended the tapings of the various shows that were featuring Janet protégés: Buckaroo Kristyn Harris, Canadian Naomi Bristow and Buckaroo Chelsea Beck. They were unable to attend the next week's shows when another Janet protégé Alexa Whipple would perform.

They also received word that stories and photos of Janet, Devon

Dawson and the Buckaroos were included in a new book by Holly George-Warren called *The Cowgirl Way* (*Houghton Mifflin Harcourt*).

Also in October, the couple traveled to the home of Tex and Mary Schutz near Streetman, Texas, where they met and spent time with Roger Tibbs, New Zealand's most popular country singer and yodeler. "This handsome man can yodel like Elton Britt and Slim Clark," said Janet. "It was a thrill to meet a fella I had admired for years. What a fantastic singer and yodeler!"

ᛒ

Through November and early December John seemed to be "perking up," his energy level was better and he felt reasonably well, although he continued to take meds for infection.

On Monday, December 20, they entertained at an assisted-living facility in Mesquite. John played his harmonica and the residents loved the music. But by Tuesday morning, it was obvious he was having problems again. This time, the doctors prescribed new antibiotics, surmising that the infection had flared up again.

Then on Wednesday morning, December 22, Janet could see that John was in serious trouble. Again she took him to his doctor, who diagnosed possible dehydration and sent him to the Emergency Room at Doctors Hospital in Dallas. They treated him, gave him intravenous antibiotics, and, when his vital signs looked good, they released him. That afternoon, while he was lounging in his easy chair, he asked Janet to fix him some chicken soup. Then he slumped down in his chair and died.

He was 79 years old. "It was just that fast! The Lord had called John home," said Janet.

She was a widow for the second time and would soon be opening the next chapter of her life.

19
Mentoring and Coaching

Six-year-old Cora Wood learns her "yodel-ay-ee-ooos"
during a 2006 coaching session with Janet. Cora went on to win
"Best Youth Yodeler" at WMA in 2010.
(Photo by Lori Faith Merritt, www.photographybyfaith.com)

Janet recognized back in the late 1960s that her chances for a starring role in the world of country music were growing slim. She loves the music and loves to share her music with her fans. But the true "curtain call" of Janet's career may well be her dedication to helping young entertainers as they learn their own style of performing.

As she's moved through the phases of her life, Janet has grown to love working with young entertainers, teaching them such things as stage presence, musicianship, singing technique and especially yodeling technique.

Janet actually began this labor of love during the Mesquite Opry days, in 1981 to be exact. Through that 15-year excursion, she worked with many a youngster and gave them the chance to perform in front of a large audience and to work with veteran entertainers.

She remembers how it was when she was young, with no one around who could teach her to sing, yodel, or even play the guitar to accompany herself. She's doing her best to make sure that no hopeful young performer goes without the kind of guidance and advice that a seasoned entertainer can give them. After all, these youngsters may be the country and cowboy performing stars of tomorrow!

Her work with a very young LeAnn Rimes during the Opry years and Rimes' subsequent success on the international music stage greatly increased Janet's visibility as a yodel coach and showbiz mentor.

Young entertainer Tiffany Jo in a yodeling coaching session with Janet at the 2003 Festival of the West. (Janet McBride Collection)

Many youngsters (and their families) find Janet through workshops at festivals or schools across the country and many find her on the internet and come to visit her at home.

Sometimes conducting as many as six coaching sessions each month, Janet works with her young students on technique, showmanship, musicianship and more. "It's so fulfilling," says Janet, "to give these kids a glimpse into something different, something more that they can do with their music. I love being able to share this stuff with the kids, listen to them, see what they want and where they want to go from there."

LeAnn and Janet at a special Johnnie High concert featuring LeAnn in Arlington, Texas. Janet McBride Collection)

Her work with the Buckaroos is an ongoing group-coaching session, a program that she and fellow performer Devon Dawson established through the Cowtown Opry. Each second Sunday, Devon and Janet conduct a teaching/rehearsal session for the kids. Then they all gather on the front steps of the Livestock Exchange Building in the Fort Worth Stockyards District and perform for tourists visiting the area.

Several of Janet's "students" have gone on to bigger and better things in the field of entertainment. Here are stories about a few of them:

LeAnn Rimes...LeAnn came to the Opry in 1989 at the age of seven. Although she was already an experienced singer by that age, she asked for help in putting a yodel into Patsy Montana's award-winning song "I Want to Be a Cowboy's Sweetheart." LeAnn quickly learned the "Sweetheart" pattern and sang it several times during the Mesquite Rodeo parade and again that evening on the Mesquite Opry show. Like Janet, she was "hooked on yodeling" and for several years, used it in her show. With more than 40 million CD sales, two Grammy Awards, several books, many TV appearances, and lots of other awards, LeAnn has become a music icon in both the USA and Europe—not bad for a little gal who learned to yodel from a gal named Janet, who never even appeared on the Grand Ole Opry!

Taylor Ware...Janet began working with seven-year-old Taylor in

192

2002, when her mother Suzanna was looking for someone to teach young Taylor to yodel. They corresponded at first by e-mail, and Janet sent her a couple practice tapes to work on and gave her suggestions on technique. Later, Taylor and her family moved from Illinois to Tennessee where she worked with Margo Smith, who helped her further develop her own yodeling style. In 2003, Taylor won the Yahoo! yodeling contest, and her voice became part of the logo of the huge Internet search engine. In 2006, Taylor was in the finals of the *America's Got Talent* television competition. In 2008, Taylor again started working with Janet in an effort to learn the nuances of cowboy yodeling. Taylor has gone on to gain national and international praise for her performances and her star is still rising.

Chelsea Beck...When eleven-year-old Chelsea Beck from Oklahoma decided in February 2004 that she wanted to learn to yodel, her singing teacher told her she needed Janet McBride, so her grandmother Micki Robinson got online and found her. "Chelsea had a very strong voice and picked up easily on the art of yodeling and left my house that day a yodeler with a plan," said Janet. That year Chelsea attended the Patsy Montana International Yodeling Competition and left understanding that, if she was to be able to perform the types of songs she wanted to, she needed to learn to play guitar. Being young and talented, she quickly learned to play and returned to that same competition in 2005 and took home the gold medal. Chelsea won the Western Music Association's youth yodeler championship in 2005, and in 2007 won the Academy of Western Artists Will Rogers award for "Best Yodeler." In 2010, her CD "Way Out West" was presented an award for "Western CD of the Year" by the Rural Roots Music Commission. Also that year, Chelsea was invited to tape a segment in Branson for the *Shotgun Red Variety Show*, to be broadcast during 2011on RFD-TV.

Terrina Hope...Young Terrina first sang at the Mesquite Opry in September of 1990. Janet could see that she loved entertaining and had a passion for the stage. The youngster took a summer singing spot at Six Flags in Arlington, Texas, then went on to Six Flags in San Antonio. When she received an invitation to appear in Dolly Parton's "Fire on the Mountain Show" at Dollywood, her family relocated to Tennessee. She continued to perform at Dollywood for the next five years, ending her stint there only when she married and moved to California. Now living in Alabama, Terrina is writing and performing gospel music with her home church.

Kata Hay...A tiny, red-haired child when Janet first met her at the Patsy Montana Yodeling Competition, Kata also already had a love for the stage. A singer/yodeler from Oklahoma, she was taken to all the music events around by her parents. By 2000 she had already won the Gold Medal at the Patsy Montana International Yodeling Competition and the Western Music Association's youth championship. With another of her mentors, Dobro player Tom Swatzell, Kata participated in two different musical tours of Australia. As soon as she graduated from high school, Kata was

Emalea Dell, Maura O'Brien, Chelsea Beck, Aly Sutherlin, Kata Hay and Janet in a performance at the 2003 Gene Autry Oklahoma Film & Music Festival.
(Janet McBride Collection)

invited to perform at the Fiddlers' Feast Chuckwagon show in Pigeon Forge, Tennessee. She left that gig when she married and built a band called "Kata & the Blaze" with her husband and went on the road nationwide. In addition to working at the new "Hatfield & McCoy Dinner Feud" show in Pigeon Forge, Tennessee, she's currently writing and recording new songs and often tours with a bluegrass/rock fusion band called the "Grassabillies."

Emalea Dell...Janet and a five-year-old Emalea met at the Patsy Montana Festival in Missouri, when the young girl was already a seasoned entertainer. Soon she became a student of Janet's. She won the Patsy Montana Yodeling Competition when she was eight years old and three months later made an appearance on *The Ellen Degeneres Show* where she taught the star to yodel in front of millions of people in the national television audience. She became a regular on the Gene Autry Oklahoma Film & Music Festival where she often got to meet some big names in show business. When she was about 11, Emalea and a few other talented youngsters started a new/bluegrass band called "Rockin' Acoustic Circus," giving her lots of experience in working with a popular performing group. She's also a regular entertainer at Jana Jae's Music Festival in Oklahoma. She traveled through Europe performing with a young group of singers called "American Kids" when she was 14. Now 16, this Oklahoma girl is in high school and looking forward to college.

Mallary Hope...Janet traveled to northern Georgia in early 2001 to meet and coach Mallary and several of her friends in a personalized two-day workshop, then returned later for a second session with that same group of youngsters. Mallary went to Music City when she was 17 as a demo and session singer. She is now recording for MCA Records, based in Nashville, and has released three CD albums. (Justin Tyler Wilson, Lindsay Harper and Brandi Nicole Coleman, three other kids who were students during that Georgia coaching session with Mallary, are all working in the entertainment business today.)

Carin Lechner...Janet met this young Colorado lady in 2004 in Scottsdale, Arizona, during the Festival of the West. Western singer Jeanne Martin had been mentoring Carin and encouraged her to come to this event where Janet was performing, and to talk with her about helping with yodel patterns. Janet invited Carin's family to attend the Patsy Montana Yodeling Competition for further coaching and gain experience in a national yodeling event. Carin won the contest that year and took home the coveted gold medal. Her performing group is known as "Carin Mari & Pony Express" and is comprised of Carin, her brothers and parents. The multi-talented siblings have won numerous awards including the North America Country Music Association Traditional Country Entertainer of the Year (2009). Carin Mari won the annual Colgate Country Showdown for Colorado during the summer of 2010 and was first runner-up in the national competition. Carin is still attending college and plans to continue her education at Belmont University in Nashville.

Naomi Bristow ...This young Canadian contacted Janet in 2009 and the two worked together online over a period of several months. With encouragement and pointers from Janet, Naomi went on to win several honors, including the "Fans Choice Award" from the Havelock (Ontario) Country Talent Show, the "Rising Star Award" from the British Columbia Cowboy Heritage Festival and the Western Music Associations' "Youth Yodeler of the Year" honor. She and Janet finally met in person in Branson at the taping of the *Shotgun Red Variety Show* in 2010.

The Prairie Twins...Kalani and Kalea Bray met Janet at the Gene Autry Oklahoma Museum after that facility's big film and music festival in September 2000. These Oklahoma girls, then eight years old, were already experienced singers making excellent use of their sibling harmonies in their performances, but they wanted to learn to yodel. After that initial meeting, Janet began sending the girls practice tapes over the next couple of months. Like she had done with many other young singers who like the western style, she encouraged them to learn to play guitar and to participate in the Western Music Association's festival in Tucson, Arizona. When Janet saw them at the WMA event, only about eight weeks after her last session with them, the girls were already yodeling and learning to play. "You can imagine how proud I was when these two girls learned to play their

Naomi Bristow from Canada was one of Janet's e-mail students. They finally met in person in 2010. (Janet McBride Collection)

guitars," said Janet, "and later after Kalani had a serious accident and was no longer able to hold her guitar, she learned how to play a fiddle." Now young adults, Kalani is teaching school in Texas and Kalea is married with a daughter and finishing her studies at the University of Oklahoma at Norman.

Jake Simpson...One of only a handful of Janet's protégés who are not yodelers, Jake, also from Oklahoma, is an extraordinary fiddler, as at home with big name entertainers as he is in a small community opry show. When Janet met Jake, he was just learning to play his fiddle. She invited him up on stage to sit in and get the feel of the stage and to play if he wanted to. "It wasn't long before Jake was playing fiddle with the best of them," said Janet. Through his middle and high school years, Jake won several summer scholarships to fiddling camps around the country. He became a regular performer on the Cedar Depot Festival in Kansas, the Miles of Memories Country MusicFest in Nebraska and the Gene Autry Oklahoma Film & Music Festival, as well as several smaller events. Currently, Jake is playing for up-and-coming Oklahoma-based star Kyly Morgan.

Catherine Bowler...Another find at the Patsy Montana International Yodeling Competition, young Catherine attended Janet's workshops and entered the yodeling contest at the 2003 event. Although Catherine did not take home a yodeling medal that year, she was hooked on the unique sound of yodeling and even wrote a song about her experience and entered it in the songwriting competition. She returned for the 2004 and 2005 events and won a medal each year. Then in 2006 she took home the gold medal for first place. After winning that "Patsy Montana" award, Catherine was featured in

*Students at the Patsy Montana Yodeling Workshops, 2009. Back row: Marina Pendleton,
McKenna Crabtree, Emma Pendleton, Paula Cravens and Janet.
Front row: Regina Scott, Lydia Epps, Anna Epps and Joel Epps.
(Janet McBride Collection)*

a top teen magazine and appeared in several TV shows, one of them in
Hollywood. The family has now relocated to Louisiana where Catherine is
attending college.

Alexa Whipple...Alexa and Janet got together at the Cedar Depot
Festival in Cedar,
Kansas, where Janet
was conducting yodeling
workshops for both
adults and youngsters.
Cheryl, Alexa's
grandmother, contacted
Janet when looking for
someone to help her
grand- daughter learn to
yodel, and they made
arrangements to meet at
the Cedar Festival.
Alexa is in high school (in

*Alexa Whipple learned to yodel from Janet at the 2007 Cedar
Depot Festival. (Janet McBride Collection)*

197

Arapahoe, Nebraska) at this writing, and plans to attend college to study some aspect of music. She already has two CDs out, is writing many of her own songs, and has appeared on RFD-TV's *Shotgun Red's Variety Show*.

☙

Through the years, Janet performed several times for Cowboy Church in the Stockyards District of Fort Worth. Then in 1998, Jean Marlowe and the Cowtown Opry folks asked Janet and Devon Dawson to head up a program that would encourage young people in the performance of any form of western music, and would help those youngsters learn about such things as pitch, timing, appropriate songs, performing on stage, and more. The program, known as **The Buckaroos**, is conducted the second Sunday of each month, and is the perfect training ground for young people who wish to learn more about performing traditional music.

The first Buckaroos performance, featuring only four youngsters, was on February 8, 1998. The group, with both Janet and Devon as coaches, continues to this day, with as many as 20 young performers participating at any given time.

Janet and Devon bring different experiences and talents to the

The 2011 crop of Buckaroos (Devon Dawson in center on fence, Janet is center on the ground, next to Janet on the right is celebrity rodeo announcer Pam Minick). (Photo by Lori Faith Merritt, www.photographybyfaith)

Buckaroos, but each believes strongly in working with young people to keep traditional music alive, and hope that some of these youngsters will grow up to help other young performers, passing the music on for generations to come.

In addition to the mentoring program, the Buckaroos organization offers scholarships each year to youngsters for such projects as music seminars, college programs, instruments, etc. The recipients are chosen by the board from numerous applications submitted by Buckaroos participants.

Some of the youngsters who have excelled in the Buckaroos program through the years include: Chelsea Beck, Brooke Wallace, Ginny Mac, Aly Sutherlin, Kacey Musgraves and Jess Meador.

"The kids come and go, some we see often, others not so often," said Janet. "Then sometimes we hear that they've accomplished something wonderful. It's all very gratifying!"

20

Colleagues and Colorful Characters

*Doug Green of "Riders in the Sky" with young Janet protégé
Kalea Bray, taken in 2001. Kalea and sister Kalani
were a popular duo known as The Prairie Twins
and were often invited to perform with the "Riders."
(Janet McBride Collection)*

Janet's life has been filled with colorful, talented and wonderful characters. Their personal comments about Janet tell much more than a recounting of her history could ever share.

Bill Mack (DJ/country music promoter/friend)...Janet McBride has always been on a super level as an entertainer. Most of the world is aware of her blessed ability to sing, yodel and entertain. She has always had the ability to "bring the house down" with applause from a loving, adoring audience. However, most of the world may not be aware of the Janet I have known for almost a half-century. I met her for the first time at the Big D Jamboree in the old Sportatorium in Dallas in 1964. From the beginning, it was a bonded friendship with a beautiful lady I will always admire for her sincere and constant wish to make everybody happy! As mentioned, she can always do this with her music, but it's that sincere, loving smile that really grabs the attention of those who have had the opportunity to meet her.

I love Janet McBride—and will always be thankful to God for placing her in a special avenue of my life.

Betsy Gay Cashen (singer/actress/friend)...I received a letter from Janet McBride in which she told me she learned to yodel listening to me on the Stuart Hamblen radio show and other shows I had been on. Janet also encouraged me to write my autobiography saying, "Do it for your children and grandchildren so they will know all the things you have done." I sat down to write and everything came back to me. It helped that my mother, Helen Gay, a songwriter under contract to American Music, kept a journal of everything I had ever done. I sent a copy of the book to Janet and she sent it to Jay Taylor who puts out the *Country Music Trails Less Traveled* magazine. He put a big article on the front page about me. I was thrilled, and it was all thanks to Janet.

She also encouraged me to put some of my old records out on a CD and gave me much good advice. I finally got that done. My CD is called "Betsy Gay, The Early Years." Recently Janet contacted Dave Sichak who runs Hillbilly-Music.com, about me, and he put a huge article on his website.

Janet has been a great friend, helping me and others, always encouraging me, plugging me, and inspiring me to do things. I've never *asked* her to help me; she just does it on her own.

Rusty Richards (cowboy singer/songwriter, 20-year member of "Sons of the Pioneers")...I have been lucky enough to have known Janet through the WMA Festivals and other events as well. I always enjoyed her performances and especially her great yodeling. She is always smiling and friendly and has never known a stranger. I will always treasure our friendship.

Junior Knight (steel guitar player for many top acts, with Mesquite Opry Band from '86 to '94)...Some of the best years of my musical life were spent at the Mesquite Opry. A lot of great memories that I will never forget. Thanks to John and Janet and all the cast for eight great years! And, oh yeah...The MOB...Mesquite Opry Band, the best bunch of musicians in Texas.

Tommy Wiggins (music promoter, entrepreneur, performer, MC)...We first met back in 1963 when Janet won a top award at our *DJ's Digest* first award ceremony, then saw her again when she won another award at the next year's event. I worked a few of the Cal Worthington shows with her, then our paths didn't cross for several years, until we met again in the late 1990s at a WMA event. Now we've become close friends and I try to catch as many of her activities as I can, including those wonderful Buckaroos programs that she does with the Cowtown Opry. She's a gal who gives more of herself than she'll ever receive, just a damn nice person!

Laverne Van Hutson (fashion buyer/singer/friend)...I met Janet some 20 years ago. At the Mesquite Opry show one night I was sitting beside Effie Robertson (Granny) and I started singing along with some of the songs. Granny liked my singing and told Janet about me and she called me to the stage. I auditioned and to my amazement was booked on the Opry! It was love at first sight and I became a regular!

Later, I was honored to supply Janet with many of the gowns she wore for Mrs. Senior Texas and was so happy to be able to do that! I also made sure she was dressed to the hilt for her Patsy Montana Award in New York City. My husband Gary and I went to NYC with John and Janet to show them around. It was a wonderful trip! Janet is the "Mother Theresa of Music." She planted footprints in my heart and they are there to stay.

Hal Spencer (CEO, Manna Music)...I first heard about Janet McBride—and also got a chance to meet her—when we both were involved with music on the West Coast. She was hot right then and receiving all kinds of awards. I served on the Board of Directors of the Academy of Country Music and noticed that she was definitely the "darling" of female country singers.

It wasn't until we both became involved in the Western Music

Association based in Tucson, Arizona, that I had an opportunity to find out what a talented performer she was—and what a great gift she had for being able to help both newcomers and established artists.

Janet never forgets what it takes to be a top professional singer and songwriter, and she continues to be a great role model for those who are serious about their role in western music. Her latest CD is entitled, "Still Loving The Ride,"and I believe her.

Ruth Dennett (President of Patsy Montana Fan Club)...Janet is not only the top female yodeler (my personal opinion) but she spends many, many hours helping young people perfect their yodeling and stage appearance. As President of the now dormant Patsy Montana Fan Club, I know Patsy would be very proud of her. Ego has never been part of her career.

Vern Stovall (singing partner to Janet)...Janet McBride, what a little trooper she is! We worked as a duet several years on the road and made several good records together. She is one fine songwriter and singer. One song we did together that comes to mind is "Wild Bill Tonight," which was written while we were on the road somewhere. The idea came when this guy stood up in the audience and yelled "I'm Wild Bill Tonight." His little wife stood up and said, "but you'll be Sweet William in the morning!" I knew we had a winner, and we wrote it in the car on the way to our next job. The road was a hard life, but that little gal handled it real well. She's tougher than a rodeo goat and is a good friend.

Christine Whipple (mother of Janet protégé Alexa Whipple)...Janet McBride is one of the best mentors Alexa will ever have! Janet's words of encouragement, gentle nudging and genuine interest in Alexa (as well as our other children Alayna and Eli) has made the Cedar Depot Memorial Celebration one of our favorite festivals to attend. Janet has been helping out her good friends Lowell and Nan at the festival for the past nine years and provides yodeling workshops for any eager individual who wishes to partake.

Janet invited Alexa to the festival after we sent her an e-mail regarding yodeling instruction. That was the beginning for us! We've loved Janet ever since! This year, 2011, marks the 10th and final celebration the weekend after Memorial Day. We look forward to seeing Janet (and will sorely miss John) and being part of this final celebration! Besides mentoring young people, Janet is an awesome entertainer and I love to watch and hear her perform! She has such a graceful and professional air of confidence and her sincerity and good-hearted nature make it easy for her to connect with her audience. Janet and John together...I think they complimented each other perfectly! Besides all the teasing that went on between the two it was always fun to listen to John play his harmonica! Janet and John went really well together and if they didn't adore each other they put on a pretty good act. I feel blessed that we have had the chance to be a part of Janet's life! Thanks for everything Janet! You're a doll!

Rose Lee Maphis (performer with "Joe & Rose Lee Maphis")...I can't recall when I first met Janet. I can only say it was somewhere in California, and we probably worked together on some show. She made it easy to remember her because of her distinct yodeling! Each time we met or worked together, I felt a sincere friendship developing. I was so glad to be able to attend the Western Music Association's gathering in Tucson a few years back and appear on a panel with Janet and Marilyn Tuttle. We surprise each other once in awhile with a phone call. I'd like to believe Janet and I have a few more meetings and hugs in years ahead.

Lowell Lydic (festival producer/music promoter)...The first time I had contact with Janet I learned quickly that this gal could make things happen. As entertainment coordinator for the Rex Allen Days event in Arizona back in 1999, I had made plans with Rex Jr. to do a Tribute of the Century show during the event that would honor Western stars or performers who have made a major contribution toward the promotion of the Western arts. When the plan was presented to the event board, the group felt it would be too costly and that we'd have to sell programs and advertising to cover all the expenses. The next day we received a letter from Janet (whom we had contacted to be a part of the show). She told us that Rex Sr. had been her idol, that her dad had bought her Rex Allen records when at a young age she had shown a strong interest in western music. Bottom line, she wanted to be part of the Tribute and would support it in any way she could. We were able to find enough sponsorships to cover all our expenses, thanks to Janet's help and enthusiasm. And, I'm so glad we did, because we went ahead with the Rex Allen Tribute of the Century Show...and two months later Rex died.

Tommy Horton (singer)...What I remember most about Janet was that she is very *unselfish and giving*. I was a guest on her Mesquite Opry many times and saw how Janet always worked closely with her guests. For example, she taught me not to sing so high, not to be afraid to sing in lower keys. In other words, save the throat! She was especially good with young entertainers, teaching them how to improve their performance and many times, she'd teach the young ones to yodel. Janet is a good singer, a good guitar player, a good teacher, a good songwriter and a fine Christian person. On a scale from one to ten, I'd give Janet a ten! She's a dandy!

Pat Boilesen (Janet McBride Fan Club president and performer)... My admiration for Janet began many years before I met her, with a song she wrote called "I Think I Heard a Yodeling Bird." I attended my first WMA Festival that year, with the hopes of meeting the lady who wrote that song, and was not disappointed. I was introduced to Janet and John and that is about all I remember!

Our close friendship began in 1999 when it happened that both Janet and I were to be inducted into the NTCMA Hall of Fame, which took place at the organization's annual festival held at that time in Avoca, Iowa. Bob Everhart, director of the festival, asked me if I would act as "hostess" to Janet and John, and of course, I was thrilled! During that festival, a bond formed between the four of us that will never be broken.

As our friendship grew, my admiration grew, for the closer I became to Janet the more I realized what an extraordinary person she is. Her life's struggles and disappointments she considers "blessings." She's used them as stepping stones, but more importantly, she's used them to make sure that countless others have benefited from lessons she's learned. Her mentoring has touched countless musicians—some young, some not so young—and it's been given so freely!

I remember how much nerve it took for me to ask her if she would allow me to form a "Janet McBride Fan Club." Her answer is something I will treasure as long as I live. I think of it as I begin putting together each Fan Club Newsletter. After some thought, Janet's answer was "Yes, that would be wonderful, but you are the only one I would allow to do it."

I learn from Janet continuously. I'm a better musician and entertainer because of her; but more than that, I've learned what it takes to be a beautiful human being, and though I may try, I will never be the person that Janet McBride is. God has blessed us with all she is to so many people on this earth!

Jeannie Seely (singer)...My memories of Janet go back many years to the early days in our careers in the Los Angeles area. Through the years, whenever someone comes up to me and says "I met Janet McBride and she said she has many memories of your times together," it always makes me smile and I would think back to those times when we were both trying hard to make it in the business. It wasn't easy back then. She's a good friend and a wonderful lady.

Bobby Newton (director, Academy of Western Artists)...I consider it an honor and a privilege to know Janet McBride. Not only is her talent immense, but so is her desire to help others and to have the music she so loves continue and improve. She exudes style and grace, as well as the desire to help the younger generation get involved in her life's work. My life has been enriched because of Janet. There are few like her, just as there should be, for some stars just shine brighter than others, but few get to that level.

Douglas Green (performer with "Riders in the Sky," author and saddle pal)...I have been privileged indeed to have known Janet for a number of years, and have been endlessly delighted by her talent, her commitment, and her warm and gracious personality. As if this weren't enough for any one human being, she has also famously mentored and tutored a whole new generation of performers, her incredibly generous gift to the coming generation. She is one of a kind, and I, like so many of her friends, am honored and grateful to know her.

Ralph Mooney (steel guitar player)...I believe it was in the late '50's when I met Janet in Long Beach, California, at "a rowdy club called George's." I was working with Wynn Stewart and Janet came up to sing with us. When she came to a certain part of the song, she broke into a yodel that knocked my socks off. Janet let me record some songs with her, too. Forty-some years later, I was playing at the Steel Guitar Club in Mesquite, Texas. I really needed a singer and she jumped up on the stage and sang up a storm with me. She is a great lady!

Barbara Musgraves (grandmother of a Janet protégé, friend)...My admiration knows no limits when it comes to all that Janet does to promote kids and love of music. She gives her heart! Known as the "Yodel Queen of Texas," Janet has taught the art of yodeling to children and adults throughout the United States. Her songwriting and yodeling talents are art forms that will live on way into the future of western music. She's a legend!

Mike Shirley (singer/performer)...When I met Janet, I was singing occasionally in church but she encouraged me to sing anywhere and everywhere I could until I got used to stage performing. One day she asked me to sing on the Mesquite Opry and later let me tag along to the Gene Autry Oklahoma Festival and used me as part of her band. I thank her for her encouragement and opening so many doors for me. She is a great friend and a great lady.

Johnny Western (singer/songwriter/radio celebrity)...I have known Janet McBride for 50 years! Who can say anything but good things about her? She is one of the best and is one of the finest people we have ever had in the music business!

Jeanne Cahill & Jerome Campbell (instrumentalists/singers/ performers with "Call of the West")...Much of our musical life began with the friends we made at the Gene Autry Oklahoma Festival. Janet was one of them. She was one of the "bigger-name" entertainers that we watched to learn about pleasing the fans who love western music. That event became like a family reunion. When we were around Janet and John Ingram, it was all lots of fun. We were honored that Janet wanted us to do harmonies for some of her recordings. We are greatly blessed by John and Janet's example of what a loving couple can be! She "bossed" him and he "bossed" her, and they got along lovingly! Peace, love and harmony to you and yours, Janet!

Paul L. White (webmaster)...Of all the historic moments during my tenure as a Mesquite Opry fan, the greatest was most likely Janet's uniting of Patsy Montana and LeAnn Rimes. When LeAnn burst onto the stage with a surprise rendition of "Cowboy's Sweetheart," Patsy's hands went up in the air with applause, she was so overjoyed!

Perhaps the single greatest attribute of the Mesquite Opry was that there was so little focus on Janet McBride herself. Yet, in every performance, every note of music, her influence was quietly there. She had moral and professional standards of the highest caliber, and always that caliber was present.

My fondest memory of Janet at the Opry is a simple one, and it involves her husband John. When it was time for Janet to descend from the lobby to the stage, down that long aisle between seats in the auditorium, John would not let her walk alone. He would leave his seat in the sound booth, put his hand on her back, and walk her forward to her backstage spot where she would wait to make her grand entrance. It was an elegant gesture, and I hope never to fail to remember or imitate that kind of respect and love. Thank you both, Janet and John, for all of your influence, all of your inspiration, and all that continues to arrive with the privilege of being your webmaster.

Al Krtil (radio DJ)... I first heard Janet when the late Bob Lockwood played "Yodeling Jan" on WJRZ Radio/Hackensack, New Jersey, in the mid-'60s. Bob played many great artists who were not part of Nashville's Top Forty group. Janet and I corresponded through the years, and finally met in 1987 in Mountain View, Arkansas, where she was one of the stars of a weekend tribute to Patsy Montana and Elton Britt.

In the early 90's Janet and the late yodeling star Ethel Delaney shared their talents with WMA (Western Music Association) audiences in Tucson, bringing a whole new sound to the WMA! It became almost an annual get-together for these two yodelers, and Janet's contributions to the WMA are priceless. She has not only preserved and perpetuated the music and careers of Patsy Montana, Carolina Cotton and Rosalie Allen, but she has also created an entire new world of yodeling for countless talented youngsters.

As far as I'm concerned, Janet McBride is worthy of induction into both the WMA Hall of Fame and the national Country Music Hall of Fame in Nashville.

Bob Everhart (NTCMA festival director/ performer)...Sheila and I first met Janet when she booked us to be part of the Mesquite Opry just outside Dallas, Texas. The night we were to do her show, some big-time entertainers were playing at the local fairgrounds, not far from the Mesquite Opry. They were so loud, we could hear them all the way to Mesquite. We brought that to Janet's attention, and she said, "we may not be as loud as they are, but we're better, so you'd best do a good job." We had a most fascinating night with her. The Opry, which probably held right at 400 people, maybe more, was full, and the crowd didn't care what was going on at the fairgrounds.

It was much later, in 1999, that we had the opportunity to induct Janet into America's Old Time Country Music Hall of Fame. She had done (and still does) so much to attract young people to traditional and classic country music, especially yodeling; she is herself an icon to many of us in the Midwest.

Chelsea Beck (Janet protégé/performer)... *"The thing always happens that you really believe in; and the belief is the thing that makes it happen." (Frank Lloyd Wright)*

That's a quote that describes my dream and Janet's belief in me. From the first time Janet came into my life seven years ago, she had that wonderful smile and those encouraging words pushing me to do what she knew I was capable of. Because of Janet I am now walking down a new road in my life. Back seven years ago, I was 11 years old and into what all the other girls were doing. It was about contests and pageants and beauty. I wanted to learn to yodel for a beauty pageant and Janet worked with me out of the goodness of her heart and for no charge, of course. And, thanks to Janet's help, I won the talent portion of that beauty pageant.

Janet knew what I was capable of and encouraged me to always be myself. She'd say to me "Never look in someone else's garden, but instead, tend to your own and watch it grow." I have tried to be a good example to my fellow musicians and friends because Janet has always been a good example to me and I know this is what she would want. Janet encouraged me to learn to play the guitar for myself. She said, "Any little girl can get up there and sing, but not every little girl can get up there *and* yodel *and* play the guitar!" Because of her belief in me and her nurturing, I now have an award from the Academy of Western Artists for Yodeler of the Year, as well as the Patsy Montana International Yodeling Champion and other yodeling awards. I have released three CDs and have been featured in *American Cowboy Magazine* and have had numerous recognitions and invitations to perform all over the United States. It's all because I had a dream and Janet helped me achieve it and believe in myself.

I have met so many wonderful people and have had so many wonderful opportunities because of Janet and John. I am so thankful that they are a part of my life and for opening up all these opportunities for me. As Janet would say, "This is too cool!"

Leon Rausch (member of "The Texas Playboys")...I've known Janet since the mid 1960s when we sometimes appeared on the same bill at festivals or concerts around the country. The Longhorn Ballroom was really hot in the early '70s and I worked with Janet several times during that era. We also played Bill's Silver Saddle Club in Grand Prairie on the same bill from time to time. She's a great lady and yodels like a bird!

Lou Curtiss (event director, music historian)...I first saw Janet during her years performing on the West Coast (it might have been *Town Hall*, or maybe one of those Cal Worthington shows) but it was really at The Adams Avenue Roots Festivals that it was my pleasure to book and present her in San Diego several times. As owner of a collectors record shop (Folk Arts Rare Records), I have seen a resurgence in interest in western style music and Janet has been an important part of that revival. I'm not doing festivals right now but I hope to again and perhaps bring Janet back to San Diego one day.

Phil York (recording studio owner/technician and digital specialist)... I first crossed paths with Janet in 1963 or '64 at Dewey Groom's recording studio, Echo Sound, in Pleasant Grove, Texas, where I was a recording technician just learning my craft. She was a charming, young, attractive country singer and yodeler. When I had the nerve to speak to her on occasion, she was always gracious and very pleasant. And, standing in the studio control room one day, when I heard her yodel, my jaw dropped nearly to the floor! She never missed a lick. Really good female country singers were more common than good singers who could also yodel!

I knew of her fame in the country music arena and in particular about her time operating The Mesquite Opry. But our paths didn't connect until much later, when she came to my own recording studio, Yorktown Digital Works, in Irving, Texas. It was probably late 1990s or early 2000s. I am known for my quality audio cleanup and restoration, as well as recording a few gold records for Willie Nelson, including the Grammy winning single, "Blue Eyes Crying in the Rain".

Janet brought me several yodeling recordings in various different formats. There were two very worn and scratchy one-of-a-kind 78s, some half-inch reel-to-reel tapes and some 45s recorded in the early 1960s, plus cassettes from more current sessions on various sizes of recording tapes. We put them altogether in a creative and organized way and the result was a showpiece called "50 Years of Yodeling," a double CD set, an awesome treasure.

Then in 2004, Janet was given a box of reel-to-reel tapes from the late Patsy Montana, with permission from the family to do what she pleased with them. We did some fancy clean-up, some new recording with Janet's voice and some fancy editing and the result of this work is "A Cowgirl's Dream."

And more recently, I recorded a CD for Janet in my studio which contained a song titled, "Mama, I Got Here As Fast As I Could." It is the ideal country song for Mother's Day, or for anyone who appreciates all that our mothers do for us. The entire CD is a charmer, but this one song brings loving tears to one's eyes. Janet's husband, John, got to perform on a song on this CD! He did quite well, even though he aspires to *not* be a professional musician.

I hold Janet McBride in very high regard and am privileged to add a few words about her to this book!

Les Gilliam (singer/performer known as "The Oklahoma Balladeer," Oklahoma Hall of Fame inductee)...I have admired Janet McBride for many years, both as a country music artist and as a kind and warm human being. Some time back, she was a major recording star and yodeler on the West Coast. After moving to Texas, she became the owner/producer of a very successful country music show. During those days, she began to identify, teach and inspire young persons who had talent and love for the music, and she helped them to improve their skills, stage presence and self-confidence. Whether they became a major force in the music business, such as Le Ann Rimes, or someone who just sings for the love of the music, she treated them equally and loved them all the same. Along the way, she has been a Grammy nominee and an outstanding contributor to the success of the Gene Autry Oklahoma Museum and its Film & Music Festival. With her magnetic personality and contagious smile, she has been a blessing to untold numbers of folks across the land. It has been my good fortune to call her friend.

Wayne Boilesen (friend)...We all have friends and friendships, but no friendship could have come easier or been more sincere than my friendship with Janet McBride and John Ingram.

Janet's willingness to share her life stories, talent and mentoring with both young and old only strengthens that friendship. John's wit, humor, and a touch of oneriness only complimented those qualities and strengthened our friendship. Their friendship has made my life richer with something that money can't buy.

Marc DeNicolai (friend, Fan Club member)...We were in Nashville enjoying all the music and raving about the yodeling that was abound. Up came Ernie, who we never saw before, and said "You haven't seen anything about great yodeling until you come to Texas and listen to Janet McBride." We were doubtful but said "O.K, where and when does she yodel, and we'll stop there on our way home to California and see if you tell the truth." That we did, and Ernie was not only telling the truth, but was understating Janet's talent for yodeling, entertaining, MC-ing, organizing the show...and she has an all-around great personality!

It's been years since then. When my wife was alive, she and I played Janet's music quite often, both in our car and at home. My wife passed away a while back, but I assure you that Janet's yodeling still fills my home and I have many good memories of her yodeling and her friendship.

Karol Dyess (producer for Rodeo City Music Hall, Mesquite, Texas)...Janet McBride is an inspiration to me. Her work with the children is admirable. When I grow up I want to be just like her.

Jane Frost (author of Patsy Montana biography, festival director)... Janet McBride makes friends easily and they last a lifetime. From her music, yodeling, songwriting and sense of humor she has garnered herself among the world's greatest entertainers. Always sincere, Janet has coaxed several generations of hopefuls into budding and successful performers. As the sole recipient of the Patsy Award, in honor of her friend, Patsy Montana, Janet is recognized for a lifetime of living her dreams, making music history the passion of her life and sharing it with the world. For this, the world has become a better place and we thank her for her unwavering commitment.

Art Greenhaw (multi-instrumentalist and manager for "The Light Crust Doughboys")...Professional performing talent that people will pay for is a rare quality composed of many parts. Some performing talents are recognizable by audiences, but the rarer, more lasting ones radiate from within. I can say that the moment I first performed with Janet McBride, I felt and recognized her outward and inward talents as a performer, songwriter and singer. These talents were born out in the fact that the Mesquite Opry during the Janet-John ownership was the most successful entertainment venue in the history of the Mesquite, Texas, region. We'll probably never see its like again.

In the more than 12 years of our association, Janet and I worked together for the good of the show as a harmonious team. Her dedication, hard work and determination were all factors in her success in a tough field. And I've always loved Janet's singing as evidenced by the fact that I'll record anywhere anytime in order to sing duets with Janet with her golden vocal pipes and skill in harmony.

I thank Janet for the 12 years of music and entertainment and our time together at the Mesquite Opry during its greatest and glory years. I also thank her for the happiness that she, the band, the performers, and all the others brought to thousands upon thousands of people during those years.

Janet, I'm proud to be in your book, and here's to our next recording and duet together. See you again real soon in the studio, OK?

Larry and Shirley Shipman (Friends for life)...In April of 1982, Shirley and I were blessed to meet Janet McBride Ingram and her husband John. My daughter Jamie and I were asked, on very short notice, due to someone's last-minute cancellation, to be on the Mesquite Opry. Janet opened the show with her signature song at that time "Best Dern Yodeler." I knew at once that her beautiful, crystal clear voice was something very special, and then the yodeling started and I immediately recognized her superstar qualities and that she was a "real deal" professional performer. Later, I would have the opportunity to be at the Opry many times during the day, before the shows (taking reservations etc.) and had the unique privilege of watching a master songwriter at work. Janet has that wonderful ability to express her ideas in catchy, heartfelt, meaningful lyrics and compliment them with original, beautiful music, usually topped off with her world-class yodeling skills. What wonderful, God given talents! Her massive catalog of music will keep her young yodeling protégés in recording material for years to come.

If one could find the definition of "Good Salt of the Earth People" in the dictionary or on the internet, you would find a picture of Janet and John. Almost immediately, we became family and John my best friend. We were so much alike it's scary, and I loved him like a brother. Besides sharing our love for music and our Christian moral views, family values, politics, and our love for good food, it was almost a clone-like situation. Some of our most fun times through the years were our great weekly meals and trips to the Shepler's Western Wear store to look for some bargain prices on show clothes, or a trip to a thrift store to find treasures. The most important treasure was the wonderful quality time we spent together.

Almost everyone knows about Janet's mentoring of young people, but Janet and John, being the caring, giving persons they are, donated many, many hours of their time to perform at nursing homes, senior citizen centers and funerals, not for a fee but because it was the right thing to do. We were always blessed when we came away from those visits.

To those of you who may not be aware, Janet was once selected to be on the national TV show *Queen for a Day*. She became the "Queen" and was awarded prizes and her crown. She and John will one day both be wearing very special permanent multi-star-laden crowns.

We love you Janet .We are so looking forward to the new book and consider you "friends for life."

Judy T. Hamilton (Janet protégé, Fan Club member)...I would like to give a great big THANK YOU to our dear Janet for teaching me and so many others how to yodel. I'm one of her "older" students and learned at the ripe young age of 50! Just goes to show that you're never too old to learn!

Janet has been so gracious and kind. What a dear friend indeed. It is also a privilege serving on her Fan Club committee. I couldn't think of a more deserving lady who's kept our western heritage alive and well all these years. Thank you Janet! I wish you love and happy trails!

Gerald Mason (Mesquite Opry performer, friend)...When I wandered into the Mesquite Opry in 1982, I thought to myself, "I might could do that." Always having more nerve than talent, I introduced myself to Janet McBride and asked if they held auditions. A few weeks later, I began a fifteen-plus-year relationship with the Mesquite Opry that will forever be etched in my memory. I had many great moments, such as appearing on shows with Patsy Montana and Charlie Louvin, not to mention sharing the stage with the many then unknown entertainers who went on to have successful music careers of their own.

Performing on the stage at the Opry gave me the chance to work on my performance skills, something that has greatly benefited me in my "day" job. Cold nights, hot nights, wet nights, lots of hot dogs, friendly fans and friends that I met there will always be cherished. Janet has no idea how many lives she has touched, both those on the stage and those in the audience. Though work had taken me away from Mesquite for many years, I never missed the chance (and was always given the opportunity) to perform when I was back home for a visit. Thanks for all you have meant to me.

Denise Vermett (Janet's daughter)...Being the oldest, some of my first memories were of us living in Southern California. I remember going with Mama on Sundays when she sang at many of the local venues. Seeing her on stage was always a thrill! We could tell that she loved performing. When we moved to Texas, she performed at Panther Hall and the Longhorn Ballroom in Dallas. I remember hearing her record, "I'm Wild Bill Tonight," played on the radio—how exciting! My mom always was, and still is, a star!

Claude McBride (Janet's older son)...For as long as I can remember Mom's music has been a big influence on my life. The family decisions that Mom made had music in the equation, and her family in mind. From helping Mom carry the guitar into a show, to spinning the old records and singing along, to the Mesquite Opry, Mom's music left an impression. My wife Devri and I are active choir members at our church, as are our children Kaitlin and Mallory. Kaitlin is an accomplished flute player and a great singer, and Mallory is a member of the Mesquite Children's Chorus. The decisions that you made early on have greatly affected my life and my family's life for the better. I know your legacy will last for generations to come. Thanks, Mom. We love you!

Mark McBride (Janet's younger son)...Growing up listening to my mom's music and country music in general was something that I will always cherish. To this day I still like the "old stuff," especially that steel guitar twangy sound that you just don't hear much anymore. Growing up following my mother's career was instilled early and made me want to sing on the Opry and be in the spotlight like she was. It certainly has been a fun ride!

Ray & Susan McBride, Sr. (brother-in-law and sister-in-law)...I was nine years old when I met Janet while she was dating my brother Claude, who was in the Navy. Claude would come home on weekends and Janet, her brother Danny and others would sit around and play music and sing. And of course, she would yodel. I was eleven years old and in the seventh grade when she won on *Queen for a Day* and we received a lot of clothes, shoes, and other necessary items for me, my brother Clyde and my Mom and Dad. We were trying to make a living picking cotton around the Walcott, Arkansas, area during that time and having a hard go of it.

I'm the youngest of six boys and Janet has always been like a sister to me. When we were growing up, she was out in California making records and we saw her as a country star. She is still the best yodeler ever as far as we're concerned. We pray that God will continue to bless her in all her endeavors.

Belinda Miller (LeAnn Rimes' mother, Janet's friend)...Janet is a wonderful, selfless woman who loves to use her God-given talents to help others. I believe Janet has enjoyed her life to the fullest, and it's a beautiful example for all of us to follow. We will always appreciate all Janet has done for LeAnn. I remember when LeAnn was asked to be part of the Mesquite Rodeo parade, it was Janet we went to for help. She taught LeAnn the yodel part in "I Want To Be a Cowboy's Sweetheart" and LeAnn performed it in the parade that very day.

Bill Rogers (Mesquite Opry performer, friend)...I never will forget the day I auditioned for the Mesquite Opry. I was scared out of my wits, but thankfully, Janet had a way of making me feel at ease. I sang two lines of "Heartaches by the Number" and Janet said, "That's all I need." Boy was I relieved. Janet and John made being on the Mesquite Opry such a pleasure as did the members of their super band, Paul, Junior, Thomas, Jerl and Art. Those were the best of times.

Mary Rogers (friend, Mesquite Opry volunteer and supporter)...I worked at the Mesquite Opry for years and had some of the best times of my life there. It was a sad day when it closed. People came to me and said "Mary, what are we going to do?" Janet operated the best Opry for all those years. She was the best and I love and respect her very much.

Larry Scott (DJ, friend)...I met Janet and Claude while working at KUZZ in Bakersfield, California, sometime in the early sixties. Her singing and yodeling impressed me but the one thing that impressed me about Janet, then and still does, she's a first class lady.

Going to Texas was a great move. While working at the Longhorn Ballroom, Janet had the opportunity to share the stage with the best in country music. After Claude died she met and married one of the nicest guys in the world, John Ingram. Then came the Mesquite Opry and an opportunity to do something she loves to do and that is to help others. Ask LeAnn Rimes.

During all of this Janet stayed busy in the studio, recording album after album and now CD after CD. Her music is not only loved in America but around the world. Janet McBride, you're a class act.

Curtis and Barb Smith (friends, Mesquite Opry volunteers, occupants of seats J-3 and J-4)...We attended the Opry for about eight years or so every Saturday night. We enjoyed the great music and performers. It was like our second family. We couldn't wait for Saturday night to come around.

Sherry Trosper (Fan Club member, protégé)...Janet is the very essence of what western music is all about. Her love and devotion for western music shows through her many acts of kindness as she encourages and teaches others how to yodel, myself included. She is a gracious and talented treasure, who has left her mark in the music industry. Thank you Janet, for your many years of selfless dedication and service to others, striving to keep western music alive for generations to come. I am honored to call you my dear friend. Love, with a yo-da-la-ei-ti-oh!

Annie von Trapp (mother of the current singing Von Trapps)... We had such a great time with Janet and her husband when they came to visit us at our home in Montana and when she came to our concert in Texas. In Montana we sang songs together and I made them huckleberry pie. We told them all about the grizzly bears in Glacier National Park where we go hiking and she taught the kids a western style of yodeling. She is a great lady.

Jim & Doris Garling (Cowboy singer/friends)...Janet McBride adjectives...kind, generous, daring, dazzling, resilient and friend. Thanks for what you do for us all.

Jay Taylor (editor/publisher of *Country Music Trails Less Traveled*)...Jim Derr and I had arrived early at the 1996 Western Music Association Festival in Tucson, Arizona, and were seated near the performers' entrance. As one of the couples came through the door, the lady looked at me and called out "Jay Taylor! Am I glad to see you!" That lady turned out to be Janet McBride, someone I'd heard of through Patsy Montana, but had never met.

Then in 1998, I visited my collector friend Jack Palmer in Michigan and together we attended the Prairieville Farm Days event. We had just arrived and Jack wanted to sit in the back row. My friends, Stew and Marge Clayton and their daughter Juanita from Manitoba were on stage, so I walked all the way up front to take some photos of them. As I returned to my seat, someone called out "Jay Taylor!" It was Janet...and I got a great big hug!

I have encountered Janet and her late husband John Ingram at numerous western music festivals in the intervening years and actually became quite good friends of theirs. Janet has provided me with ideas and materials for quite a few articles for my bimonthly newsletter *Country Music Trails Less Traveled.* Janet herself has put in a lot of time and effort helping kids learn to yodel and to sing western songs...and I'm certainly proud to call her "friend!"

Bill Goodman (Opry comedian)...On behalf of Morgan Buildings, I would like to thank you, Janet, for the three 8' x 10' buildings in my back yard purchased through the years to store the various comedy items I have purchased, made possible by the chance you gave me to perform at the Mesquite Opry. I am just one of many people you have helped to do something they love and enjoy: entertain! And thanks for allowing me to win all those "comedian of the year" awards at the other north Texas oprys after the Mesquite closed!

Doug Edwards (Opry singer)...Janet and the Mesquite Opry gave me a chance to sing in front of people with a band behind me and gave me the courage to go to Branson to try my luck in the professional arena. With great experience and several awards under my belt, I finally decided that being a full-time road singer was not really what I wanted to do, so came back to Dallas and got into full-time real estate sales, doing music on the side. It's a good life!

Jerl Welch (Opry musician)...After playing music on the road for years, I got so burned out that I quit music totally. Years later, I was invited to sit in with the Mesquite Opry folks. I stayed for over ten years. The Opry was so much fun, everyone knew each other and it was a clean show. And best of all, it allowed me to get back into my music, but not on the road. Thank you, Janet.

Jamie Shipman Kassab (Opry singer)...I can't tell you how I felt the first time I heard Janet yodel. I wasn't very old, barely 15, but I knew she was someone I had to meet. I was in awe the first time I met her. She was a lady of distinction and grace.I could just tell from looking at her that she had class and had what it took to run a super-duper opry show. I was all excited (when she asked me to perform), for it was my dream to sing on her stage.

Through the years, Janet and I have made many wonderful memories and built a strong life-lasting friendship. Bruce and my daughters, who are also in music, know who Janet is and look up to her. Our oldest daughter, Kaylen, used Janet as a mentor and, through that relationship, has accomplished the art of yodeling.

It's so amazing to think that Janet has taught and shared her love of music and yodeling with so many young artists to make sure that this unique art form doesn't die. Thank you, Janet, for being such a wonderful music mentor to me and our daughter. You will always have a place in my heart.

John & Ann Buttram (friends)...Genuine and generous...those words describe Janet perfectly. Both Janet and I (Ann) are members of the Saddle Vamp Club, a group of gals who regularly attended the Gene Autry Oklahoma Film & Music Festival. We had wonderful times being in that crazy group. We love spending time with Janet and will miss John for the rest of our days!

Elvin & Flo Sweeten (directors, Gene Autry Oklahoma Museum)...Janet has given so freely of her time and talents to help the Museum that we can't say enough about how much we appreciate her. She's helped with the Museum's annual fundraiser by lining up entertainers and collecting raffle items, and she sings and yodels for the crowd, and always brings a great group of followers to our events. We appreciate her immensely!

Kacey Musgraves (singer, Janet protégé)...Janet is one of the most patient, encouraging and inspiring people I've been fortunate enough to meet on this musical journey. She's the reason I've got calluses on my fingers from playing guitar. She's the reason I even picked it up in the first place, instilling in me the importance of songwriting and learning to play an instrument. She taught me how to yodel and shared her knowledge and love for western swing. I, along with countless other kids who need some (no nonsense) nurturing and a stage to grow up on, thank you. We need more teachers like Janet McBride!

Ron & Penny Carrabis (fans, friends)...Hey, let's go have dinner in Scottsdale again one of these days! We're your forever fans, friends...and oh yes, Ron is still your "wannabe" nephew!

Walter Nevada (fan, friend)...As president of the Vienna Country Music Club, I was proud to have Janet visit Austria and perform on our country music festival. She also helped me to invite numerous other American country artists to our country. What a great gal!

21

Family, Friends and Fond Memories
(from Janet's Perspective)

*John and Janet prepare to hit the road in Ron Carrabis' semi
in this "just for fun" pose.
(Janet McBride Collection)*

Mama

(Aurelia Marquis Lister)

Mama was a special person. I didn't realize it at the time but I now know that she could have made a million dollars by selling her secrets on how she survived to be 92 years of age, given her start in life. Every strike was against her from birth in 1909. She was one of eight children who found themselves without a father when he walked away and never looked back. In order to survive, the older children went to work and brought home their pay to help the others. Mama completed the 8th grade and like her siblings, found a job. Hers was in the cafeteria of the Veterans Home in Togus, Maine. She married my father in 1927 and bore three children by 1930 and had already buried two of them. She had four more children and buried one of them before 1939.

December 1941 brought Pearl Harbor and a move back to Maine and by the middle of 1942, the family of six moved to a small home on a dirt road where there was no electricity, an outhouse and, in winter, a potbelly stove to fight the cold. Summer was easy and sometimes even fun. There were fish to catch and eat, berries to pick and can and, if it was a good year, there were potatoes in the cellar, pickles in a crock and plenty of dry beans to eat. But the winters were harsh and with only a kerosene lamp for light, they would drag on and on. Winter meant six people moved into three rooms to keep warm but still, Mama never complained.

A return to California in January 1947 brought an 18-feet-long trailer

Dan, Janet, Joan, Don and Mama. 1997. (Janet McBride Collection)

that made those three small rooms in Maine seem like a mansion.

Mama could have written a "How to Survive" book. She could tell you how it felt to pull up stakes and move across the country more than once, without a complaint even if when Christmas came there was nothing to give. She explained it well and we always had hope that somehow Santa would bring something and surprise us.

She never failed to come home from work, fix dinner and call us all in to the table to eat as a family. She could have a chapter on how it felt to face her day without all of her front teeth and then smile like it didn't matter. She could show you how to make a braid with your hair and "wrap it in a circle around neatly" which hid the fact that she couldn't afford to go to a beauty shop or a barber. She could give lessons on how to tell your children that she wouldn't be going to parent-teacher conferences because she didn't want to embarrass anyone. It didn't make any difference to us kids, of course. She was our Mama.

She could give lessons on how to hold yourself together when your husband died. She could tell you how to take control, sell the trailer home and rent another one on a street along a bus line and ride the bus to work to the shoe factory in downtown Los Angeles. She might also add how she used Daddy's insurance money to find a dentist who made her a beautiful set of false teeth and how it felt to smile again at the age of 46. She could sell hope to anyone who felt like all hope was gone. She could say with a smile that there could be life again for someone who always gave and never asked for anything in return but their love.

What did I learn from Mama? I learned how to survive. Mama was strong. She loved my music. If she thought I was wasting my time trying for a recording career she never said a word. Ever. Did she like Claude? She never said a bad word to me about him. Daddy did, but only once.

For those who wonder if I thought Mama was pretty. Mama's inside beauty always shone through even moreso as the outside faded.

Mama married again some years after Daddy died and enjoyed a contented home life. She outlived her second husband Emmitt French and was able to live comfortably until she died in 1999. It was always nice to know that for all of the years without even the bare necessities, Mama had everything she needed and a lot more than she wanted. She didn't spend much of what she had and was actually able to leave something to each of us four kids.

Was she beautiful? Oh yes, she definitely was! Her name was Aurelia Julia Marquis and she was My Mama.

ߏ

Daddy
(Victor Ulman Lister)

Daddy did his best in a world where his lack of education would catch up with him. The shoe factory jobs he had mastered were disappearing and he still needed to work. Don and Joan were gone by that time, and I'm sure he gave a lot of thought to what would happen to him and Mama if he couldn't find work.

I don't believe Daddy ever drew an unemployment check. His work ethic was passed on to me for sure. He always had a job of some kind as long as I can remember.

Daddy didn't have a tooth in his head but he never talked about seeing a dentist for false teeth. He never seemed to let it bother him. I remember when I was in the ninth grade, he took me to the dentist for a series of appointments to fix my bad teeth, but he and Mama never spent money to fix their own problems. Us kids came first.

Daddy taught us all how to enjoy life without spending any money. We fished often, using a stick with a string and hook, no bobber. I remember one time when we were looking for lady slippers, he came upon a deer and it jumped right over us kids. What a thrill that was!

It was Daddy who shaped my life. He gave me the love of flowers and nature. We spent many spring and summer hours walking in the woods and stopping to see the smallest violets, the "jack-in-the-pulpits" and the pussywillows, that bloomed even when there was still snow on the ground. The May flower, the lady slipper...these were all free gifts...and I cherish them.

Daddy loved the horse races and would go to the track whenever he could. I think of Daddy when the big horse races are on TV. If he were alive today, he'd have the horseracing channel, if there is one.

After I graduated from school and had a car, I remember one time I accidentally backed the tailpipe into a mountain of dirt. The engine stalled and when I "cranked 'er up" I blew out every gasket in the engine. My Dad had it ready for me to drive it to work on Monday morning. He was an exceptional mechanic.

Daddy and Mama didn't let us girls work until we were out of school. Then it was "You gotta have a job." After Daddy died, I wondered how Mama would make it. It had always been the two of them.

cx

My Siblings

Donald Francis Lister (born May 17, 1929)

Don is the oldest of my siblings and has always been pretty quiet. He really got tired of my yodeling noise fast. He has always been "Mr. Steady." He and his wife Dorothy worked hard, raised their family and retired. He loves to go to gospel concerts and is a Sunday school teacher. He is a wonderful cabinet maker and is great at making wood crafts.

Joan Lister Dearborn (born October 3, 1932)

Joan is 18 months older than me. She married Larry Dearborn in 1954 and lived in Southern California until they both retired and moved to Big Bar, California. She is now a widow and has filled her life with family and friends...and still has that beautiful Martin guitar.

Daniel Richard Lister (born March 8, 1936)

Dan is the youngest. He married Jean in 1955 and they raised three children of their own plus a niece and a couple grandchildren. He worked his whole life and is now retired. He is a genius when it comes to re-building or restoring old cars and trucks.

cx

My Children

Denise McBride Vermett (born November 8, 1955)

Denise was an absolutely beautiful baby. When I left the hospital with her, I went to the McBride's house and stayed there a few days until I was able to make it alone. She was an independent child, and

Mark, Denise and Claude Jr.
(Janet McBride Collection)

226

always the "big sister." She made good grades in school and has grown into a wonderful wife, mother and even grandmother! Denise is an executive assistant for a money management firm. Married to Stanley Vermett, she has two children, Stephanie and Shannon, and three grandchildren, Dylan, Reese and Hadley.

Claude Edward McBride, Jr. (born February 1, 1959)

Claude Jr. was "Mr. Dependable," always where he said he'd be when he said he'd be there. He joined the Dallas Police Department in 1981 and plans to retire in a few years. He's married to Devri and has two daughters, Mallory and Kaitlin.

Mark Stephen McBride (born January 15, 1961)

Mark was so lucky to have his grandmother Ruth cook for him for so long. Now working as a telephone system instructor, Mark has his father's good looks and charm. He is married to Kim and they have four children: Madeline, Abigail, Caroline and Johnathan, plus Mark's three older children: Marcee, Chad, and J.B. plus Maxwell (deceased). He has one grandchild, Kade.

ભ

John's Children

Gary Dwain Ingram

Based in Fort Worth, Gary has worked for the railroad in Texas for 37 years. He is married to Jamie and is a proud grandparent to Katelynn and Emmalee, and lives in Aurora, Texas.

John Patrick Ingram

John lives in Bedford, Texas, and has three daughters: Jessica, Reanna and Rachel; and two granddaughters: Riley and Alix. He's very involved with his church.

ભ

Nieces and Nephews

Patty, Larry, Kathy, Vivian, David, Donna, Dale, Danny Allen, Kenny, Randy, Ricky and several others from the McBride side of the family.

and Cousins

Leona, Elmore, Dot, Arlene, Norman, Bob, Louise, Christine and Jackie, plus many I've lost track of.

cx

Some of My Dearest Friends

Pat & Wayne Boilesen...You meet a lot of people in life, especially in the music business. Some of them you may keep for life and some only for the moment (or festival) and then they are gone. In 1994 at the Western Music Festival in Tucson, Arizona, I met Pat and Wayne Boilesen from Albion, Nebraska. As it happened, the nighttime stage show we were all to attend was being held in the old movie town called "Old Tucson." We all traveled to the location that night in a limousine shuttle, which in itself was pretty neat. Then Pat and Wayne and their group "Cowboy Rhythm" all got in the limo with us and Pat's friend Lee Ann Frame introduced us. Pat's group backed Patsy Montana that night and I was jealous.

Fast forward to 1999 and Bob Everhart's Annual Old Time Music Festival in Avoca, Iowa. I was able to talk with Pat during this event, between talking to fans at our product tables. The year 2000 found us together again at that same event and we got to know each other better.

I'm not sure when Pat first mentioned a "Janet McBride Fan Club" to me, and I am sure I asked her if she had been out in the sun too long. We talked about stuff we could do to make the newsletter interesting. She had listened to many of the stories that I had told over my lifetime and career and asked if I would write them down and send them to her and we'd start putting them into the newsletter by chapters. Then in 2003, she sent the first Fan Club Newsletter to a list of fans I had put together for her.

Pat and Wayne invited us up to their home in Albion, Nebraska, and the visits began in 2005 between the Cedar Depot Festival and the Patsy Montana International Yodeling Competition in

Janet and John with Pat and Wayne Boilesen at a WMA festival. (Pat Boilesen Collection)

Missouri when we had a few days to wait before the 'Patsy' began. They were great hosts and we enjoyed each other's company...and those visits became a standard routine every year, which was a blessing for us.

Pat and others had often said that I needed to write a book, but books don't just happen. Someone has to step up and say "I'll do it," so when Mary Schutz said she'd like to do it, the work began right then. It was a natural fit to have Pat join in the project since she had been working on bits and pieces of my story for so long with the Fan Club Newsletter.

We began gathering the stories together and funneling them all to Mary, as well as put to paper some of the newer stories. The project was larger than anyone thought, and life keeps going on, so the stories keep coming. All the while, Mary and Tex had their own careers and bookings to keep and medical problems to handle. Pat also has a very active booking schedule but found time to work on fact-checking for Mary, while she dealt with her own family illnesses and events. Each of these ladies has put in countless hours on this chore called a book with the title *Still Lovin' the Ride.*

The Good Lord put the three of us together and I am sure at the time we met, none of us could have guessed that this is what we'd be doing as a project. I can't thank these ladies and their husbands enough for the time they have spent on this book. When you try to put your life into words, it does take time. John spent lots of hours watching the History Channel or the Western Channel, while I gathered information, dug out photos and tried to answer all the questions Mary was asking. I appreciated his understanding and patience so very much.

Larry & Shirley Shipman...These fine folks started out as Opry supporters and volunteers and grew to become dear friends and traveling companions. Larry would give us the shirt off his back if we asked for it. Whenever we were unable to host Patsy Montana because of our work schedules, Larry and Shirley jumped in and took care of her. Every Saturday night when the Mesquite Opry show was over, Larry and Damon Withrow were the first to grab a trash bag and go through the theater picking up trash, so we could all go to breakfast together.

Shirley is the perfect partner for Larry and the perfect friend. She's a great cook, a creative crafter, a good organizer...and she raised five kids. As a woman friend, she is supportive, fun to be around and just a great gal! We seem to like to do the same kinds of things, especially when it comes to traveling...and that's not easy!

Larry and Shirley have been dear friends both to me and John, as a couple as well as individuals. They are tireless, dependable, trustworthy and fun-loving people.

John, Janet, Shirley and Larry Shipman, a nice dinner out.
(Larry Shipman Collection)

Lowell & Nan Lydic...These sweet people came into my life at the Festival of the West in March 1999. I saw a flyer for the Rex Allen Days Celebration and sought out the guy in charge of entertainment for that event. From that time on, Rex Allen Days became one of the highlights of our year. John and I visited with Lowell and Nan whenever we were anywhere close to Kansas and one day, while we were all sitting on the porch of Cedar's antique shop, Lowell asked whether I knew of anyplace they could "throw a music festival." I looked out over the town of Cedar, Kansas, and said, "Why not here?" They laughed, but a few weeks later, we got a flyer in the mail announcing the first annual Cedar Depot Celebration. That was May 2002. Lowell, Nan, Francis and Loretta worked together to clean up the vacant town square and turned it into Depot Park and made improvements each year for the event, which lasted ten years (the last one held in June of 2011). There was space for RVs, car parking, vendors, workshops and lots of lawn chairs.

Lowell felt like I did about the young talent and he wanted to offer a stage to as many of the kids as he could. From the very first festival he offered free instruction to all at workshops covering such subjects as fiddle, Dobro, harmonica, guitar, songwriting and, of course, I conducted several yodeling workshops there through those ten years.

Lowell and Nan Lydic are not only fans but they are also dear friends. John and I always had a great relationship with them and always enjoyed just hanging out with them.

JoAnn Tucker Page...This sweet and wonderful gal was there from the beginning of my Seagoville days. I met her at the beauty shop. She loved

Lowell & Nan Lydic, Janet & John at Fiddler's Feast Chuckwagon Theater in Pigeon Forge, while visiting Kata Hay, who was working there.
(Janet McBride Collection)

country music and we just hit it off! She loved to dance and go to the Longhorn Ballroom with the gals to hear country music and see the guest stars. She particularly remembers a night when Conway Twitty was performing and we had a table just in front of the stage, where we could almost touch him! All the gals were in Hog Heaven that night.

It was so hard on their family when they had to watch their daughter suffering with cancer, and I tried to be there for her, but always felt inadequate. When they lost her, it was a tragedy felt by the whole town.

I would put JoAnn in the "good ol' country gal" category. She's a good cook and knows how to do everything! When we were both a bit younger, she just loved playing softball and often played on a team. She and Robert stood up for John and me when we got married. We often did things as families...my kids and her kids. After she and Robert divorced and she married Ralph, it seemed that I was so busy with my job and the Opry, that we weren't able to get together as often as we would have liked. And though we haven't been together much lately, I still think of her often and cherish our friendship. She's happy-go-lucky, smart and fun to be with. She's got a positive outlook, she's trustworthy, a hard worker and a phenomenal organizer. And she drives *really fast!*

231

🙂

Other Friends

Maine: Mary, Clara and Stanley and the Carters and all my other friends from my school days in Whitefield, Maine.

California: Janice, JoAnn, Jolene, Carol, Sally and Mary, plus other friends from Narbonne High School in Lomita. Also Joe, who was my favorite mechanic, and Evie, my boss at the aircraft plant.

Texas: The early years: Quinlan (Dewey's wife), Jessie and Mary Helen, plus others from the Longhorn Ballroom days. More recently: Co-workers from the Sheriff's Department; fans and friends from the Mesquite Opry, Country Church and Cowtown Opry; Crystal and Steve (who were always there to help), Kelly, Karen and Craig Musgraves, Barbara and Darrell Musgraves.

From WMA: Hank and Sharon, Jeff and Debbie, plus all the other wonderful folks I've met through my involvement with WMA.

🙂

Lots of Other Music Friends

I just can't go without mentioning some of the wonderful folks I've met through the music, whether at a festival or other event, at the Opry, at Buckaroos, whether you're a performer or a fan. You all know that I love you and that my life is fuller for having known you!

From the Entertainment Industry...Cheryl Rogers & Larry Barnett, Marilyn Tuttle, Tom & Bertha Swatzell, Rose Lee Maphis, Rex, Jr. and Deanna Allen, Dale Berry, Jeanne Cahill & Jerome Campbell, Judy Coder, Tex & Mary Schutz, Jim & Jeanne Martin, Rollie Stevens, Liz Anderson, Lynn & Casey Anderson, Roger & Denise Tibbs, Joyce Simone, John & Ann Buttram, Dick & Dixie Goodman, Billy Joe Rogers, Ethel Delaney.

Festival Friends...Hazel & Don, Darline & Bob, Marge & Jack, Leslie & Barbara, Shiloh, Micki & Dick, Mike & Linda, Flo & Elvin, Stan & Alma, Galen, Shirley & Harry, Loretta & Francis, Jim & Doris, Buck, Jane & Larry, Chris & Rodney, Louie & Georgia, Sharon & Tom, Ron & Penny, Wilbur & Sherry, Bill Tune, the Whites.

Special DJ Friends...Marvin O'Dell, Al Krtil, OJ Sikes, Mike Gross, Art Kneeland, Darwin Lee Hill, Herb Sudzin, Marshall Alan Bailey, Ed and Jolene Bullard, Joe Baker, Enola Gay, Waynetta Ausmus, Graham Lees,

Tommy Tucker, Tom Wardle, Irv Simner, Rick Huff, Hugh McLennan, Barb Richhart.

Generous Supporters...Terry Lee, Susan and Bill Montgomery, Don and Dee Duncan, Barbara and Don Stevens, Wilbur and Sherry Watts, plus various Opry regulars and performers.

ଔ

Musings and Memories

Showing affection...There weren't many hugs, kisses or "I love you's" in our lives as we were growing up. It just wasn't said, but Daddy and Mama did show us they loved us by their actions. They gave us their lives. This silent affection carried over into each of our lives. My first trip to Texas to meet the friends of the Longhorn Ballroom and record company group, when everyone hugged me, I nearly freaked out! I was not expecting it and I was very suspect of each of them. Of course, as time went by, it became easier to give a hug, and now I'm a true hugger when I greet people, but I always say "In Texas we hug," so I won't scare them off. Nowadays, I hug my kids and tell them I love them often, but it did take several years to get good at it.

About Claude...It wasn't love at first sight in any way. He did grow on me, however, and before long we became a couple. He was handsome and I was so in love. He told me he loved me and I fell hard. He could make me feel beautiful and I had low self-esteem, so that meant a lot. I had no experience in dating or guys, but it probably wouldn't have changed anything if I had.

Getting married was a great idea, I thought. Claude was 18 and I was 20. He was a new sailor and I was working. I was living with my mom and he lived on the naval base in San Diego. I had a car payment and he had his uniform. What was I thinking? I wasn't thinking, obviously, and we got married on our second try. He was too young to marry in California, so we went to Mexico.

We had pretty babies, but as a husband, he'd get a bad grade for sure. He should never have married anyone. Ever!

About being a young wife...Wow, I was unprepared, for sure. I had no clue how to cook anything, had never cleaned a house, never washed a load of clothes, never ironed, never held a baby, and on top of all that, I had to work to eat and pay a car payment. Claude was a sailor and wasn't any smarter than I was. I expected life to be tough because I watched Mama and Daddy, but reality was way beyond anything I could imagine.

About Claude's death...The night Claude died...I was still trying to bend over backwards for him, and had never given up hope that he could become a good husband and father. After 18 years and a lot of tears, I just couldn't cry. All I could think was, "It's over. It's finally over."

Things didn't change so much without him. We had learned to do without him years ago. We all just wanted a dad and husband, but really didn't ever have one.

It took nearly three years for me to "hit the wall." I was very close to a breakdown. I had finally faced the fact that I was "looking for love in all the wrong places." I realized I needed the Lord's hand to lead me out of the hole I had dug for myself and my kids. I turned my broken world over to God and asked Him to guide me to a better way of life. In turn, I agreed to walk away from my past.

Venues that mean so much to me...It was 1996 and I was performing at the Cowboy Symposium in Lubbock, Texas. There I met Les Gilliam from Oklahoma. He asked if I had ever thought about participating in the Gene Autry Oklahoma Festival and I said "Where's that?" He told me all about the Gene Autry Oklahoma Museum and that there was, in fact, a town named Gene Autry. He invited me to drop in at that year's event, but when he told me that Johnny Western would be performing at the upcoming festival, I decided to make every effort to get there. We got to see Johnny and others perform in this wonderful museum dedicated to the singing cowboys of the western movies. It was magic! Through the years since, I've given as much time and energy as I could to the Museum and its events, and have developed a good friendship with Museum owners, Flo and Elvin Sweeten. Through the Museum, we also made good friends with Ed and Jolene Bullard and Don and Hazel Sargent. Then, in 2009, I was presented the Museum's Lifetime Achievement Award. What a treasure!

The Hank Snow Festival in Nova Scotia, Canada, holds such special memories for me. I was invited several times to perform there by our friend Bob Paulin, but couldn't really make the trip until we'd retired. It's a wonderful event dedicated to all things Hank Snow. It's a large and very successful festival with contests for Hank Snow sing-alikes, Hank Snow dress-alikes, and Hank Snow guitar picking-alikes, with great prizes and very colorful contestants as well. The Hank Snow Music Centre is in Liverpool, Nova Scotia, and we did a performance there—but the other events we attended were held in Caledonia, Nova Scotia.

Another festival that was dear to my heart was "The Patsy Montana

Music Days &
International
Yodeling
Competition."
This one was, of
course, devoted to
the memory and
talent of Patsy
Montana, the
singular yodeling
female icon in the
world. The event,
held every June,
began in 1998 in
the small town of
Havenhurst,
Missouri. The

Mr. Mukai, a longtime fan from Japan, came to visit on two separate occasions.
(Janet McBride Collection)

entrants never ceased to amaze me at how hard they worked to be "Patsy Montana for a day." Each year I conducted yodeling workshops and performed as many Patsy songs as I could. I held my yodel camp on Fridays of the three-day festival and taught a *bunch* of kids to yodel! Festival director Jane Frost's husband Larry became quite ill at one point. The festival became more than they could handle, and after the tenth annual event, it ended. What wonderful memories I have of this festival and all the youngsters who would follow in Patsy Montana's footsteps!

A wonderful "fan" story...A man from Japan, who said he was a huge Janet McBride fan, tracked me down through a Japanese-speaking Texas friend. He said he owned some of my early records and wanted so badly to meet me. Then one day he asked where we could meet, because he was planning a trip to America. Through the Texas friend's e-mail correspondence with me, we arranged to meet at a Buckaroos gathering in May of 2005. John and I got there early and, sure enough, there was Mr. Mukai with all four of my LP covers under his arm for me to autograph. He couldn't speak much English but we were able to communicate quite well. He brought me a beautiful music box with two revolving swans, and I gave him some of my CDs and publicity photos. He asked me to sing one of my old songs, "Almost Three" (a great "mommy song"). I amazed myself and John, too, when I sang the song without missing a word. We learned that Mr. Mukai had flown directly from Japan, stayed two nights at the Stockyards Hotel and would fly back to Japan on Monday morning. He made that trip

just to see Janet McBride! And, if that one long trip weren't enough, he came again, about a year later. Now, friends, *that* is a fan!

Daddy's Bible...In 1942, Mama ordered a mail-order Bible for Daddy for Christmas. It had a leather binding and his name was written in gold on the front. I remember pressing four-leaf clovers and a violet or two in its pages. Before Mama died, I found Daddy's Bible in her closet, with the body intact, but the leather cover was totally worn and nearly gone. I carried it home to Texas in a big envelope and finally took it to The Book Doctor (in Dallas) in 2010 and had it restored. It's so special having it whole again! And some of those four-leaf clovers are still pressed between its pages!

Who would play me if they made a movie of my life...Who would do a movie of my life? I don't have a clue. To play me in the early years, it would have to be someone who could look like a waif—with tight French braids and a cat in her arms. As a young woman, when I was beginning to find "Janet," when I had the cancer surgery, then finally realized that make-up was a good thing, had a few stylish clothes and blossomed—that would have to be someone who could play the part of a plain Jane turning into an attractive young woman, but still struggling to deal with personal problems. When I was a young widow, looking for love and stability, raising two teenage boys—that needs an actress who can portray insecurity, toughness, tenderness, vulnerability, tenacity and so much more. Then when I met John and at last found the stability I was searching for, it would be someone who could portray my dedication to building a real American life, where a man and woman work hard together and are able to retire and enjoy what they worked for.

My proudest accomplishment...my family. Even with all of the ups and downs, I tried to be a good mom for the kids. I'm not sure they understood why their mom always had to work, but in order to keep food on the table and the electricity on and have a place to call home, I had to work.

What I'd want people to remember about me...That I had my yodel...and I gave it away. That I was a mentor for kids who wanted to learn how to get that gift, and helped them every chance I could.

Kids...I see kids in my future still. The Buckaroos program will always bring me new kids to help.

My single greatest moment...Wow, that was a pretty easy choice, actually. It would be meeting Billy (John) Ingram.

22

John and Beyond
(from Janet's Perspective)

*Billy John Ingram (July 3, 1931-December 22, 2010), the man who
was (and will always be) the love of Janet's life.
(Photo by Ron and Glenda Shipman, from Janet McBride Collection)*

John Ingram

John was the reason I started singing on a stage again. I knew my age was a problem but John kept saying I could perform at Grapevine Opry and just have fun...not "star stuff" but certainly fun stage-show stuff. So I started back singing in 1979 and loved it. We'd drive to Stephenville on a Saturday, sing and drive home in time to make shift change at work. It was hard on us...functioning without much sleep...but great fun!

Through all the Opry years, John was right there with me. I don't know where I would have ended up without John Ingram in my life. John helped me along my path, no doubt with the Lord's hand. We talked about that many times during our 34 years together. With the Lord in our lives we learned to totally trust each other and we found a lasting love that few people find. Everyone saw the change in each of us over the years. There was a peace within that wasn't there before. We worked together from Day One. It was always "us" and never "me" or "you." It was always "me *and* you." When someone asks who made the biggest change in my life, for me it was John. Who had the biggest impact on my life? That, too, would be John.

I found love with John Ingram that I had never before known. He loved me for me, a bit of a challenge at times, I'll wager. He never tried to change me, never told me *not* to do something. He let me fly as high as I could.

On December 22, 2010, my world stood still. It didn't stop, but it certainly stood still. I can't say for sure what I will be able to do. Losing John will change where I sing, for sure, but I hope to continue traveling as much as I can.

The Next Chapter

Yes, John is gone from my life, and I'll re-invent myself in a life without him, but always with his spunky spirit that I know will stay with me forever.

I am not sure what is in store for me. I've never done much alone so I have some big decisions to make.

I may not want to travel as far to sing, but I am very aware that I can perform as often as I like locally, at senior centers, kids' events, church get-togethers and opry shows. Sometime those are even more rewarding than the ones you play for money.

Someday, I may just decide to be a stay-at-home Mom to my three kids and a Grandma and Great-grandma to Stephanie and John, Shannon and Wes, Marcee and Kirk, Chad, J.B., two Mallorys, Kaitlin, two Madelines, Maci, Abigail, Caroline, Johnathan, Kade, Dylan, Reese and Hadley. Maybe I'll make peanut butter and jelly sandwiches and keep a pantry full of three-minute mac and cheese and a freezer full of ice cream cups. That is some of the most fun...as long as my rules apply and I'm in charge. Does that sound familiar?

I'm sure that I do want to continue with my music in some way, however, and will definitely continue to be a mentor to as many young performers as possible. Plus, I'll want to share this book with as many old and new friends as I can, and, while I'm at it, I'd just love to make even more friends. Because there's nothing quite as special as a music friend!

The End

Photo by Lori Faith Merritt (www.photographybyfaith.com)

Appendices

Persons and Organizations Mentioned in this Book

Academy of Country & Western Music grew out of discussions in 1963 between trade journal publisher Tommy Wiggins (*DJ's Digest*) and three other country enthusiasts, Eddie Miller, Mickey Christiansen and Chris Christiansen. Before the Academy became the Academy, this group began presenting awards for musical accomplishments on the West Coast, under the aegis of their *DJ's Digest* magazine. Janet won two of those awards, one in 1963 and one in 1964. The group's efforts attracted the interest of several bigger name entertainers and producers who began working with Wiggins and the others to create a national organization called the Country and Western Music Academy. Continuing its awards program, the Academy helped to propel country music into the national public spotlight for the first time. During the early 1970s the organization changed its name to the Academy of Country and Western Music and finally to the Academy of Country Music (ACM). The Academy of Country Music continues to promote and support the industry and engage country music fans not just in the western states, but from coast to coast.

Allsup, Tommy (born November 24, 1931) is an American musician, arranger, producer, and live and session guitarist, who served as an A&R man for Liberty Records for a time and operated Metromedia Records. As a musician he worked with Buddy Holly, Ronnie Smith and Roy Orbison. As a producer he worked with Bob Wills, Leon Rausch and Willie Nelson.

Anderson, Bill (James William Anderson III) (born November 1, 1937) is an American country singer, songwriter and TV personality. He has released more than 40 studio albums and has reached Number One on the country charts seven times. Twenty-nine more of his singles have reached the Top Ten.

Atkins, Chet (Chester Burton Atkins) (June 20, 1924–June 30, 2001) was an American guitarist and record producer who created, along with Owen Bradley, the smoother country music style known as the "Nashville Sound," which expanded country's appeal to adult pop music fans. Atkins received 14 Grammy Awards as well as the Grammy Lifetime Achievement Award and nine Country Music Association (CMA) Instrumentalist of the Year awards. He was inducted into the Country Music Hall of Fame in 1973.

Bailey, Jack (September 15, 1907–February 1, 1980) was an American actor and host of the *Queen for a Day* daytime television game show. He was awarded two stars on the Hollywood Walk of Fame—one for his radio career and one for his work in television.

Big D Jamboree was an American radio program broadcast by KRLD-AM in Dallas, Texas. The show consisted of appearances by famous country music performers as well as comedians. It was also carried by KRLD-TV during the 1950s. The *Big D Jamboree* began in 1947 as *The Lone Star Barn Dance*, but was renamed soon after.

Buckaroos, a project of the Cowtown Opry of Fort Worth, Texas, that helps young people learn to perform traditional music and gives them a stage where they can perform.

Burton's Bend Music Festival, a music festival established in 2010 and presented in the renovated school house in Holbrook, Nebraska. Burton's Bend was the name given to the community when it was established in 1870 by Isaac Burton near a bend of the Republican River at the 100th meridian. Once the railroad came to the area, the town changed its name to Holbrook. *www.burtonsbendmusicfestival.com*

Cagle, Buddy was an early Southern California singer signed with Capitol Records, best known for "Tonight, I'm Coming Home."

Campbell, Glen Travis (born April 22, 1936) is a Grammy and Dove-winning and two-time Golden Globe-nominated country and pop singer, guitarist and occasional actor. He is best known for a series of hits in the 1960s and 1970s, as well as for hosting a TV variety show called *The Glen Campbell Goodtime Hour* on CBS television.

Cedarwood Publishing Company, at one time the most important publishing house in Nashville, was formed in 1954 by James Denny, booking agent and long-time manager of the Grand Ole Opry, and Opry star Webb Pierce.

Clark, Roy L. (born April 15, 1933) is a versatile American country musician and performer. He is best known for hosting *Hee Haw*, a nationally televised country variety show, from 1969–1992, and still popular in syndicated re-runs.

Compton Brothers, a group comprised of Tom Compton, Bill Compton and Harry Compton plus Dave Murray. They were country music singers/recording artists of the 1960s and '70s.

Cooper, Wilma Lee & Stoney Cooper (Nee Wilma Lee Leary, born February 7, 1921). Wilma Lee Cooper is a country entertainer who married Dale Troy Cooper (October 16, 1918 - March 22, 1977), known professionally as Stoney Cooper, master of fiddle and guitar. They were members of the Grand Ole Opry, with their strongest stardom evident from the 1940s through the 1970s. Wilma Lee continued to perform on the Grand Ole Opry through 2009.

Country Music Trails Less Traveled is a bimonthly newsletter dealing with all things related to the preservation of traditional country music: events, performers, history, trends and CD releases. Published by Jay Taylor.

Dawson, Devon was named the Academy of Western Artists' Female Artist of the Year for 2009, and has received two Grammy nominations. Devon performs with The Texas Trailhands and provided the singin', yodelin' voice for Jessie, The Yodelin' Cowgirl on the Grammy Award-winning "Woody's Roundup featuring Riders In the Sky" CD released by Walt Disney Records in August 2000. Her singing, yodeling and songwriting have been compared to those of Dale Evans and Patsy Montana. Devon was the first winner of the "Patsy Montana International Yodeling Competition."

Dickens, Little Jimmy (James Cecil Dickens) (born December 19, 1920) is an American country singer famous for his humorous novelty songs, his small size, 4'11", and his rhinestone-studded outfits. He has been a member of the Grand Ole Opry for more than 60 years and has also been inducted into the Country Music Hall of Fame.

Gene Autry Oklahoma Museum, located in the tiny town of Gene Autry, OK, houses a large collection of western film memorabilia and hosted the Gene Autry Oklahoma Film & Music Festival from 1991-2009. It was founded by and is directed by Elvin Sweeten.

George's Round-up. This country music club in Long Beach, California, was a frequent showcase for singer Wynn Stewart and his band The West Coast Playboys. George's was one of biggest nightclubs in the area and was in competition with the famous Palomino Club in North Hollywood.

Gibson, Donald (Eugene) (April 3, 1928–November 17, 2003) was an American songwriter and country musician, as well an inductee into the Country Music Hall of Fame. Gibson penned such country standards as "Sweet Dreams" and "I Can't Stop Loving You," and had several country hits from 1957 into the early 1970s.

Gilliam, Les (born October 18, 1934) is a cowboy and country singer from Oklahoma. Known as "The Oklahoma Balladeer" and a member of the Oklahoma Music Hall of Fame.

Groom, Dewey (April 30, 1918-March 31, 1997) was an early performer in the Dallas area who appeared regularly on the Big D Jamboree and in nightclubs. For several years, he was owner/operator of the Longhorn Ballroom, which opened in the early 1960s and soon became *the* place to hear big name acts in the Dallas area. Groom also established the Saran Music Company.

Haggard, Merle (Ronald) (born April 6, 1937) is an American country singer/guitarist/ songwriter and instrumentalist. He was inducted into the Oklahoma Music Hall of Fame for his song "Okie from Muskogee" and into the national Country Music Hall of Fame in 1994.

Husky, Ferlin (December 3, 1925-March 17, 2011) was an American singer who became well-known as a country-pop chart-topper under various names, including Terry Preston and Simon Crum. In the 1950s and 60s, Husky had several hits, including "Gone" and "Wings of a Dove." As a member of the US Merchant Marines, he entertained the troops on his ship during World War II.

Jones, George (Glenn) (born September 12, 1931) is an American country singer known for his long list of hit records, his distinctive voice and phrasing, and his marriage to Tammy Wynette. He was inducted into the Country Music Hall of Fame in 1992.

Leach, Curtis (October 10, 1928-December 14, 1965). This singer/songwriter recorded under the Longhorn label, with his best known songs being "The Highway Man" and "Golden Guitar." He died after a stabbing incident.

Longhorn Ballroom is a music venue and country western dance hall in Dallas, Texas. It was formerly the Bob Wills Ranch House. Prior to 1978, performers such as Loretta Lynn and Patsy Montana performed there.

Lydic, Lowell is a festival producer and country/cowboy music promoter who presented the Cedar Depot Festival from 2002 to 2011 and before that, worked as entertainment coordinator for the Rex Allen Days event in Wilcox, Arizona, for several years.

McDonald, Skeets (October 1, 1915-March 31, 1968). Best known for his self-penned chart-topper "Don't Let the Stars Get in Your Eyes," Skeets McDonald was a honky-tonk singer and songwriter whose work helped bridge the gap between country and rock & roll.

Metromedia was a media company that owned radio and television stations in the United States from 1956 to 1986. They entered the record business in 1969 when they launched the Metromedia Records label, whose biggest-selling artist was Bobby Sherman. The label went out of business in 1974.

Miles of Memories Country MusicFest is an annual traditional country music festival held in Hastings, Nebraska, each September. Directors: Tex and Mary Schutz. *www.texandmary.com, www.milesofmemoriesmusic.com*

Montana, Patsy (October 30, 1912-May 3, 1996) was born Ruby Rebecca Blevins. She was an American country singer/songwriter/yodeler and the first female country performer to have a million-selling single for "I Want to Be a Cowboy's Sweetheart." She is a member of the Country Music Hall of Fame.

Mooney, Ralph (Sept. 16, 1928-Mar. 20, 2011) was the steel guitarist credited with creating the "Bakersfield Sound," also known as the "California Style" or "West Coast Style" steel guitar. Mooney played on the early recordings of Buck Owens, Merle Haggard, Waylon Jennings and many other country artists.

Mosby, Johnny & Jonie This husband-and-wife duo charted 17 times on the country music charts between 1963 and 1973, in addition to releasing six albums for various labels (Columbia, Starday and Capitol). Five of the duo's singles made Top 20 on the country charts, with the highest peaks being "Trouble in My Arms" and "Just Hold My Hand," both at number 12.

Nail, Rusty was a female songwriter who had some success on the Toppa label, a West Coast-based label. Janet recorded Nail's "Let Those Brown Eyes Smile at Me" as a demo and Capitol artist Rose Maddox later recorded that song. Janet also recorded Nail's "Is it Pity" and "I Just Can't Stop Loving You," which she released in 2008 on her CD called "Still Loving the Ride."

National Traditional Country Music Assocciation is a non-profit organization dedicated to the preservation, perpetuation and performance of America's rural music. Robert Everhart, Director.

Neal, Bob, Elvis' first manager, Neal had great success in talent managing and booking since the early 1950s. He also owned radio stations and produced and promoted country music package shows. He later sold his agency to the William Morris Agency.

Nelson, Willie (Hugh) (born April 30, 1933) is an American country singer/songwriter, author, poet, actor and activist. He reached his greatest fame during the outlaw country movement of the 1970s. Nelson was inducted into the Country Music Hall of Fame in 1993

Patsy Montana Yodeling Competitions occurred from 1998 to 2009 (except 2007) in Pineville-Havenhurst, Missouri. It was produced by Jane Frost, who was also the co-author of Patsy's autobiography, *Patsy Montana: The Cowboy's Sweetheart* (McFarland, 2002).

Paulin, Bob was a guitar player for a short time in Hank Snow's band and a local entertainer playing in eastern Canada and the northeastern United States from the 1930s through the 1950s. He worked to book The Listers (Janet's childhood singing group) locally in the Gardiner, Maine, area.

Peebles, Hap (1913-1993) was a music promoter whose acts included Elvis and Loretta Lynn. He started booking entertainment events while still in high school in Kansas and went on to found the Harry Peebles Agency. He was a longtime president of the International Country Music Buyers Association.

Pierce, Webb (Michael) (August 8, 1921–February 24, 1991) was one of the most popular American honky tonk country vocalists of the 1950s, charting more Number One hits than any other country artist during the decade. He was a member of the Grand Ole Opry and an inductee into the Country Music Hall of Fame.

Queen for a Day was a radio and television show that helped to usher in Americans' fascination with big-prize giveaway shows when it was born on radio (1945), before moving to television (1956-64). The radio version was hosted by Ken Murray and the TV version was hosted first by Jack Bailey, and later by Dick Curtis.

RCA Records (originally The Victor Talking Machine Company, then RCA Victor) is one of the flagship labels of Sony Music Entertainment.

Riley, Jeannie C. (born Jeanne Carolyn Stephenson on October 19, 1945) was a country music singer of the 1960's whose biggest hit was "Harper Valley PTA". The song made her the first female singer to have a song go to No. 1 on both the country music and pop music charts simultaneously.

Robbins, Marty (Martin David Robinson) (September 26, 1925–December 8, 1982) was an American singer, songwriter and multi-instrumentalist. One of the most popular and successful country and cowboy singers of his era, for most of his nearly four-decade career, Robbins was rarely far from the country music charts, and several of his songs also became pop hits. He was also an avid race car driver, a Grand Ole Opry star and an inductee of the Country Music Hall of Fame. He won three Grammy Awards, and was inducted into the Nashville Songwriter Hall of Fame.

Rodeo City Music Hall is the opry-style show that resides in the building in Mesquite, Texas, that once housed the Mesquite Opry. It is owned by Clara Walker and operated by Karol Dyess and features country, gospel, fifties and pop shows on Friday and Saturday nights.

Saran Music Publishing was established and owned by Dewey Groom in Dallas and is now owned by Groom's family.

Seely, Jeannie (born Marilyn Jeanne Seely July 6, 1940) is an American country singer and Grand Ole Opry star as well as an actress. She is best-known for her 1966 Grammy award-winning country hit, "Don't Touch Me," which peaked at No. 2 on the country charts. She is a Grammy Award winner and nominee for four CMA Awards.

Simpson, Red (born March 6, 1934) is an American country singer/songwriter best known for his trucker-themed songs. He performed from time to time on the Grand Ole Opry during the '60s and '70s and charted with one of his numerous truck-driving songs as late as 1979.

Sims Records Russell Sims had been associated with country music in the late 40's and early 50s and became a touring manager for T.Texas Tyler, who was a Four Star Records artist. He established Sims Records in Los Angeles in the early 50's and recorded primarily local country musicians and singers.

Snow, Hank (Clarence Eugene "Hank" Snow) (May 9, 1914 – December 20, 1999) was a Canadian-American country music artist. He charted more than 70 singles on the *Billboard* country charts from 1950 until 1980. Snow recorded with RCA and was a regular on the Grand Ole Opry. He was inducted into the Country Music Hall of Fame, the Nova Scotia Hall of Fame and The Canadian Country Music Hall of Fame. A victim of child abuse, he established the Hank Snow International Foundation for Prevention of Child Abuse.

Stewart, Wynn (Winford Lindsey Stewart) (June 7, 1934–July 17, 1985), was an American country singer who was one of the progenitors of the Bakersfield sound. Although not a huge chart success in his own right, he was an inspiration to such greats as Buck Owens and Merle Haggard. Stewart was part owner of a popular Las Vegas, Nevada nightclub called "Nashville Nevada" during the early 1960s. Wynn Stewart's big hit was "It's Such a Pretty World Today."

Stovall, Vern (Born October 23, 1928) Vern and Bobby George wrote such hits as "The Long Black Limousine," recorded first by Vern, then by Bobby Bare, George Hamilton IV, Rose Maddox, Glenn Campbell, Gordon Terry and Elvis Presley. Then "Who'll Be The First?" recorded by Ray Price and "One More Memory" recorded by Wynn Stewart. In 1961, his band, which included Phil Baugh, Bobby George and Freddy Rose, worked in and around the Los Angeles area for about four years where he built up a strong following. In 1964 Baugh and Stovall recorded the album "Country Guitar," which contained two major hits, "Country Guitar" and "One Man Band." Longhorn Records in Texas signed Stovall and he moved to the Dallas area, where he began working with Janet, first in a trio with Curtis Leach, then when Leach was killed, Stovall and McBride worked as a duo, mostly in the south and southwest. Their biggest song together was "I'm Wild Bill Tonight."

Stringbean (David Akeman) (June 17, 1916–November 10, 1973) was an American country banjo player and comedy musician best known for his role on the hit television show, *Hee Haw*. A member of the Grand Ole Opry, Akeman and his wife were murdered by burglars at their rural Tennessee home in 1973.

Sunbeam Music Publishing, owned by Metromedia, based in Nashville, active in 1960s.

Sweeten, Elvin (Born April 2 1942) Owner/operator/curator of the Gene Autry Oklahoma Museum in Gene Autry, Oklahoma.

Town Hall Party was an American country radio and television show broadcast over several Los Angeles area stations beginning in the autumn of 1951.

WPA—The Works Progress Administration (renamed during 1939 as the Work Projects Administration; WPA) was the largest New Deal agency, employing millions to carry out work projects, including the construction of public buildings and roads, and operated large arts, drama, media and literacy projects. It fed children and redistributed food, clothing and housing. Almost every community in the United States had a park, bridge or school constructed by the agency, which especially benefited rural and Western populations. Expenditures from 1936 to 1939 totaled nearly $7 billion.

Wells, Kitty (Ellen Muriel Deason) (born August 30, 1919) is an American country singer. Her 1952 hit recording, "It Wasn't God Who Made Honky Tonk Angels," made her the first female country singer to top the U.S. country charts, and turned her into the first female country star. In 1976 she became only the second female to be inducted into the Country Music Hall of Fame.

Western, Johnny (born October 28, 1934) is an American country singer-songwriter, musician, actor, and radio show host. He is a member of the Western Music Association Hall of Fame and the Country Music Disc Jockey Hall of Fame. He performed with Gene Autry's band and then for nearly 30 years was a part of the Johnny Cash road show. He wrote and performed the theme song "The Ballad of Paladin" for the television program *Have Gun—Will Travel* and co-wrote songs for TV shows *The Rebel* and *Bonanza*.

Wiggins, Tommy (born May 29, 1928) Singer, cowboy, actor, publisher, and co-founder of the Academy of Country and Western Music, with Eddie Miller, Chris and Mickey Christianson. Later re-named the Academy of Country Music.

Worthington, Cal (Calvin Coolidge Worthington) (born November 27, 1920) was a well-known car dealer with businesses located all along the West Coast. He is best known for his unique radio and television advertising for the Worthington Dealership Group.

Wray, John (November 30, 1926-April 24, 2008) was the originator of the Clifton-Vining Country Music Festival held in Clifton, Kansas, during the 1990s.

Janet McBride Discography

1951   "He Taught Me to Yodel" and "Let's Pretend"...Garrison Studio, Long Beach, California, Two-song 78 RPM, with siblings Joan and Dan on "Let's Pretend."
    "My Echo and I" 78 RPM, (Garrison, first time)

1952   "My Echo and I" 78 RPM (Garrison, second time)

1960   A: "I'm in Love with Another Woman's Man" and B: "Help Me Forget Him" (Toppa Records, 45-2013)
    A: "Sweethearts by Night" and B: "Can You Love Us Both?" (Toppa Records, 45-1029)
    A: "Home Away from Home" (Also on Binge LP 1003) and B: "Crazy Heart" (Toppa Records, 45-1043)

1962   A: "Your Nights in Charlie's Shoes" and B: "Heaven is for Sale" (Toppa Records, 45-1059)
    A: "Holding On to You" and B: "Why'd You Do It?" (Toppa Records, 45-1072)

1963   A: "Even If I Win" and B: "Home Away from Home" (Galahad Records, 45-G-528) ("Home" also on Binge LP 1001)

1964   A: "Almost Three" and B: "Swiss Cheese" (Sims Records, 45-163)
    A: "You'd Better Go" and B: "Cannonball Yodel" (Brookhurst Records, 45-004, 45-003) C: "What Did She Do?" and D: "I Want to Be a Cowboy's Sweetheart" (Brookhurst Records, 45-0017)
    A: "Stranger at the Funeral" and B: "The Girl Who Invented Mistakes" (Brookhurst Records, 45-0015)

1965   A: "A Letter to a Fool" with Billy Barton and B: "The Arms of a Child" (Sims Records, 45-244)
    A: "Common Law Wife" and B: "The Guy Here with Me" (Longhorn Records, 45-564)

1966   A: "Yodelin' Jan" and B: "Outside of That" (Longhorn Records, 45-568)
    A: "I'm Wild Bill Tonight" with Vern Stovall and "Not Worth the Paper" with Vern Stovall (Longhorn Records, 45-571)
    A: "Where Did the Other Dollar Go?" with Vern Stovall and B: "Tell Me Again" with Vern Stovall (Longhorn Records, 45-575)
    LP: "Country Dozen" LP with Vern Stovall. (Longhorn Records, 005)

1967   A: "It's the Truth That's Killin' Me" and B: "Play Like You Love Me" (Longhorn Records, 45-585)
    A: "A Woman's Point of View" and B: "Mass Confusion" (Longhorn Records, 45-582)

1969   A: "That's Not Like Me" and B: "My Johnny Lies Over and Over" (Metromedia Records, 45-MM-161)

1981   A: "Yodeling Tribute" (Recorded at Sumet Bernet Sound) and B: "Best Dern
             Yodeler" with Tommy Allsup and his band. (Brookhurst Records, 45-
             BR-20)

1984   A: "The Mild Side of Life" (recorded as a duet with Emma Herron and a recitation
             by John Ingram) and B: "There's a Silver Moon on the Golden Gate"
             (also a duet with Emma Herron) (Brookhurst Records, 45-BR-21)

1985   "The Pride of Mesquite" LP, (Binge Records, LP1001, and Bronco Buster,
             West Germany)
         "Texas Yodel Lady" (Brookhurst Records, Cassette:001)

1986   "Yodelin' Jan" LP, (Binge Records, LP1003, and Bronco Buster, West
             Germany)
         "Yodeling at the Grand Ole Opry" LP with Dexter Johnson, (Cattle Records,
             LP93, West Germany)

1988   "Texas Yodel Lady" LP with Dexter Johnson, (Cattle Records LP118, West
             Germany)
         "My Kind of Country" (Brookhurst Records, Cassette:002)

1989   "By Request" (Brookhurst Records, Cassette:003)

1990   "Mesquite-Flavored Country" (Brookhurst Records, Cassette:004)

1991   "Always Country" (Brookhurst Records, Cassette:005)

1992   "The Yodeling Side of Janet McBride" (Brookhurst Records, Cassette:006)

1994   "The Gospel Side of Janet McBride" (Brookhurst Records, Cassette:007)

1995   "The Yodeler's Dream" (Brookhurst Records, Cassette:008)

1996   "Mesquite-Flavored Country" (Brookhurst Records, CD:001)

1997   "Yodeling Favorites" (Brookhurst Records, Cassette:009)

1998   "Yodeling Classics" (Brookhurst Records, Cassette:010)
         "Classic Yodeling Songs Collection" (Brookhurst Records, CD:002)

1999   "Yodeling Texas Cowgirl" (Brookhurst Records, Cassette:011)
         "Yodeling Texas Cowgirl" (Brookhurst Records, CD:003)

2001   "Wyoming Rose" (Brookhurst Records, CD:004)
         "Wyoming Rose" (Brookhurst Records, Cassette:012)

2002   "50 Years of Yodeling with Janet McBride" A 2-CD set. (Brookhurst Records,
             CD:005)

2004   "Gospel Country" (Brookhurst Records, CD:006)

2005   "Happy Yodeling Cowgirl" (Brookhurst Records, CD:007)

2007   "Honky Tonk Ballads & Classic Yodeling" (Bronco Buster, CD:9060, Germany)

2009   "Still Loving the Ride" (Brookhurst Records, CD:008)

Janet received two awards from the DJ Digest *organization, which was later expanded into the Academy of Country Music. Janet is fourth from right in the front row and Tommy Wiggins is second from right in the second row in this shot taken after one of the award ceremonies. (Janet McBride Collection)*

Awards and Honors

1963 "Female Artist of the Year." Presented by *DJ Digest*. (Precursor to Academy of Country Music).

1964 "Most Promising Female Artist." Presented by *VIP Magazine*. (Precursor to Academy of Country Music).

1989 "MC of the Year." Presented by Dallas-Fort Worth Metroplex Country Music Association.

1990   "MC of the Year." Presented by Dallas-Fort Worth Metroplex Country Music Association.

1991 "Female Yodeler of the Year." Presented by Western Music Association.

1991 "Front Person of the Year." Presented by Dallas-Fort Worth Metroplex Country Music Association.

1992 "Humanitarian Award." Presented by The Terry Awards.

1993 "Hall of Fame Award." Presented by Dallas-Fort Worth Metroplex Country Music Association.

1996 Top Ten Finalist and Talent Winner, Mrs. Senior Texas America Competition.

1997 "Yodeler of the Year." Presented by Academy of Western Artists.

1999 "Patsy Montana Cowgirl Spirit Award." Presented by Patsy Montana Family.

2001 "Lone Star State Country Music Hall of Fame Award." Presented by Lone Star State Country Music Association.

2002 "Western Song of the Year" for "Wyoming Rose." Presented by Western Music Association.

2005 WMA "Hall of Fame Pioneer Award" for dedication to the teaching and preservation of western music and ideas. Presented by Western Music Association.

2005 Grammy Award nomination for "A Cowgirl's Dream" for "Best Country Music Collaboration" (Janet McBride and Patsy Montana).

2006 "Yodeler of the Year." Presented by Academy of Western Artists.

2008 "Special Achievement Award" for her work with young talent. Presented by Cedar Depot Association.

2008 "Special Recognition Award" for her work with The Buckaroos. Presented by the Cowtown Opry, Fort Worth, Texas.

2009 "Lifetime Achievement Award" for her continuing work with young people in the field of music and entertainment. Presented by Gene Autry Oklahoma Museum, Elvin Sweeten, Director.

2010 "Living Legend Award" for her long performance career combined with her commitment to nurturing young performers. Presented by Burton's Bend Music Festival, Christine and Rodney Whipple, Directors.

2010 "Yodeler CD of the Year" award for "Still Loving the Ride." Presented by Rural Roots Commission, Bob Everhart, Director.

Fun Stuff

Song on Stage

Janet's and Gwen's song "Yodeling at the Grand Ole Opry"
was used in *Honky Tonk Laundry*,
a hilarious musical about two heartbroken women.
The play was performed across the country in 2004 and 2005.
(Artwork from Steele Spring Productions)

Through a Child's Eyes

Kathleen Juhl of Shelton, Nebraska, a ten-year-old student
of Janet's, created this artistic impression of Janet and
presented it to her at a 2010 festival.

In the Most Unlikely Places

"The Yodeling Tribute," Janet's song that paid homage to her many yodeling heroes, was included in *Lipstick & Dynamite*, a documentary film about women wrestlers. The song was sung by retired professional wrestler and singer Ida May Martinez, a fan whom Janet called "Miss Ida." *(Shown in photo). (Images from Ruthless Films)*

259

Fun Awards

In 2007, the Gene Autry Oklahoma Museum and its Film & Music Festival presented Janet with a pretty normal "Queen of Musical Mentors" award and John with a hilarious "Sassiest Sidekick" award. Just a couple of the many special memories from that wonderful event!

GENE AUTRY OKLAHOMA MUSEUM

Certificate of Award

This document certifies that
the
Queen of Musical Mentors
Award
is
conferred upon

Janet McBride

The above mentioned individual is recognized
for believing in and sharing the legacy
of the Singing Cowboys of the "B" Western films
of the 1930s, 1940s and 1950s.

Gene Autry Oklahoma Museum
PO Box 67
Gene Autry, OK 73436

Elvin R. Sweeten, Director

OKLAHOMA MUSEUM

Certificate of Award

This document certifies that
the
Sassiest Sidekick
Award
is
conferred upon

John Ingram

The above mentioned individual is recognized
for believing in and sharing the legacy
of the Singing Cowboys of the "B" Western films
of the 1930s, 1940s and 1950s.

Gene Autry Oklahoma Museum
PO Box 67
Gene Autry, OK 73436

Elvin R. Sweeten, Director

Sweet Publicity

Every now and again, Janet was featured on the cover of a regional or national magazine, or maybe in an article inside. It didn't happen as often as it should have, but it was all fun while it lasted. Many articles about Janet were included inside other magazines, but front covers were pretty special.

Photo by Lori Faith Merritt. (www.photographybyfaith.com)

A Few
Favorite Photos

Photo by Steve Covault. (www.rockmusicphotos.com)

Top left: "It's not *all* about you, John!" *Top right*: Janet, Art Greenhaw and Jamie Shipman. *Center*: At the Adams Avenue Roots Festival. *Bottom right*: Pickin' and grinnin' at Old Tucson. (*Janet McBride Collection*)

John's favorite (Photo by Glamour Shots)

Photo by Ron & Glenda Shipman

Publicity Photo number three, 1966.

Photo by Ron & Glenda Shipman

Publicity Photo number one, 1960.

Publicity Photo number two, 1962.

Photo by Ron & Glenda Shipman

Publicity Shots...Through the Years

Index

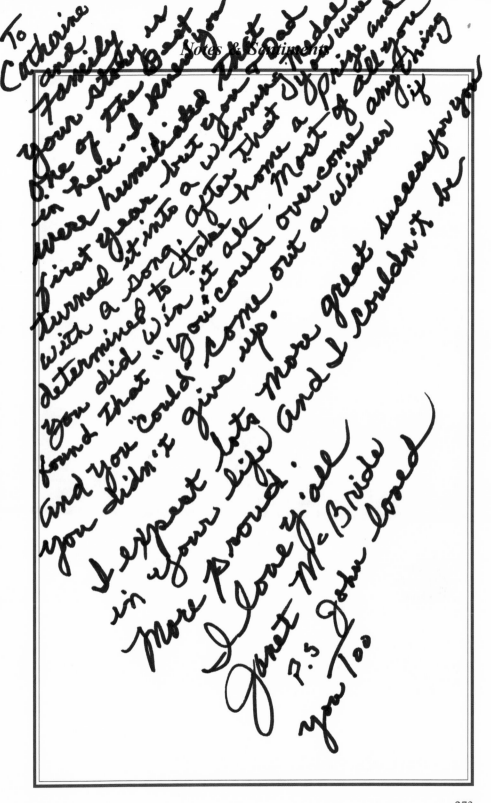

To Catharine and family we enjoyed your story that you were one of the best in here. I knew that you were humiliated that your medal first year but you turned it into a winning with a song after that I found that determined to stake it. Most of all you did win it all. You could overcome anything if and you "could" come out a winner you didn't give up.

I expect lots more great success in your life and I couldn't be more proud.

I love y'all

Janet McBride

P.S. John loves you too

Made in the USA
Charleston, SC
22 July 2011